Worth

ALSO BY MARISA G. FRANCO, PhD

Platonic: How the Science of Attachment Can Help You Make—and Keep—Friends

Worth

The NEW SCIENCE *of* SELF-ESTEEM *and* SECURE ATTACHMENT

Marisa G. Franco, PhD

G. P. PUTNAM'S SONS
NEW YORK

PUTNAM
— EST. 1838 —
G. P. Putnam's Sons
Publishers Since 1838
An imprint of Penguin Random House LLC
1745 Broadway, New York, NY 10019
penguinrandomhouse.com

Book design by Patrice Sheridan

LIBRARY OF CONGRESS CATALOGING-IN-PUBLICATION DATA
has been applied for.

ISBN: 9798217046591
Ebook ISBN: 9798217046607

Printed in the United States of America
1st Printing

To Alyssa—
for a love so unyielding that it made even the darkest
parts of me fathom there was light,
and for helping me become who I always was

Contents

Worth

Introduction

As I walked on a lush path with my boyfriend by my side, trees canopying our trail, birds literally tweeting, I felt deeply alone.

Perhaps it was the darkness that had fallen over our relationship that explained why, to resuscitate it, we sought the sun. As we hiked, I marveled at how my life could be fraying at its seams while light still gladdened my skin, water still whooshed like a song, and the leaves twirled in the breeze. Like, *Hello, nature, haven't you heard that my relationship is crumbling?*

But to be honest, I was acting more like the light, water, and leaves—gladdening, whooshing, and twirling—than I was myself. I'd wake up, greet my then-boyfriend good morning, ask how he was doing, and only hear grunts and one-word answers in response.

When I gently brought up a favor he'd said he would do for me but had neglected for the past month, he refused to speak to me for days, his silence showing me that weapons are made not just through the presence of something, but also by the absence. In reaction to his brooding, I stayed sunny, soft, and accommodating, hoping that as long as *I* was steadfast in my commitment to the relationship—which he seemed to have psychologically extricated himself from months ago—I could entice him back to it.

Yet even as I tried to present a secure exterior, on the inside, I was torn up. When I'd greet him good morning and he'd just stare—my mood plunged. When he'd snap at me, I'd implore him to tell me more about what he needed from me—instead of acknowledging what I needed from him, which was more gentleness. And as I tried to give him his space when words and emotions deserted him—I actually took too much space from the part of *me* that needed communication, affirmation, and resolution.

I tried to exude an anchored, secure facade amid a situation that was increasingly seeming doomed. (Picture me like that meme dog with the dilated pupils who says "This is fine" while the room burns around him.) I knew something was terribly wrong. But I couldn't understand what. For the majority of our relationship, he'd been caring and responsive, and, well, he'd *talked.* He'd made me feel seen, appreciated, and loved. Now that things were suddenly very different, I persisted in my old behavior—grimly playacting happiness and normality—because I didn't know what to make of his pivot.

Why was this happening? Was it because we had spent the last few months cooped up together during the COVID-19 pandemic? Did my demands for pandemic caution, warning him to avoid restaurants and hanging out unmasked indoors, feel too controlling? Or did my surge of anxiety when someone hacked a cough around me ambush him like a brick to the face? Did he transform into this mute stranger because of the situation . . . or was this our new normal?

I spent a lot of time and energy worrying about his reactions and feelings. *Why is he doing this?* But hindsight has revealed that I should have been just as curious about *my own.* Why was *I* so composed in the face of neglect? So able to be okay with what was not okay? So invested in getting an A in being a "secure girlfriend" that I was willing to abandon the emotions that I thought would mark me as otherwise—the anger, the hurt, the betrayal, the confusion?

As that relationship withered, I began my search for a version of being secure that didn't require me to abandon myself.

ATTACHMENT THEORY WAS SUPPOSED TO SAVE US

When I referred to my "secure" exterior above, I intentionally chose that word in reference to a popular, long-standing, and science-backed framework called attachment theory. I have a PhD in psychology, and I specialize in relationships. I've read all the popular psychology self-help books; my favorites are underlined and tattered from use. And the concept that resonated most with me—the one that informed much of my work as well as my personal life—was attachment theory.

Attachment theory has recently broken out of the ivory tower of academia and made waves in popular culture—among online self-help gurus, in parenting discussions, and in popular books like Amir Levine's *Attached*, which applied it to romantic relationships. I even wrote a book myself about friendship through the lens of attachment, called *Platonic: How the Science of Attachment Can Help You Make—and Keep—Friends*. Attachment theory has gone mainstream, and you might already be familiar with the different attachment styles.

Securely attached people, well, they're the gold standard of attachment styles. The securely attached have had loving and supportive parents, which has made them experts at giving and receiving love. They are good at initiating new relationships, reaching out to maintain them, and bringing up conflict while staying levelheaded, and are generally the least rattled when relationships go south.

Anxiously attached people, according to theory, struggle to depend on themselves for comfort and often must demand it from others. Their parents were too preoccupied by other things, perhaps their work or their marriage troubles, to focus on them, meaning they were never taught how to regulate their own inflamed emotions. They fear others will abandon them unless they work to earn their love, like they did with their parents. They cling to others, dive into relationships at warp speed, and sacrifice their needs to ward off any chance of abandonment.

Avoidantly attached people, in contrast, only rely on themselves. They had parents who fed and sheltered them, but who stifled or shamed their emotions. They don't trust people, avoid being vulnerable, withhold affection, and keep others at a distance.

People with a *disorganized attachment style* had parents who were highly unsafe or abusive. They use a mix of strategies to get their needs met, flipping between the strategies of avoidantly and anxiously attached people but displaying even more intense versions of these strategies. They might switch between idealizing and then hating people close to them, or toggle between struggling to tolerate being alone and struggling to tolerate company, for example.

A key tenet of attachment theory is that early relationships shape an internal template we use for every relationship that follows. So as adults, we project the qualities of our parents onto others. A more recent study, however, found that the link between childhood and adult attachment is modest, suggesting that our template continues to get updated throughout life. Nonetheless, our attachment styles push us to re-create dynamics from previous relationships in new ones because we look to *verify our past* more than we do to *see current reality clearly.*

Our lives, as a behavioral scientist might say, are an extended emotional confirmation bias—or as the writer William Faulkner put it more eloquently in *Requiem for a Nun*, "The past is never dead. It's not even past." So anxious people cling. Avoidant people detach. Secure people connect.

All the research finds that secure people are thriving in their relationships. But there I was, performing what I now realize was a *pantomime* of security . . . and somehow, my relationship was still crumbling. What was I doing wrong? If attachment theory couldn't save my relationship—or, more importantly, myself—then what could?

WHAT WE GET WRONG ABOUT ATTACHMENT THEORY

In the current zeitgeist, attachment theory has become an obsession. Secure-attachment influencers abound, getting hundreds of thousands or even millions of followers. Think pieces galore break down the nuances of attachment styles. A recent essay in *The New York Times* Modern Love column, "An Anxious Person Tries to Be Chill," describes a woman who hopped from an avoidant partner to a secure one, whom she—spoiler alert—married. Online dating profiles share requests for the elusive "secure partner" or seductively proclaim to be one. Secure attachment has become something close to a status symbol.

There's a good reason for this obsession. Finally, we know why the one who got away ghosted us (they're avoidant), why that friend came on super strong and then petered out (anxious), and how to talk through conflict in ways that keep us close (by using the playbook of the securely attached). Attachment theory feels like a relationship cheat code.

My first book, *Platonic: How the Science of Attachment Can Help You Make—and Keep—Friends*, shared many of these secrets. In it, I taught people how to act securely in friendships, skirmish sans vitriol, tilt on the tightrope between distrust and oversharing, and love freely yet flexibly, so as to adapt to how others need to be loved. I knew that the tips I shared in *Platonic* were helpful in navigating friendships—I saw it in my own life, and I heard from hundreds of readers who put these ideas into practice to help build connection in their lives.

But the more I learned (and lived), the more I was coming to suspect that, when it comes to our complex relationship with ourselves, we need more than secure strategies . . . and that sometimes these strategies can backfire, like they did in my relationship.

The problem is that secure attachment is easy to perform and a lot tougher to internalize. If we *act* secure without also doing the deliberate internal work to *become* secure, we are left to desperately perform attachment, even when our nervous system hasn't caught up. We can say all the right things but still feel untethered. When conflict arises, our anxiety kicks in. When we're vulnerable, we feel pathetic.

As psychologist Marion Woodman put it, "It is easier to try to be better than you are than to try to *be* who you are." Ultimately, in feigning security, we abandon what we truly feel—which only makes us more insecure, no matter how well-therapized we sound. I should know.

I wrote *Worth* to offer you something more penetrating, something that doesn't just help you change what you say but also what you *feel*, deep down. We need a version of security that goes beyond relationship scripts and weaves itself into the contours of our nervous system.

A NEW MODEL OF SELF-WORTH

The first step to becoming secure is to stop calling yourself "secure."

Ironically, *calling* ourselves secure can, in itself, make us more *in*secure. When I think of myself as secure, and my nerves jangle about being left behind, for example, I might ignore these feelings because they don't align with the story of my security. In ignoring an anxious feeling in myself, I become *less* secure, because I can't heal what I don't acknowledge.

True security comes from recognizing when you feel anxious or avoidant so you can care for those parts of yourself. When we ignore them, instead, we internally reenact the original harm of neglect that made us insecure in the first place. So we must be honest about what we're feeling—even if that's insecurity. That truthful reckoning with our emotions is how we actually find our sense of worth.

So in this book, we strive to become not secure, but secure-*ish*.

What is "secure-ish"? We'll explore that concept throughout this book. But simply put: Being secure-ish is more about becoming *real* than it is about living up to a set of expected behaviors. It's about accepting the full range of your emotions—secure, but also anxious and avoidant—and inviting them *all* in. It's about being honest about what you feel and who you are.

As I developed the secure-ish concept that underpins this book, I began to conduct a psychological inventory of my own feelings, prioritizing knowing myself fully instead of putting forward my best self. Who would I be if I didn't put any pressure on myself to be—and seem—okay? What would happen if I let go of who I *thought* I should be, what I *thought* I should feel . . . and I simply let myself *be* who I was and feel what I felt? I started to let in my weakness, resentment, hostility, judgment, anger, and, yes, insecurities. These emotions were uncomfortable; they made me feel shame. I wished I could just release them into the air like balloons floating into outer space, but they weren't floating anywhere. Denial is like trying to mend a broken bone by pretending it is unbroken.

When I stopped trying to sieve my personality through the strainer of acceptability, I could see feelings of dependency, vulnerability, neediness, and downright self-pity. These feelings threatened my greater sense of who I am. I tried to sock away those feelings, to run from them, white them out. It's only now that I'm realizing that's quite a cruel way to treat a part of you that needs your help. It's only now that I'm realizing the depths to which what we suppress never quite leaves us.

So in this book, I'm offering you a relationship with yourself that goes beyond being securely attached. I'm offering a sense of *worth*. This came from me realizing some of the limitations of attachment theory. As I did, I loosened the boundaries of what I read beyond attachment, using studies on related concepts to fill in gaps. I sought out science on self-compassion, self-esteem, authenticity, self-actualization, and resilience. (Now picture me as Charlie in the conspiracy meme with papers pinned across the bulletin board and a thick red string connecting all the dots.)

What I've ended up with is something much more expansive and complex than I expected I'd find. I use *worth* as a catchall term that encompasses secure attachment and adjacent terms. Yet I also use these alternative terms—*worthy*, *self-esteem*, *self-actualization*, *secure-ish attachment*—when their specificity helps me more accurately reflect data or reference a particular aspect of worth.

When we feel worth, we are willing to feel all of our emotions and face all sides of ourselves in a centered and compassionate way, just like the securely attached kid has learned to do from their parents. We do not try to deny, mask, or shame parts, like we might be tempted to do when we think of ourselves as completely secure. We're able to look at our prickly side, our failures, and the parts of us we dislike and treat them with dignity because every part of us offers a precious opportunity for us to know ourselves more fully.

What this ongoing work of finding worth looks like for me—and what I'll invite it to look like for you through *Worth*—is a change in relationship with my insecurities, the ones that cause me shame and make me want to look away, since I've realized I'm only as insecure as the parts of me I leave in the shadows. So I'm no longer asking parts of me to disappear. I'm saying to them, *I'm so sorry I've neglected you. I'm thankful for the ways you have carried the pain I wasn't willing to see. I never want you to stop crying, raging, and screaming out about how hurt you are. I want to create an environment within myself where pain isn't something I ignore and shame myself for. Because without this pain, I may have never known these depths of love.*

WHY SEEK SECURITY

Finding worth requires us to face all sides of ourselves, and yet technology allows us to regularly escape ourselves. Anxiety, instead of being faced, gets smothered by a TikTok video of cats; despair gets disregarded for the latest news ping. In light of this trend, two related crises have embroiled us: those of plummeting mental health and self-worth. A 2022 report found that many young people, steeped in technology, exhibit a troubling constellation of traits: lacking a sense of who they are as individuals and withdrawing from the social world. Taken together, this causes what psychologists call a "disintegrating social self"—a poor sense of self and withdrawal from relationships. On the mental health front, from 2009 to 2021, the number of high school students in the U.S. who said they felt persistently sad or hopeless surged from 26 to 44 percent.

The "vulnerability model" of self-esteem also suggests there is a tango happening between mental health and our sense of self. The lower our self-esteem, the more likely we are to succumb to mental health issues. One study found that the lower our self-esteem in adolescence, the more likely we are to be depressed at age forty-five. Similarly, studies of attachment find that our childhood insecurities influence our physical health later in life. Compared with secure babies, avoidant infants are three times more likely to later report inflammation-related illness (think asthma, heart problems, diabetes) at age thirty-two, and anxious infants are 7.5 times more likely.

These harrowing health findings may have to do with insecure people perceiving the world as more threatening. In *The Antecedents of Self-Esteem*, Stanley Coopersmith imparts that issues with our sense of self lie at the root of anxiety. He writes that anxiety involves the constant perception of threat, but what is being threatened is our sense of self. When we don't feel worth, we don't feel capable of coping; threats expand; anxiety surges. Our insecurities reduce our sense of reality, twisting our psyche into a sonar system for real or suspected psychological pain. Studies find that the lower our self-esteem, the more likely we are to "dramatically" (in the words of the study) underestimate how much others love us, ignore blatant signs of acceptance from others, and misremember past experiences as being less positive than they were.

When we feel worth and can register the good that's happening all around us, we end up with better relationships. People who are more secure have higher-quality relationships, a meta-analysis found. They will absorb love and safety more easily, choose healthier relationships, and improve on existing ones. To reach out to someone, work through conflict, or tell someone how much we love them, we must be confident enough to take these risks.

Our sense of worth, then, benefits not just us but also everyone around us. And yet, some think of the pursuit of worth as a selfish journey that involves focusing on yourself at the expense of everyone else. But people who feel worthy don't just focus on themselves; they stand up for the good of all, like August Landmesser did.

In a photo taken in a shipyard during the Third Reich in Germany, nearly all the workers are shown heiling Hitler, except Landmesser. His arms remain folded, his face disapproving. He had abandoned the Nazi Party years earlier, after witnessing the lies it spewed about Jews. The Nuremberg Laws forbade him from marrying his Jewish wife.

In the face of a Holocaust, we would all like to be Landmesser. Yet Isabel Wilkerson, author of *Caste: The Origin of Our Discontents*, asks us to consider that "unless people are willing to transcend their fears, endure discomfort and derision, suffer the scorn of loved ones and neighbors and co-workers and friends, fall into disfavor of perhaps everyone they know, face exclusion and even banishment, it would be numerically impossible, humanly impossible, for everyone to be that man." Wilkerson is of course right: Not everyone will be that man. But some people will. The question then is, what does it take?

A robust body of research suggests that it takes worth. Worth acts as the inner kindling we need to have the audacity to make social progress. According to one study, people who are primed to have self-esteem transcend, rather than conform to, norms, as did Landmesser. Studies find secure people are more likely to be compassionate and altruistic, to do things like donate blood or care for the elderly, and they are less likely to discriminate against others.

Security also spurs the creativity we need to tackle the world's greatest social problems. In Austrian psychoanalyst Ernst Kris's study of creativity, he proposed that creativity involves having enough worth to be able to regress to a more primitive and chaotic version of ourselves without being debilitated. It allows us, in his words, a "regression in the service of the ego." Similarly, in the pursuit of social change, we must have enough worth to surrender ourselves to a larger movement, the ability to shed self-centeredness without feeling evaporated.

Of course, no single person should bear the brunt of an entire system's failure. We assign blame to individuals when they don't feel good enough without scrutinizing how society creates the conditions for them to feel insecure. For individuals from marginalized identities, our culture's emphasis on individual responsibility means they must somehow transcend not only the more typical experiences that lead to insecurity—rejection from parents, bullying from peers—but also experiences that are unique to their identities such as racism, sexism, classism, ableism, etc.

Discrimination is meant to put people in their place so they'll no longer resist continued discrimination. It impacts worth, by design, and it is part of how injustice sustains itself. Learning how not to internalize those assaults on your worth is how you resist, how you maintain the audacity to envision a system that involves better treatment for us all. The more work we do on ourselves, the better we'll be at changing, rather than adapting to, unfair systems. "When wounded individuals come together in groups to make change, as the feminist thinker bell hooks writes in *Sisters of the Yam: Black Women and Self-Recovery*, "our collective struggle is often undermined by all that has not been dealt with emotionally." And as author Toni Cade Bambara reminds us, "Revolution begins in the self and with the self."

HOW TO FIND WORTH

If, as attachment theory suggests, our insecurities are rooted in our past—in the rejection, neglect, or abuse we've experienced that we superimpose now—how can we ever recover our sense of security? The good news is that, in *Worth*, you will learn that you *can* change the past, or at least how it lives within you. In the chapters that follow, I'm going to introduce you to a remarkable new concept called *memory reconsolidation theory*—the idea that our memories update when we bring them new information. This allows us to literally rewrite how those memories live in our consciousness . . . and subsequently revise how they affect our lives. Finding worth, then, is not about changing ourselves—finding that high-status job or optimizing our appearance. Instead, it's about facing the painful memories that made us forget we've been worthy all along.

Throughout this book, I'll share exercises, drawn straight from the best research, that help us find worth. I have done these exercises myself, with people I feel safe with, and the impact has been transformative. I recommend you gather others to do the exercises with, too, as studies find that being around others intensifies our emotional experience. Of course, you can do them solo, too, if you prefer.

Even though *Worth* will bring you all the best tools to feel worthy, this will still be a process, one I haven't always been patient with. I've sometimes treated insecure parts of me like a shy dog that is scared to cross the street and that I've dragged along by a leash, tugging it across the crosswalk on its hind legs. I have repeated my complaints about not having made more progress to my therapist so many times that I've had to reassure myself that I pay her, so I'm allowed to be draining and repetitive when talking with her! (If I treated my physical health the way I treated my mental wellness, it would look like me scrunching my face at a deep gash on my leg and scolding, "Epidermis, why are you not regenerating more quickly?")

I've acted as if a fully developed sense of worth was the norm and struggling was an unacceptable deviation. But I'm starting to see that this is not true. In their essay "Sick Woman Theory," writer Johanna Hedva challenges the assumption of "health" as the baseline by citing the philosopher Judith Butler's work, which proposes that the body is defined by its vulnerabilities, not temporarily affected by them. "What is so destructive about conceiving of wellness as the default, as the standard mode of existence, is that it *invents illness as temporary.* When being sick is an abhorrence of the norm, *it allows us to conceive of care and support in the same way*," Hedva argues.

Hedva has a point. Many of us struggling with insecurity have been "sick" with it our entire lives, and yet we have been expected to act as if we're fine, and we haven't permitted ourselves to consistently care for ourselves. Behind closed doors, we battle imposter syndrome, question whether our romantic partners or friends really love us, or ruminate incessantly on a scrap of feedback.

What if we take Hedva's advice and admit to ourselves that perhaps wellness, or worth, isn't the default? That finding a sense of worth may be a lifelong journey for some of us? What if we took care of ourselves, continuously, as we do when we are sick? We would take special time out of our day for mental health care, pausing before we respond to that curt email to feel our pain. Our self-talk would be more forgiving and tender, letting us know that how we feel is okay. We would prioritize our joy, pause and not push through when we need a break, take a few more seconds to savor the sunrise.

Knowing that finding worth is a practice—perhaps a lifelong one—impels us to avoid the healing equivalent of a one-night stand, where we do one exercise to work on our worth and never text our pain again. To make strides toward security, to really feel our own worth, we'll have to do the exercises in this book over and over again. In other words, we will enter a committed relationship with our pain, so that deep care for ourselves becomes our new normal.

Security, I've realized, is not about learning the tools to sacrifice yourself and build a facade of harmony. It's about becoming *all* of who you are so you can find people who harmonize with the truest version of you. Sometimes finding worth means shedding relationships like molting dead skin, or embracing more friction in them rather than curling into a constricted version of yourself.

On that hike to save our relationship, the light was still gladdening, the water was still whooshing, the leaves were still twirling, and my then-boyfriend was still stonewalling. Finally, something broke in me, or broke through me. First came the tears, as my body spoke before I did. And then the words came, like an out-of-body experience, from a me I had tried to suppress so long she seemed foreign. "I don't want to be the shock absorber for your moods anymore. I can't keep doing this."

Looking back at that relationship, I can see how my attempts at *acting* secure in my relationship made me less secure. Doing whatever I thought would fix the relationship alienated me from what I needed for myself. I was still hurting, which demonstrated to me that true security, in that situation, meant I had to ask a partner to step up. In this case, no amount of self-regulation would make up for neglect. The most secure thing I said in that relationship was that I needed to leave it.

In *Worth*, we will come to appreciate our insecurities, to see them not as meddlers infringing upon our existence but as messengers alerting us to the pain we must face to exist more deeply. We will stop interpreting pain as a threat and instead see it as an open-palmed plea for love or a closed-palm prayer for it.

"Stay in here as long as you can. Here is where the healing happens," my friend Sigal once told me when I was in pain. We'll stay in the territory of our insecurities and learn how to summon healing from there.

Part 1

Understanding Worth

1

Defining Worth

The best and worst people both have high self-esteem.

By *high self-esteem*, I mean that they score high on a classic assessment of the concept. Yes, they say, I am satisfied with myself. Yes, I have a number of good qualities. Yes, I'm a person of value. No, I don't think I'm a failure. No, I don't feel useless. No, I don't think I'm no good at all.

And yet, as you look closer at these high-self-esteem havers, you'll start to make out two very distinct groups of them. People with high self-esteem are either the kindest, calmest, most generous people you know *or* the meanest, most hostile, and most selfish. Self-esteem, it seems, is not a purely "good" or "bad" trait. And yet most of us would agree that self-esteem is a defining—perhaps *the* defining—characteristic of worth.

So how do we know if we have enough (and the right kind) of self-esteem?

WHY DOES SELF-ESTEEM LOOK SO DIFFERENT IN SOME PEOPLE?

When I came across these clashing profiles of high self-esteem, I thought of a party I hosted where I served two specialty drinks with identical ingredients, except one contained alcohol and the other didn't. We called the nonalcoholic drink the "good friend" and the alcoholic one the "toxic friend."

My guest Heather asked, "Did you do it on purpose, make the toxic and nontoxic friend look the same?" Another guest requested a good friend but was accidentally served a toxic one. She began to feel loose and woozy. "Are you sure that was a good friend?" she asked.

Although both kinds of people with high self-esteem can appear identical at face value, there *are* tells. Some high-esteem individuals use their sense of worth for good . . . others, not so much.

- Ask someone with high self-esteem about a time they did something bad, like broke the rules, acted unethically, or disappointed their parents. One will tell you why their behavior was someone else's fault, one study found. The other will admit they were wrong and share how they honestly felt. They'll reflect on their remorse, regret, and growth.
- Imagine this person with high self-esteem was your romantic partner, and one day, you were too engrossed in your work to acknowledge that they entered the room. One would interpret this as a sign of disrespect and ignore you back. The other would assume you're invested in something important and go on with their day, as revealed by a study where people were exposed to those scenarios.
- High self-esteem affects how people interact with the wider world. It can either make them angrier and more hostile than the average person, or it can make them less so, another study found. Because of this, according to another study, one type of high-self-esteem haver has the smoothest and most intimate relationships of all, while the other has the least.

In other words, while you might find no difference in how these high-self-esteem people speak of themselves—as worthy, confident, special—you will find a stark difference in how they treat *others.* One group treats others the best, and the other, the worst.

I call these two groups the "good" and "bad" twins of self-esteem because this same trait expresses itself so differently. Michael H. Kernis, the late psychology professor who studied self-esteem, referenced these twins of self-esteem when others critiqued his ideas and he jokingly replied: "I could respond to these commentaries by thoughtfully assimilating their meaning and modifying my position . . . or I could begin my response with a resounding #%+$@&*! OFF."

I explored this research on self-esteem to help me define worth. Yet I found that the concept of self-esteem was not necessarily aligned with how I see worth, or, to be more specific, the bad twin's kind wasn't, while the good twin's was. This is why it's important to have precision in my understanding of self-esteem. If I wasn't able to understand the differences between these twins, I might inadvertently lead us to become the bad twin, springing off the backs of others to lift ourselves higher. To truly understand worth, I had to distinguish the good twin's kind of self-esteem, so I could lead us to develop the type of self-esteem that doesn't come at everyone else's expense.

The stakes here are everyone we will ever love.

Good Twins Acknowledge—and Accept—Negative Feelings

How could two types of people, who say they feel the same about themselves, treat other people so differently? My mind was working overtime to figure out this puzzle when I ran into Beth. Beth had supervised my graduate school teaching years ago. She had insisted on paying me, even though I was teaching the class for credits to fulfill my grad school requirements. Beth also listened like she left her body to live in yours. She felt what you felt, knew what you knew. She wielded this uncanny empathy when a colleague had something to celebrate. She would eagerly proclaim "Mazel tov!" and her face would light up so much, you'd sense your win was hers, too. I intuited a good twin before me.

As I told Beth about these two twins of high self-esteem, I expected us to commiserate over the orneriness of the bad twin, and in doing so, mark ourselves as a cut above the rest. But to my surprise, Beth didn't follow my lead in othering the bad twin. Instead, she began to reflect on herself. "I'm trying to think about what's going on with me when I feel defensive. I am usually feeling unseen, unheard, insecure."

Beth's words led me to a flash of insight. We all have the same urges the bad twin does, to blame or get defensive, hostile, or vengeful. The difference, Beth showed me, is that good twins, like her, can acknowledge this is happening. Renowned therapists who were teaching me about how to become worthy, like Erich Fromm, Carl Rogers, and Karen Horney, sang in Beth's choir. They say we should acknowledge our every feeling—annoyance, anger, judgment, desperation, weakness, hurt, pity—as a welcome guest. Then, we won't need to hot-potato them to someone else. As psychologist Abraham Maslow put it, the secure exhibit a "lack of fear of their own insides of their own impulses, emotions, thoughts." Carl Rogers advised us to "admit [our] real self with its childish patterns, its aggressive feelings, and its ambivalences" because "we cannot move away from what we are, until we thoroughly accept what we are."

As I interviewed more people who were referred to me for having a strong sense of worth, they emphasized the importance of knowing their feelings, of welcoming the bad twin's urges within. They weren't just unafraid of their emotions. They sought communion with them. No feeling was too small to attend to. They'd search for them, cordoning off time for contemplation, justifying this act in their busy lives because they realized that in each feeling, they would find a part of themselves, too precious to let diffuse into oblivion. And that was their biggest priority—more important than resetting their bones to cast themselves into someone's definition of important—they wanted to know themselves, one sliver of feeling at a time.

Many of us squirm away from our hard feelings because we worry that if we acknowledge them, they'll grow. And this is a fair assumption. People who observed their feelings were *more* depressed months later, one study found. When people with panic disorder monitored their sensations, like heart rate, during a panic attack, they only felt more anxiety and panic. Acknowledging our feelings will make us feel worse—if we freak out about them.

But acknowledging our feelings is helpful if we use it as an opportunity to regulate them. While people who only observe their feelings experienced the highest levels of anxiety in one study's sample, people who observe *and* accept their feelings experienced the lowest. In another study, people who monitored *and* accepted their feelings had a more stable mood, less depression, and less anxiety than those who monitored alone.

Good twins aren't threatened by their feelings, because they regulate these feelings after they arise. This is the secret behind their kindness. While the good twins have hostile feelings, too, it is only when those feelings aren't regulated that they lead to hostile behavior. Some—like the bad twin—may confuse regulating feelings with suppressing them, a way many of us have been taught to deal with big emotions. But regulating them is more like turning toward them with open arms, allowing them in, feeling them through their ebb until they flow again. Good twins don't try to exile a feeling because it isn't "rational" (feelings are not subject to the rules of rationality), generalize them to mean something about them as a person, or label their feelings as bad. They wouldn't mark their defensiveness, hostility, or resentment as evidence of a "bad twin" within them because doing so would alienate the part of them in pain. Instead, no matter how small, uncomfortable, or even antisocial the feeling, they make space for it on the couch, comfort it, and thank it for showing up and revealing their deeper needs. And once they gather their feelings, they then infuse them with the faith that everything will be okay. It's this compassion for the self, one study found, that's linked to having more good twin–

like qualities—such as being slower to anger and not particularly self-absorbed* —more than self-esteem in itself is.

Good Twins Regulate Negative Feelings

Good twins I interviewed shared insights with me on how they practiced acknowledging and regulating their feelings. Helen, a woman in her early thirties who works in policy, reflected on how she listened to music to welcome her tears. "After a couple of songs ugly crying, I felt way better. A friend of mine says, 'Find a way to say it that makes you cry.' And I resonate a lot with that. Can you find a way of articulating it that just, like, brings tears to your eyes?" she said.

Another interviewee, Dr. Skyler Jackson, a forty-year-old professor, imparted his practice of attuning to his emotions. "I think you have to slow down and explore yourself . . . meditate on these things that may seem small . . . that can allow you to learn what small things are really small things and what small things really matter and have stuck with you. . . . Run your hand over these small things just to see if there's energy somewhere."

But why do bad twins struggle so much with being compassionate toward their negative emotions? To understand the psychology of the bad twin, imagine a friend who hides their mess—a metaphor, here, for their negative emotions—in their closet. All their dirty clothes, shoes with worn soles, near empty bottles of lotion are tossed in their closet. Their room looks organized, and they can say they're an organized person. They wouldn't even be lying, by all appearances. But just because the mess is hidden, doesn't mean it is not there.

"Hey. What happened to that hoodie you borrowed?" you ask this friend one day, innocently. It's crumpled in a heap in the closet. But your friend doesn't say that. Instead, to your surprise, they get feral,

* By *not particularly self-absorbed*, I mean that people who are more compassionate, in the study, were less likely to compare themselves with others, ruminate on things that happen to them, or focus on how they're being perceived.

"What hoodie? I returned it months ago. Why don't you remember? Are you dumb?" They're so incensed because you didn't just bring up a hoodie. The hoodie symbolizes the heaps of shame locked behind that closet door.

Eventually, because none of their shame has been processed, it becomes so colossal that any slight can trigger it. When the trigger arises along with the mountain of shame it's attached to, the bad twin's self-esteem plummets. They get feral, again. In Safiya Sinclair's memoir *How to Say Babylon*, she describes how this dynamic was true for her father when she was growing up in Jamaica. Sinclair recounts how the "chaos of [her] father's interior life" manifested as cruelty toward her: "He was never good at managing his disappointments or tempering frustration without firebombing the nearest person." One night, while she was writing in her bedroom, her father came by to harangue her for not taking more physics or economics classes in high school, so she'd be more successful now. When she told him she was writing poetry, he said, "You're really worthless." When her poetry was later published in Jamaica's newspaper, the *Jamaica Observer*, he accused her of writing for white people and hurled the newspaper at her.

Denying that your negative emotions exist is the modus operandi of the bad twin, studies find. That's why bad twins *say* they have high self-esteem; they simply ignore any feelings that suggest they don't. And yet, it's a costly defense mechanism. Because they have no practice being with their negative feelings, they struggle all the more when situations force them to. One study found that when emotional compartmentalizers were rejected—playing catch with others and not getting thrown the ball—they felt *more* rejected and their self-esteem fell *more* than non-compartmentalizers. Because they compartmentalize, bad twins—unlike people with low self-esteem—feel great about themselves when everything is copacetic. But at any hint of rejection, the avalanche of clothes forces open the closet door. When they're confronted with the mess that is locked away, their sense of self will violently swing to the negative . . . and their civility will follow suit.

Of course, all of us wig out like bad twins sometimes, when it's been a tough day, or we're in a bout of depression or burnout. Having to confront our feelings all the time is exhausting work. To see the good and bad twins as mutually exclusive categories, then, is too simplistic. And even for those of us who hover around bad twin–like behaviors more regularly, that category doesn't define you. It can shift. I'll teach you how throughout *Worth.*

Maybe understanding the bad twin's experience makes you feel some compassion for them, whether you are them or have known them. As we'll explore more later, when bad twins are slighted, they are gobsmacked with a lifetime's worth of shame, as all the humiliation locked in their closet bursts out. They feel like they're lit on fire. No wonder they have to pass that torch to someone else. Here's how this all plays out internally for the bad twin: Let's say the bad twin hurt someone's feelings and that person told them so. The bad twin's body interprets this to mean that they're bad at their core, all unprocessed feelings of unworthiness firing at once. The negative reaction punctures the bad twin's sense of self so deeply that it's all there is. It feels like being stabbed. The pain of the person they hurt doesn't exist on its own, as valid, but as mere prologue for the bad twin's pain. The bad twin's primal anger leaps out to close the wound. The anger moves in so quickly, so desperately that the bad twin can't make out their own vulnerable feelings underneath. So they respond—*They're dramatic, sensitive, pathetic. That's why they're hurt.* That feels better.

Meanwhile, the good twin soothes their shame every time it arises, so it's not contagious. Good twins have learned that what lurks in their closet is not to be escaped. The closet is just another room to explore in the house of yourself. The bad twins board up the closet, neglecting what happens within it, to the peril of themselves and others. What makes the good twin so kind, and distinct from the bad one, is that they *know how to be with pain.*

WHAT IT MEANS TO FEEL WORTHY

The secret to the good twin's kind of self-esteem, the one aligned with how I see worth, is found in facing your emotions, or being with pain, as I've referred to it. Secure-ish people have learned to do this, too, through a process of sensitivity and responsiveness. When they were kids, their caregivers practiced *sensitivity* by recognizing and validating their feelings, rather than denying them, and *responsiveness* by acting to meet the needs revealed by their feelings. Their sense of worth came from someone consistently treating their feelings and needs and thus themselves as if they mattered.

Sensitivity means you know when you're tired. Responsiveness means you ask your body if it prefers to rest on its back or its side. Sensitivity means picking up on your dread at an unachievable deadline. Responsiveness means bargaining for more time. Sensitivity means you're aware that you chronically feel crummy after hanging out with that friend who communicates in backhanded compliments—*That new haircut is so interesting. So kind of you to give an amateur stylist a chance.* Responsiveness means you ask them to stop. Cultivating sensitivity and responsiveness doesn't mean you always get your way. But it does mean that if you have the privilege of options, you don't habituate to your discomfort. Nor do you get lost in the shuffle of your own life, living for someone else, as you're churned into jobs, relationships, or identities that never feel like home. To feel worth is not an end state and more of an exercise. It means to practice sensitivity and responsiveness within, treating your inner world as if it matters. These steps, collectively, are called attuning to yourself.

It's culture-clashing enough for me to recommend that you be sensitive and acknowledge and feel through even your most seemingly trivial feelings. But responsiveness means that it is not enough to have a feeling. You must *use* the feeling. Far from seeing feelings as a nuisance, I'm suggesting that feelings are the guides we need to pay attention to to live our most authentic, worthy life. Here is an example from a friend who shared her rough dating situation with me: The guy she was seeing slid in and out of her life, his presence as reliable as pulling three cherries on a slot machine. She said she *did* have high self-esteem—she really did feel good about herself, she claimed—but somehow, she kept finding herself in these painful dating situations.

I shared with her something I learned from bell hooks's *All about Love*: "To have high self-esteem," I told her, "is not just to feel good about yourself, but to demand others treat you in a way that reflects that." It's this connection between feeling her pain and then following through into changing her dating situation that turns sensitivity into responsiveness.

I reject defining self-esteem as simply "feeling good about oneself," knowing that relying on this simple description can lead people to harm others who threaten this story of their own goodness. It can also lead people to suppress their negative feelings toward themselves. My definition of self-esteem is rooted in awareness of feelings. This is called *attunement*—being able to notice, identify, and acknowledge the feelings (good and bad) that flash by in each moment. This attunement to self is at the core of both true self-esteem and this new definition of worth that is at the heart of this book.

To feel worth, then, we must, ironically, be able to feel and then admit when we feel unworthy. Good twins, for example, told me they sometimes felt insecure, but their insecurities were okay, emotionally neutral territory. "First let me share that I don't always have high self-esteem, and I didn't always feel this way," one interviewee said to start off our interview. Without shame shrouding their insecurities, they fluidly switched back to security. The paradox of the self, therapists argue, is that the more we welcome all sides of ourselves, even the bruised and brittle sides, the more secure we become.

HOW SELF-ESTEEM CHANGES WHEN WE START TO ATTUNE

Learning about how those with high self-esteem cherish their feelings left me keen to be more aware of my own, even those I typically didn't acknowledge. I got to practice when a friend texted me to hang out. Earlier in the year, we had yearned, together, for a friend group to roll deep with, rather than spreading ourselves threadbare across individual friendships. So as we were hatching dinner plans, I proposed that we invite some other friends, too. But she didn't want to.

"Do you mind if we do a one-on-one hang/catch-up . . . and then we can all plan something sometime soon?" she wrote.

"Yes. That's fine," my fingers started to type, urgently. Urgency, to me, is a signal that I'm trying to escape a feeling. I kneaded out the dough of my emotions and recognized the bad twin's urges inside me. I felt rejected and offended that my friend had dismissed my suggestion, especially after we had discussed otherwise. That part of me wanted to insist on a group hang, to vindicate my offer and myself. But then a counterforce inside me freaked out about me having feelings I didn't want me to have. *How silly of you to get offended. Let it go,* the people-pleasing part of me said, desperate to trap me in a cage of my own kindness. I was stuck in a web between the dueling spiders of my own unacceptable emotions and the urge to abolish them.

This urge to stifle my feelings reminded me of something that occurred at a speaking event I held. This event took on the emotional tone of group therapy, as women shared their friendship struggles to faces filled with empathy.

"My friend told me they are struggling. Every time I reach out to them, they don't respond, but I see them posting on Instagram. I'm upset, but am I not giving them enough grace?" one woman asked, looking deflated.

"My friend gave me a list of all the problems she has with me," said another, "and I feel so put down that I want to take space from the friendship. Is that bad?"

Another woman shared, "I just had a miscarriage, and my friend had a baby. I want to celebrate her, but it triggers my grief. Am I a bad friend?"

These women knew they felt rejection, betrayal, and grief, but as soon as their own feelings bubbled up, they tamped them down, afraid of what these feelings meant about them.

"Women will destroy their sense of self in the name of grace for others," I said, looking out to the audience of women. This observation had been percolating inside me, well, likely since birth, but more acutely, as I heard their stories. From what I had learned about sensitivity and responsiveness, I wanted to encourage these women to be okay with how they felt and even, if necessary, to advocate for themselves on behalf of these feelings. After I conveyed this insight, the room went silent and then burst into a wave of mm-hmms so loud that my co-speaker, the friendship expert Danielle Bayard Jackson, and I had to pause so we wouldn't be drowned out by them.

Men also face these pressures to mis-attune to themselves, but often in the name of "duty" rather than "grace." "Being a man is putting everybody else first, and your needs going last . . . your needs down the toilet," Mariano Martelletti, a forty-year-old Argentine therapist told me. He was socialized *not* to rest when he wanted to, *not* to have preferences for what to eat, and *not* to listen to his own inner voice about what he wanted to do for fun. "Man up and get used to life sucking" were words he lived by. He was doing everything "right," working a fancy job as a corporate leadership trainer. It wasn't supposed to matter that he hated it—but to his body, it did. He started having panic attacks, ones that subsided only when he demoted himself and started resting and treating himself kindly.

In that moment I was texting my friend back, I realized that even as I had clocked those women months ago back at that speaking event, *I was one of them.* I didn't want to be like a graceful woman or a dutiful man. *Acknowledge these emotions*, I reminded myself. I paused to witness my emotional chain reaction. I physically felt my hurt and noticed how I carried its heft in my stomach. I detected my people-pleasing, too—

how my heartbeat hastened out of fear of what might happen if I wasn't so kind anymore.

I then set out to regulate these feelings. After calmly tracking the presence of the emotions in my body, I tried to love each prickly feeling for being brave enough to show up. *Thanks for telling me you're here. I want to hear you both. We're going to try to do something new. I'm going to unlock you from your basement and welcome you to the living room.* Once I did, my feelings freed me, no longer lording over my text response, jerking me to type back whatever calmed their frenzied fears.

It was only through this process of identifying and then feeling my emotions—attuning—that I could distinguish what I really wanted from my friend. It turns out, I *did* want to hang with this friend one-on-one, too. My knee-jerk reaction against her proposal was born of unexamined hurt (*I'm being disregarded*). But this urge did not represent what the truest version of me wanted; it represented what a *hurt* part of me did. Once I acknowledged this hurt, it dissolved, and I could see that I did, in fact, want to spend time with my friend alone. We had a private catch-up and then we met up with our larger group later, just as I'd hoped we could.

An important lesson in the process of attunement is that we must follow it through to the end—not just acknowledging our feelings but also regulating them so they give us enough space for us to see what's left over. If I'd stopped too early in this process of attunement—being aware of but not regulating my feelings—I wouldn't have understood what I truly wanted. Our neuroses, as Maslow put it, represent "not part of the inner core but rather a defense against or an evasion of it." Attunement pushes us to molt the skins of our self-protection and discover our true feelings underneath. When we engage in the process of attunement over and over, treating ourselves repeatedly as if we matter, we develop worth.

As a psychologist who could die happy drowning in a pool of self-help books, I considered myself self-aware. I was used to acknowledging my emotions when they were obvious. But this one-two punch of emotion and counter-emotion had flashed through me quickly—so quickly that I had only noticed they were there because I was prowling for them. This granular level of emotional awareness I was learning about, this come-hither openness to the minutiae of my feelings, *this* was new for me.

I was beginning to see why this precise level of attunement was necessary. Typically, these micro feelings were so threatening that my psyche tucked them away before I was even aware of them. Yet these banished emotions were where my deep healing work lay. My body vanquished these feelings because they were the ones mired in the most shame. In performing its disappearing act, my body said *I will protect you from peril, from feelings you've learned are so abominable that their very presence will mark you as rotten.* But in doing so, it was leaving that threatening emotion undigested, left there to possess me, until the next time around. What the good twin knows is that it is only through feeling even our most warded-off feelings that they will release their control over us, now and in the future.

It wasn't just these feelings my body was trying to escape, I realized. It was also the shame that had become married to them, invading these feelings like an infection. In my childhood, I was often told I was too sensitive, which has led me to hide some negative reactions from others and myself so quickly that I often didn't know they were even there. But in acknowledging and regulating them, I was proclaiming that it was okay that these feelings existed—and, thus, cleansing them of their shame. This shame had been squirreled away deep inside these emotions, and facing it meant more parts of me lived. I was on a precipice, gazing into the valley of my vitality, one I could only get to if I dove through a crust of every emotion I had never felt.

Acknowledging (and regulating) antisocial feelings is an act that challenges what many of us were taught to do with our feelings. To be good, we've been told, means to never feel annoyed, hostile, or resentful toward anyone. But to be truly loving, the good twins show us, means to become more aware of and accepting toward these negative emotions, rather than judging ourselves for having them. The regular practice of treating our every feeling as worthy—of acknowledgment and care—culminates in a sense of worth.

WHY WORTHINESS MAKES US TREAT OTHERS BETTER

Some people may claim to have high self-esteem, but the true test is found in how they treat others. True love for self amplifies love for others. Yet many thinkers saw these two forms of love as clashing. Immanuel Kant, for example, said pleasure in oneself must be "battered down" and we should feel "humiliated" so we could humble ourselves enough to be moral. Philosopher Max Stirner stated, "love knows only sacrifice and demands self-sacrifice."

But social psychologist Erich Fromm, rattling convention, thought that to be truly loving is to have a certain "readiness to love" that is freely applied to self and others. If we proclaim to love all of humankind, then why should we be our own exception? In having this "readiness to love," the more we love ourselves, the less selfish we become, Fromm argued. While other thinkers saw selfish people as self-loving, Fromm disagreed, which he implied when he asked, "Was his selfishness identical with self-love or was it instead rooted in the very lack of it?" Selfish people are self-less, he said, remixing how we typically use the term; they have no rooted self to anchor them, so they grab outward.

Part of the reason good twins treat others better is because they can see others more clearly. As Abraham Maslow put it, "This approval and acceptance of their deeper selves then made it more possible to perceive bravely the real nature of the world." Now, I know what he meant. When I acknowledged my triggers, I no longer perceived my friend's actions through the lens of them. Although I knew this intellectually when she sent the text, now my nervous system knew, too, that her wanting to hang out one-on-one was not a rejection of my suggestion, and thus myself. It was a sign of how invested she was in our friendship.

Fromm's words, my own experience of deeper attunement, and the research findings helped me understand why people with each profile of high self-esteem—with their opposing relationships to pain—treated others so differently. I imagined the two profiles of high self-esteem, one as a funnel, and the other as a corkscrew. The funnel, mouth agape at the tip, was ready to be fed by others' praise, adoration, supplication. Unable to feed its sense of self—by experiencing and regulating their emotion, in this case—it could never stay full. For its satiety, then, others had to cease to contain their multitudes; they had to become feeders. But the other profile was shaped like a corkscrew. As they went inward and anchored themselves, they came outward to check on others, chanting as they went 'round, I'm here for you through being here for me.

HOW WORTHY PEOPLE PRACTICE ATTUNEMENT

Once you start being more attuned to yourself and your emotions, you will begin to feel more authentic. You'll not only come to know who you are, but you'll also have the self-esteem to live that truth. Your relationships with yourself and with others will start to change. And those changes are going to ripple outward and affect how you view larger society.

If you're insecure, however, you may have trouble seeing the ways society is not quite sane. You've learned you're only worthy if you fulfill others' expectations. *Don't make a fuss. Be perfect. Pretzel yourself into who others want you to be.* At first, with your caregivers, and later with another all-knowing authority, society. *Yes, I won't question that policy because it's what the higher-ups want and I need to please them. Of course, I want to get married and have two children, a boy and a girl, because that's what society has told me to want, so it must be right. Yes, I'll work forty hours a week at my desk job I hate. And injustice must be okay because everyone else is okay with it.*

When we lose our authenticity at a young age and replace our inner wisdom with an ideology offered by society, we "become normal" according to Fromm. When we are "normal," we don't experience internal conflict between who we truly are and what we are expected to be. How can there be a discrepancy between our sense of self and the outside world when our sense of self has long disappeared?

Instead, we often blame ourselves for our discontent—*I'm not grateful enough; I'm too picky, too needy, expecting too much; I don't have what it takes.* This is because, as Fromm argues, society compels people to internalize an ideology of self-denial rather than attunement. *I don't like this, but it must be me. I don't know any better.* We are ready to sign the contract for an eighty-hour workweek, to become the barista who smiles at the customers who condescend to her, or the friend who martyrs herself in the name of womanly grace.

Once self-denial becomes part of our values, we don't resist it like we would if we saw it for what it is, an ideology fed to us, so we relinquish our agency. This explains why even when we might be aware of our unease, we respond to it with distrust, skepticism, and downright hostility, Fromm described. To challenge self-denial, when it has formed at the core of our learned beliefs, becomes an act of self-denial. The call must come from inside the house.

Once this sense of self is lost, and we are without a strong internal compass, we are more likely to assimilate into cultures of harm. Hannah Arendt famously emphasized the "banality of evil" when she observed Nazis and found they were "terrifyingly normal." In the late psychologist Philip Zimbardo's Stanford Prison Experiment, he had college students assume the roles of prison guards and prisoners to determine whether taking on a role could compel unethical behavior. Guards made the prisoners strip naked, use buckets as toilets, and hump each other. When Zimbardo's girlfriend, Christina, visited the prison, she ran out crying. She wasn't sure she could be with Zimbardo if he condoned this behavior. "I don't know who you are," she said. Later on, Zimbardo reflected, "And really what she's saying [is] 'do you know who you are?' And the answer is no . . . what I had become is abhorrent."

When we instead listen to our internal compass, the one pointing in a different direction from the crowd, when we tune in to the niggling feeling that a situation is not right for us, that is us tapping into our worth. We're attuning to our true feelings. Our sense of self-esteem is guiding us on another path. We'll no longer conflate what is normal with what is right. Instead, we'll ask ourselves, *Do I think this is correct?* We'll bristle against norms others have surrendered to. We'll push back against injustices others don't see. This will be bittersweet; sweet because living a more authentic life is inherently rewarding. But because you're focused on attuning to yourself in a society that impels you to conform, you may find yourself in bitter friction with those around you, like Laura was.

Laura was a twenty-three-year-old at war with her bosses. Working in a hospice center, she was encouraged to dissolve the wall of professionalism separating employee and patient and to have a genuine human experience with the dying. While she loved the approach theoretically, in practice, the lack of boundaries meant women who worked there were often sexually harassed. Laura had been spoken to disrespectfully, and she had seen others be touched inappropriately. One patient had even pulled one of the young female employees into his bed beside him. She told her bosses they needed a policy to address sexual harassment and protect her and her fellow workers, but they were unresponsive. After she repeatedly raised the issue, one boss even yelled at her.

But Laura had hit the jackpot when it came to her family. Her lineage was composed of generations of attuned parents. When Laura's grandfather asked her what she did for work, she told him she was a therapist. He had trouble understanding what that was. "Good luck on your interviews," he'd tell her. When she explained that she listened to people to help them heal from their problems, he told her, "Well, your grandma was a therapist, too, then." This emotional intelligence had trickled down to Laura's parents, who had always apologized when they hurt her, invited her to share her opinions with their friends, and listened to what she had to say. She'd been equipped with the tools to develop high self-esteem and an inherent sense of worth, and that's what gave her the strength to push back in a situation that she knew wasn't okay.

But as Laura found, many so-called professional workplaces don't enable attunement like her family did. Erich Fromm in *The Sane Society* envisioned a workplace, and even a larger culture, designed to support people, not just institutions. Imagine a workplace where annual evaluations looked like your boss asking you if you *like* the work and if it's helping you grow into who you want to become. A workplace where, when you left your job, your boss would be elated because you'd be choosing a better path for yourself. A job where, when you turned down overtime, your boss told you they're proud you're taking care of yourself. One where self-esteem was celebrated, not challenged. That kind of attuned workplace is all too rare.

Within and outside the workplace, a sane society would be one that encourages people to express who they are—in all their individual glory. In the book *Self-Care for Autistic People: 100+ Ways to Recharge, De-Stress, and Unmask!*, author Dr. Megan Anna Neff describes how unmasking, or revealing one's true, authentic, autistic self, is emotionally regulating. As autistic people twirl, clap, rock, or express themselves more directly, they also regulate how they feel. They feel calmer, lighter, happier. While this is particularly true for autistic people who must contort themselves to fit into society more than allistic people do, this is also true for the rest of us. The more authentic we are, the more emotionally healthy we are. Authenticity is not just correlated with well-being, a meta-analysis found; researchers have described it as the very *essence* of well-being.

Laura's sense of worth equipped her to speak up about the indignities of her hospice job and demand change despite a culture where she'd be prized for her silence. And in a culture pressing you to self-deny, attunement is costly. She could advocate for the sexual assault policy at her job and find herself without one. Or she could keep her head down and witness her own and others' daily indignities but still get a paycheck. Neither choice is more noble. Each fulfills different needs. Attuning to yourself is not about always expressing what you want, but about realizing you have choices, and that expressing yourself is one of them. Only when she attuned to herself could Laura even realize that she had a choice.

THE MANY FACES OF ATTUNEMENT

Up to now, I've sold you a story of attunement that's incomplete. Yes, attunement is about acknowledging and regulating your feelings. But feelings are much more than our reaction to something in the present. As I alluded to when I discussed the psychology of the bad twin, each time an emotion crops up, so does its history. When you're sad, you experience that sadness arising now, along with the waves of past sadness you haven't yet felt.

When we avoid our emotions, they compound. That's why it's so hard for the bad twin to acknowledge their flaws. It's not one imperfection they'd be acknowledging, but every instance they've felt bad and escaped the feeling by attacking someone else. It's also why anxiously attached people have trouble self-soothing. When a crush doesn't respond to a text, the anxious person is ambushed by a history of undigested abandonment. Similarly, when the avoidant person experiences intimacy, they reexperience the unprocessed feelings of danger and threat that have been entangled with intimacy in their past. If attunement means feeling not just a feeling, but also a lineage of feelings, then it can become unbearable, like it was for Ashley.

Ashley, a lawyer working with kids in foster care, would, on some days, have eleven back-to-back hearings. On her schedule, she'd put a block that said "Stop now" to get herself to stop working, and then later, another that said "Really stop." Every other weekend she was on call for emergency cases. She'd have to drop everything, find the child in potential danger, and investigate whether there was probable cause to terminate parental rights, all within forty-eight hours.

Ashley was also the only Black woman at her workplace, and she endured various indignities because of it. During her evaluations, she was told she needed to smile more, feedback she reported to her higher-ups. The diversity trainer at her organization pulled up a picture of Lil Wayne during a meeting and asked everyone if they agreed that he looked like a monkey. While her colleagues laughed anxiously, Ashley responded, "There is nothing you can do to convince me that man looks like a monkey."

And now, her colleagues, threatened by the ways she had broken convention to fight for families to stay together, were polluting the climate further. They started to review her records, reprimanding her for lapses in punctuation. They arranged for a supervisor to attend each of her hearings on the children's cases and provide feedback after each.

"I didn't even realize these things upset me until years later," Ashley reflected. In her childhood, she learned to "survive the unsurvivable," so at work, she did, too. "I was a fighter. And so, when I ran up to an obstacle, I just kept fighting." Ashley was destroying herself to succeed at work, ambling forward, disconnected from the cues, her feelings, that warned of her undoing. By year two, the stress had taken its toll. Ashley was gaunt, sipping cans of Ensure throughout the day to replace the food she couldn't keep down.

Ashley endured so much at work because she had shut off the spigot of her feelings in her childhood. As I asked her about her childhood, her vivid storytelling became hazy. Her pace went from a jog to a saunter. She offered me breadcrumbs—that she'd endured physical punishment that escalated the more she let on that it hurt—"Stop crying or I'll [*sic*] give you something to cry about"—but then she relented and said that these were memories she'd only begun to process in therapy and even there, only in bite-sized chunks. "I go back to these really painful moments where it was wrong to cry, but I can't describe what I felt in my body, because that's a different version of me. I can't get into vivid memories from my childhood because most of it I disassociated from."

Ashley underwent harm still unspeakable. And when that harm

occurred, she was not allowed to acknowledge her pain. So when pain comes now, it hits her like a wrecking ball, heavy with the history of past pain, still undigested.

When work stress exploded, Ashley set aside time to weep in the shower. As her tears materialized, so did a lifetime of tears that had been stuck in their waiting room. Yes, she wept for the mistreatment at work. She also wept for the kids she couldn't help, the ones locked in revolving doors of foster families. She wept for herself, too, because she had been a mistreated kid herself. As her tears surfaced, so did a lifetime of terror. She wept, while she shook with fear because of what she had learned that it meant to weep, how it revealed her weaknesses so they could be pressed into later. And this bulbous knot that was her feelings, the veins of grief and terror it held, was incapacitating. She crumpled on the floor crying until her body couldn't bear it anymore.

Then the numbness came, like an act of mercy.

For those of us lumbering along, weighed down by the baggage of unresolved past emotions, it's not too late. We need to return to our history, revisit the feelings lodged there, and somehow set them free. Then we can attune to our feelings in the present without being debilitated, like Ashley and the bad twin were. In part 2 of this book, you'll learn how to do this.

The same word—*attunement*—lands so differently depending on who we are. For people with low self-esteem, each feeling is braided with a sense of shame they must confront every time they feel. They are left scorched by the hot iron of their feelings, sometimes passing the iron to whoever is next in line, and sometimes just not feeling at all. They reveal that self-esteem issues are feelings issues: Feelings don't flow through but get stuck, bogging down our sense of self.

And we need another word for attunement for Helen and Skyler and Laura, whose every feeling is interlaced with its own medicine, woven with memories of *I'm here*, *I love you*, and *I want to hear you*.

"Feel your feelings" sounds simple, but not when, in practice, it means "feel the entire history of this feeling"; and not when, in practice, it means "confront the current of danger pulsing through each feeling." The work of this book is to unbraid what our body has come to intertwine with our feelings, to put the medicine there instead.

Then, we can bear to attune to ourselves.

One day in the spring of 2024, I sat with my friend Steven at a café at the university where he teaches. Between nibbles of my sandwich, I told him about this book, about the irony that people with the most thorough version of high self-esteem aren't focused on having high self-esteem at all. They're not cruising for a certain reputation, hell-bent on being right or amassing markers of status.

"Worthiness," he pondered, ". . . that sounds like you're still evaluating yourself. What you're describing seems like getting to a place where you're beyond self-evaluation, where you're just letting all parts of yourself flow."

"You're right," I replied. "The goal of the book isn't to get to a place where I can say 'I am worthy.'"

"Then what is it?"

"To get to *I am.*"

2

The Theory That Changed Everything

Do you remember diet culture in the nineties? It was a total disaster. Be grateful if you weren't alive for it (although otherwise, the nineties were pretty dope). Crash diets were all the rage, and you were supposed to subsist on things like cayenne pepper and lemon juice, or premade shakes, or grapefruit, or some other foul concoction for a period of time to drop the pounds, *fast.* You might have tried one (or all) of them. And they might have worked, for a moment. But the fine print didn't tell you that you'd yo-yo back to your original weight, plus some extra for posterity. Biology, it turns out, is stubborn.

Cue despair, because, yes, you failed. But the depths of despair came from you failing at something you were told you *should* succeed at. The only viable explanation for my failed diets, chubby younger me thought, was that *I* was a failure, and I should feel that in my big bones.

While you've been working on becoming more secure, you might be startled by flashbacks of nineties' diet culture. You are gritting your teeth, following the rules like they're the Ten Commandments. But your unwieldy body—or nervous system, in this case—still does what it wants. No matter how hard you try to be less anxious, more confident, and more secure-ish, you struggle to succeed. And it feels like it's all your fault.

I've studied this for years, and I'm here to tell you: It's not your fault. If you understand the science of the self, you'll see why our psyches fight us every step of the way as we try to feel worthy, just like our bodies fight us when we put them through a crash diet.

In part 2 of this book, we'll find a way to do it anyway.

TRIGGERED BY SUCCESS

Jerry is a pastor with a corresponding "big church-pastor look," as he puts it: a six-foot-tall, 185-pound white man with brown hair and blue eyes. Straight out of seminary school, he spoke at a church of five thousand, with jumbo screens amplifying his message. He went on to teach as a "preaching professor" and has trained one thousand pastors across the country.

To help the church reach millennials, he developed Last Call, a program of preaching from a bar. Determined to meet his congregation where they were, Jerry sermonized on a bar stool, beer in hand, to millennials listening as they packaged peanut butter and jelly sandwiches for the unhoused. When the press caught wind of these sermons, he became a sought-after speaker at churches all over the country, talking about alternative ways to worship.

With all his accomplishments, most people see Jerry as, in his words, "ragingly successful."

But he doesn't feel that way.

After he spoke at a conference for church leaders who think outside the box, Jessica Miller Kelley, a magazine editor turned book editor, approached him. "Remember me, Jerry? I published the first magazine article you wrote about your church-in-bars idea. Do you want to write a book?"

Jerry *did* want to write a book. He had wanted to for years, ever since he surrendered his dream of being a comedian to pursue a more stable one as a pastor. It'd be about people, like him, who had colossal dreams that didn't happen: the football player aspiring to play in the NFL but who injured his knee, or the lawyer who never made partner. But even with ideas swirling, and an editor courting him, something niggling held him back from saying yes. He needed to think about it. He felt uneasy about the idea.

The prospect of success activated what he calls his "negative tape" or "earworm." It butts in when he's doing well to remind him that he is, at his core, a failure. If he worked on this book idea, the earworm told him, it would get rejected. When the deal was eventually signed and he published *Last Call: From Serving Drinks to Serving Jesus*, the tape played to say it was a fluke. When he sold his second book, *Rogue Saints: Spirituality for Good-Hearted Heathens*, the earworm piped up again with, "This new book deal is smaller than your last, so it doesn't count." Success is so triggering for people who feel unworthy because it propels their internal critic to remind them that they don't deserve what they've been given. This makes their success, counterintuitively, anguishing.

Jerry's reaction sheds light on *self-verification theory*, which will help us understand why it's so difficult to feel worthy. Self-verification theory indicates that we want others to see us as we see ourselves—even when we see ourselves as failures. Self-verification theory explains why studies find that people with low self-esteem felt *worse* after compliments and were more likely to dismiss them. When they gave a speech and got positive feedback, their blood pressure spiked. And they don't even like praise coming from themselves. When they repeated "I am lovable" at the sound of a beep, they felt worse afterward.

It's reasonable to think people who feel unworthy would need approval more than other people, to assume praise would be the medicine that soothes their psychic blisters. If someone had to devise a cure for Jerry's unworthiness struggles, they might naively prescribe that he do exactly what he's done: find a prestigious job, acquire a band of followers, and secure book deals.

Yet people who feel unworthy respond to their achievements by deflecting all evidence of good in themselves. Success only leaves them sinking in a quicksand of inadequacy, roiled by hisses of self-criticism, or scampering on the hamster wheel of achievement that goes nowhere.

Tragically, signals of worth don't cleanse our feelings of inferiority but rather only reveal how firmly rooted they are.

THE THINGS WE THINK WILL MAKE US FEEL WORTHY (BUT DON'T)

Like Jerry, you may have wondered, *Maybe if I finally find the right job, get the right body, or date the right person, I'll feel good enough.* But you may increasingly find that these efforts are fruitless.

We turn to our work for that rush of worth. We become the doctor or lawyer, or leader, in Jerry's case, that our parents always dreamed of. But once we do, we find that the prestige does not heal us. In fact, one meta-analysis found that while self-esteem improves job success, job success doesn't improve self-esteem at all.*

In the Anglo-Swiss philosopher Alain de Botton's essay "The Secret Sorrows of Over-Achievers," he argues that overachievers work so hard not because they enjoy what they do, but because they are trying "to correct an aspect of a troubled emotional past . . . to solve a range of psychological problems through material or worldly means," which indicates their efforts to use their success to propel their worth are doomed. He goes on to explain that when overachievers finally achieve whatever it is they've been seeking, they are at risk of "severe

* Being employed and having a better income were each weakly correlated with higher self-esteem.

breakdown" because "so long as they are merely running, they can forget to notice that their goal is misaligned with their true inner ambition." Raise your hand, reader, if you feel personally attacked by de Botton's profile. Now, put your hand down, because we're overachievers and we don't admit weakness here. I promise I'm still in therapy.

We may try to find worth by achieving the physique we are conditioned to value. But doing that won't heal us either. While a meta-analysis found that participating in a weight-loss intervention boosted self-esteem, five of the six reviewed studies found that losing weight did not. It was *participating* in the weight-loss intervention itself, which provided camaraderie and helped people feel less alone in their struggles, that boosted self-esteem. Losing weight made no difference.

In an episode of *This American Life* called "Tell Me I'm Fat," a producer on the podcast, Elna Baker, shared how she lost more than 110 pounds from phentermine, a medication similar in composition to speed. Living as a thin person forced her to come to terms with the depressing reality of how badly fat people are treated. She got a boyfriend shortly after losing the weight. One night he told her he'd fallen for her the moment he'd seen her, a few months before at a building barbecue. But they'd lived in the same building for four years. In fact, they'd first met shortly after she'd moved in, back when she was still heavy, and she had even knocked on his door to borrow a hammer. When she'd returned it, they'd talked for twenty minutes. But he'd completely forgotten who heavy Elna was. She had deep ambivalence over her weight loss, remarking, "It's sad that new Elna gets everything old Elna wanted, because I think old Elna was a better person than new Elna."

Why won't the new job or the new body save us? Why can't we assume that gorgeous, intelligent, accomplished people feel worthy? It's because changing our sense of worth is much harder than changing our qualities. It requires us to change our theory of who we are.

WORTH AS A THEORY OF SELF

In Detroit in the fall of 1979, Jerry and his friend Tim were complaining about how they didn't have dates for the high school homecoming. As they entered Jerry's house, still commiserating, Jerry noticed that his sister, who lived ten minutes away, was unexpectedly home. If he'd paused to notice, he might have also realized his mother seemed distraught. But he didn't. He was too caught up in not getting girls. He announced, "Well, looks like Tim and I don't have dates for homecoming."

"It's worse than that," his sister said. "You don't even have a dad."

In the time between when Jerry left for school that morning and when he got home after it, his dad had left the family. He scribbled his reasons on a note that no one would let Jerry see. But the gist of it was that he was having an affair with his administrative assistant. The news hit Jerry hard. "If my friends wanted to go out and do something and my dad said 'Hey. Do you want to go with me to buy nails at Ace Hardware?' I'd go, 'Sorry, guys. I'm gonna go buy the nails.' I idolized, just worshipped, that guy." By the time his dad left, his older siblings had already moved out. Jerry was left to care for his shattered mom by himself.

His dad returned a year later, saying it was too cruel to leave your kid in the middle of high school. But then, in Jerry's senior year, he came home to another note from his father. This one said he was leaving for good, because he'd realized there's really no great time to leave your kid so he might as well leave now.

The abandonment ravaged Jerry's sense of worth. "When your primary hero symbolically kicks you to the curb, it's easy to make the leap and go . . . if he's going to walk out, anybody could. He was the one guy I thought would never do that. There's no way he would do that. And he did. And then built my confidence back and did it all over again two years later."

Our sense of worth is not just how good we feel about ourselves. It's the bedrock of our sense of reality. It's a theory about ourselves that we use to predict how others will respond to us. If we feel unworthy, our theory is that others will reject us. If we feel worthy, we assume they will accept us. We filter reality so it aligns with this theory. Unworthiness, then, acts as a kind of distorted filter on life: We internalize data confirming we're unlovable but filter out anything suggesting our lovability.

After the abandonments from his father, Jerry's theory calcified. Successes didn't "count." In fact, they became threats luring him to feel better about himself so he'd only fall farther the next time things went south. It didn't matter how many books he sold, peanut butter and jelly sandwiches he donated, or people who hung on his every word.

He was still a failure.

WHY WE NEED A THEORY

In 1845, measles swept through Hannibal, Missouri. Tiny bodies lay rigid in caskets at the funerals that took place almost daily. The rest of the kids, along with their mothers, were terrified they'd soon be stricken, too.

Jane Lampton Clemens did everything she could to quarantine her children, Orion, Pamela, Henry, and Sam. But to Sam, the constant threat of getting sick, the agonizing uncertainty, soon became worse than the disease itself. Sam had heard of another kid, Will Bowen, who had a mean case of measles. He went to Will's house and snuck up the stairs and into Will's room. But Will's mother caught him and shooed him away.

Undeterred, Sam peeked through cracks in the fence bordering Will's house until the coast was clear. He snuck back up to Will's room and scooched into bed with him, as close to the sick boy as he could. Will was too sick to notice Sam was there, but Will's mom found him, grabbed him by the collar, and personally escorted him home.

Predictably, Sam was struck with a horrific case of the measles, but also with the ironic comfort that he had controlled his fate. He no longer had to face uncertainty, to endure the existential dread of powerlessness. He was in control, and life was again predictable.

Sam Clemens became a famous author. You might know him by his pen name, Mark Twain. Twain's story reveals our deep need to know what's coming, for life to be predictable. We do this by establishing a theory of self that allows us to predict how the world will respond to us. And we look to others to verify our theory of self. If information conveys that our theory is off, it means that we can't forecast the future. Nothing is predictable. Our world feels chaotic. It means that *anything* could happen; disaster could strike at any time, and we won't be ready. In this way, uncertainty (*I might at any moment get measles*) is actually worse than knowing a bad outcome (*I have measles*).

When people treat us counter to our expectations, it can trigger what renowned psychoanalyst Heinz Kohut dubs "disintegration anxiety"—the unmoored feeling that your sense of self is crumbling. In fact, one study found that the more that positive events happened to people with low self-esteem, the more likely they were to get physically sick months later. Even though the events were positive, the conflict between their low self-esteem and the good things that happened was destabilizing. So it challenged their sense of predictability and actually compromised their health.

To escape this clash, people who feel unworthy may actively avoid positive environments where they are likely to be affirmed and their negative theory of self is challenged. For example, another study found that while people with high self-esteem were more likely to commit to an organization that treated them fairly, people with low self-esteem were less likely to do so. Why? Those with low self-esteem felt less understood, less seen in the fair workplace. Similarly, they feel less understood around loving people. In another study, people with low self-esteem endorsed statements like "When I am complimented, sometimes I feel the person clearly doesn't know me." Feeling misunderstood is so uncomfortable that the unworthy would often rather forego fair treatment or love. Better that than disprove your theory of who you are.

So when we feel unworthy, we tend to filter out love, praise, and success. But when failure strikes, we are all too willing to buy into the negative beliefs that are waiting in the corners of our mind, as revealed by a study that exposed people to an ambiguous rejection. People received the profile of an attractive stranger, whom they then chatted online with. The stranger left abruptly, ending the experiment prematurely. (The stranger was actually just the researchers, in disguise. Doesn't online dating suck?) The participant was left to make sense of the stranger's departure. Of course, she could have left for an innocent reason: Maybe she, say, got a text that her cat ate a piece of chalk and had to be rushed to the hospital? Or maybe she wasn't interested—or worse, maybe she actively hated you? People with low self-esteem hovered toward the latter explanation: *I think she thought I was probably weird due to the personal description I wrote and my photo.* They also rated themselves as *less* likable after and released *more* stress hormones.

This study is evidence that people who feel unworthy perceive reality in ways that confirm their theory of themselves as unlovable. The finding that people with low self-esteem released more stress hormones suggests that people who feel unworthy not only read rejection into ambiguous situations, but they also are more impacted by perceived rejection. Another study found that, when rejected, people with low self-esteem experienced more activity in the part of their brain—the anterior cingulate cortex—associated with physical and social pain. However, research also shows that, when they are praised, they experience less activity in the part of the brain that processes information relevant to the self. In other words, the praise was less likely to impact their sense of self.

WHY WE RESIST WORTH

Jerry knows what it's like to be especially vulnerable to criticism. Back when he did comedy, he got his big break doing a four-minute set at

LA's renowned Hollywood Improv. Based on his performance, the owner, Mark, would decide if Jerry would be hired for longer sets. After the set, Mark told Jerry, "You're kind of funny, like the way an old vaudeville comic would be funny in that schticky way. You're not what we're looking for. I don't know another way to say it, but you're not funny."

The feedback devastated Jerry so much that he left comedy.

Then he thought about it nearly every day for the next ten years.

At face value, Jerry's reaction may seem extreme. One moment reverberating for ten years? Yet feelings compound, as I mentioned in the previous chapter. Jerry wasn't reacting to one moment. He was reacting to a lifetime of moments of rejection. When we go through something in the present, our ventromedial prefrontal cortex rummages through our past to find something similar to what is happening now. Then it triggers a similar body state to what was triggered then. For people with low self-esteem, their cortisol surges at rejection, and their brain lights up with hurt, because each moment of rejection is a link in a chain of rejection that gets jangled all at once. Jerry may have been so devastated by being rejected at the comedy show because it triggered the same depths of rejection that he felt when his dad left. As author Michael Pollan puts it in *How to Change Your Mind: What the New Science of Psychedelics Teaches Us about Consciousness, Dying, Addiction, Depression, and Transcendence*, "Our perceptions of the world offer us not a literal transcription of reality but rather a seamless illusion woven from both the data of our senses and the models in our memories. Normal waking consciousness feels perfectly transparent, and yet it is less a window on reality than a product of our imaginations—a kind of controlled hallucination."

At the neural level, the brains of people who feel unworthy are sticky for criticism and slick for love. When affirmed, their blood pressure rises and their brain dissents. When criticized, their bodies surge with more stress hormones and the brain flashes with more pain. Their ventromedial prefrontal cortex grasps at their brain's past, so they constantly relive the rejection that brought them to feel unworthy, and they are stuck preparing for it by rejecting signs of love and success. Their theory doesn't just guess at their sense of reality; it determines it.*

These mechanisms are supposed to protect us against a future that will match our baggage-laden past. This past leads us to predict, at a deep level, that the world around us will be like our absent parents, ready to reject us if we proclaim ourselves worthy. The world, we think, will kick us behind our knees, leaving us crumpling. Beyond just making life predictable, our theory of unworthiness prepares us. It saves us from descent, keeping us low so there's no place to fall. Better to be at the trough of the valley than plunge off the cliff into it. We were meant to fail at becoming worthy because, in a puzzling way, feeling unworthy makes us feel psychologically safe in a world that, we're convinced, will break us down again.

But bracing constantly, preparing for harm to strike again, doesn't ultimately protect us. First, even if harm has knocked before, we can never truly know when it will knock again. And hypervigilantly anticipating it guarantees there is no peace in the meantime. Also, scanning for threats makes them seem real even when there's no reason to think they are. Although the attractive stranger left the study early because of her cat, we deduce it's because we're inferior. The drawbacks here are that we are left feeling afraid of others, bad about ourselves, and threatened by any information that suggests otherwise. We struggle to convince our brain of these drawbacks, though.

Jerry couldn't. He was convinced that shoring up his worth would only prompt a deeper plummet when he was rejected again. "Knock yourself down first before they do. Knock yourself down first before

---

* It might seem contradictory that for people feeling unworthy, negative events both feel good (triggering predictability) and bad (because they are internalized more deeply). Think of it like going to work on Monday when you don't like your job. On Monday, you're relieved, less anxious than you were on Sunday, because you're not anticipating going back to work. But you also feel crummy because you're back at work. Your reactions seem to contradict each other because they are seated in two different tracks of feelings, one for anxiety and the other for emotional valence.

they do. . . . Remember that last time in high school you let your guard down? You thought you were in this safe place and even that place wasn't safe. . . . [So] thanks, I'm just going to keep my dukes up."

OUR THEORY IN RELATIONSHIPS

It was September 2001 when Veronica finally had her meet-cute, a man who would lead her to write in her diary, "After all the years of pain where I thought I couldn't love again, my heart is healed." She met him while traveling the world on severance money from being laid off from her tech job. After a solo trip to Italy, she went to Düsseldorf, Germany, where her cousin, Maria, invited her out to dinner. Maria planned to bring her boyfriend, and not wanting Veronica to feel like a third wheel, she also invited a friend from high school, Dominik.

Dominik and Veronica were all sparks, absorbed in each other's conversation from the instant they met. As the group left the restaurant to go to a bar, the two held hands. When the World Trade Center was attacked on September 11, Veronica couldn't get back to the US on her scheduled flight, and they saw each other again; this time he kissed her "on the lips," as she wrote in her diary. "He is affectionate, funny, considerate, positive, mature, giving. I'm negative, egocentric, and shy. But despite all this, this is all very stupid because Dominik is in Bonn [Germany] and I'm in Virginia," she wrote.

In December, Veronica visited Dominik in Bonn. They went to Munich together for New Year's, and they did everything—glamorous restaurants, historical churches, squares, and landmarks. But Dominik wasn't ready for a long-distance relationship, which devastated Veronica. Bitter, she wrote in her diary, "It's amazing how much time I think about these men who are worth nothing in the sum of things."

Dominik and Veronica kept in touch with postcards and emails after Munich, but they both dated other people. Still, Veronica couldn't get him out of her head. Then, three years later, in 2004,

Dominik came to New York on a work trip, and Veronica decided to go meet him. The chemistry still pulsed. Now that these sparks had struck twice, the couple wasn't ready to give up on them. They decided to start a long-distance relationship. Veronica couldn't be happier.

When Dominik finally wanted to be with Veronica, she thought she snagged a catch, in part since he was a tall, handsome white man, and Veronica was still working through feelings of unworthiness related to her race. She is an immigrant from Peru who moved to the US when she was nine. The white boys she liked in high school never liked her, and she didn't see small Hispanic women with Indigenous features like hers as objects of desire in any of her favorite movies, like *Pretty in Pink*, *The Breakfast Club*, or *Sixteen Candles.*

When Veronica visited Dominik's family on a farm in rural Germany, she felt as impressed as she did inadequate. "A part of me has this image that I'm like a little Indigenous peasant, and here's like this peasant here to meet with all these famous people. There's this idea in my head that I'm too unworthy to be among these people. They must be so evolved to see my true beauty inside, they have a hidden agenda, or maybe I'm a project for them." Nikki Giovanni's "Woman Poem" evocatively reveals this skepticism people who feel unworthy have toward people who love them when she says that caring about her means "you ain't got no good sense / cause i ain't shit you must be lower."

Despite Veronica's feelings of inferiority, Dominik seemed to really love her. He'd fly her to Germany. He knew she liked hearts and books, so a heart-shaped paperweight arrived in her mailbox. When he heard a trance song on the radio, Veronica's favorite genre, he'd go home and burn the song onto a CD. He told her he saw a future with her, and they discussed living together.

How did Veronica feel in response to all this love? Fearful. "I get scared when people woo me, because it implies I have to change. When someone loves you, you want to put your best foot forward . . .

and that's a lot of pressure. I have a bad temper. I can be cutting or caustic. There are things about me that are hard to love. I don't like myself, so how is somebody else going to like me? It's only because they haven't seen the real me." Veronica is a neighbor who I asked to interview. I suspected she struggled with her sense of worth in moments, like this one, when I watched her say harsh things to herself.

Like Veronica, people who feel unworthy tend to really want love but struggle to sustain it. They are more likely to dive headfirst into relationships. People with low self-esteem, for example, obsess more over their lovers, one study found. They agree with statements like "Sometimes I get so excited about being in love that I can't go to sleep" and "When my love affairs break up, I get so depressed that I have even thought of suicide." Love is so urgent because there is an (often unconscious) hope that someone else's love will compensate for the lack of it they feel within. But this urgency around love sets relationships up to fail. Studies find that whirlwind courtships, those that move fast, run a higher risk of breaking up.

Unworthiness doesn't just affect how relationships start; it also affects whether they continue. For Veronica, and for people who struggle with unworthiness, to be so loved when you feel unlovable is to feel misunderstood. At times, people struggling with unworthiness are driven toward unhealthier relationships to avoid feeling so unseen. People with low self-esteem report being more committed to spouses who treat them negatively rather than positively. And when they *were* matched with a spouse who saw them positively, another study found, they were less intimate with them.

When we feel bad about ourselves, those feelings are so visceral, so woven into the nucleus of who we are, we can't fathom that someone could see us differently. As Veronica put it, "I feel like I got away with something when a guy was into me . . . I am flawed. He has seen some of my flaws. If we continue down this path, then he's gonna reject me." So it's not that people who feel unworthy don't want love. It's just that, given their theory of self, love isn't plausible, so they don't feel loved no matter how loved they are. This explains why one study found that the more we doubt ourselves, the more we underestimate how loved we are. This occurs even though, as another study found, romantic partners had equally positive impressions of partners with low or high self-esteem.

Because their theory signals they'll ultimately be rejected, people who feel unworthy respond to any hints of rejection in relationships by rejecting first. People who feel worthy, in contrast, don't believe snags in a relationship signal further rejection, so they work through rough patches.

Imagine you were a college student. You came to a lab with your romantic partner, and they were sent to another room where, the experimenter told you, they listed things they disliked about you. As the time passed, you started to feel bad. *Does my romantic partner dislike me?* No, not necessarily. The experimenter had lied to you. Your partner, at the experimenter's request, was actually in the other room listing items in their dorm room.

How would you perceive your partner after? If you feel unworthy, you'd feel threatened. To protect yourself, you might reject first, which is what people with lower self-esteem in the study did. They reported seeing their partners more negatively, as more thoughtless and lazy. High self-esteem participants (presumedly mostly the good-twin kind) did not put down their partner when threatened. Their belief is that they'll be accepted, which helps them address problems instead of escalating them.

These defensive behaviors played out for Veronica as she collected reasons why she shouldn't be with Dominik. He was an investment banker who liked a flashy lifestyle of fancy dinners and expensive clubs. She liked musicals, plays, and museums. How could that ever work? But looking back, she sees her flaw-finding as a way to escape the rejection she believed to be inevitable.

"It was almost like preempting something because you have such a certainty that it's not going to work, or that you don't deserve it," she said. "I already had these patterns in my mind about the high unlikelihood of ending up in a meaningful relationship and that becomes a self-fulfilling prophecy. . . . He's gonna reject me, right? So why [don't I] just get it out of the way before? The sabotage came from this inherent feeling that I'm not worthy of true love."

For people who feel unworthy, these studies suggest, love gets garbled. It's heard as pressure to live up to expectations, being misunderstood for who you "really" are, or living in an unpredictable world. Its integrity is questioned when even the smallest of issues arise. And love is a warning of inflated expectations—ones that they will inevitably disappoint.

Feeling unworthy, we've learned, turns life into a series of double binds. Acts that would make you feel worthy are repelled because they feel too threatening. Loving people who would make you feel worthy are preemptively rejected. You inhale, deeply, the slightest whiff of rejection. Yet when acceptance beckons, you hold your breath. Jerry and Veronica both fell victim to these pitfalls—Jerry in work, and Veronica in her relationship. They both braced themselves against the good, because they were still living in an alternative reality that was shaped by the past. *I can't trust this good. It will end. And that will devastate me, so I must escape first.* These strategies may help them navigate the people whose rejection led them to feel this way, but they're costly thereafter. We can honor our unworthiness for the ways it has tried to keep us safe, by keeping us from trusting others' love when it wasn't worthy of our trust. And we can also acknowledge that we're ready for something different.

It's been fifteen years since Veronica dated Dominik. He's married now. Veronica is single. She has what many would consider a full life, with friends, a high-power job, and a lot of healing work under her belt, like meditation, therapy, and a devotion to Buddhist teachings. It's all brought her a long way from who she was when she dated Dominik. But she still has a photo book filled with pictures of them together. And sometimes, she still thinks about him.

While flipping through old pictures, she sighed and said, "Sometimes, I look back and think I may have let things go too soon."

As I wrote this chapter, I thought about friends and lovers I failed to love. When they've gone through something rough, I've tried to send a loving text—to tell them I'm here, to tell them what they mean to me. The responses are curt, often feeling, on my end, dismissive. When I've tried to gush about the halo they wear, in my eyes, I see their goose bumps protrude. Suddenly, the air has left the room and we're both holding our breath, unsure of how love toppled us over into unease. My heart feels sore about it sometimes. I start to feel swollen with all the love I have that I know can't reach them. I want to learn to say they're great in the perfect melody or at the ideal window, so it'll dislodge all the building blocks of their theory and we can be as close as we might otherwise be if the channels of love between us were flung wide open.

When I tried to love them in these ways, I assumed that it would be easy for them to receive my love, but now I know this isn't true. There's a reason finding worth is like beating diet culture; for each, we are set up to fail. To receive blessings in our bloodstream means we must voyage into our fraught insides, face parts of us that register these blessings, and bluster "I don't deserve it," or push back "You don't think that. You must want something," or whimper "If you love me that much, I'll fail you." Feeling worthy is so hard because it means we receive the good as truth rather than threat, which requires us to change our theory of ourselves and the world.

Let's begin.

Part 2

Finding Worth

3

Memories That Bleed

When she was thirteen, something happened to Esme. Because of it, thirty-year-old Esme was sitting in a bar with a woman named Jay, worrying about whether Jay wanted to become her friend as much as she did Jay's.

Jay is a marine biologist turned documentary filmmaker bent on revealing the secrets of the ocean. Esme had moved to town a few years ago, but she hadn't really found many close friends yet. The two women met at a storytelling event, where people divulged personal stories to an audience. Esme enjoyed hanging out with Jay at the bar and wanted to see her again. So despite her insecurities, before the end of the evening, Esme gathered her courage to ask Jay to hang out again in the only way she knew how.

"Look. I want to be your friend, but I'm nervous you don't want to be mine," she said. "And because of this experience I had a long time ago, I don't reach out to people because I think they don't want to hang out with me. If you want to hang out again, I would like that, but I need *you* to reach out."

Esme recognized that this was an unusual overture for friendship. She worried she was burdening Jay. There's a fine line between asking for your needs and offloading your insecurities onto someone, she realized. Sometimes, she wondered if she lost potential friends because she didn't initiate. But it still felt easier to air her insecurities and ask Jay to suggest hanging out, rather than Esme bringing it up herself.

Esme last felt confident initiating a friendship when she was thirteen. She had been in seventh grade when she met Maya. Like Esme, Maya was bookish and an animal lover. Every day after school, Esme would sit at her desk with her computer, grab her silver cordless phone, and call Maya to spill about her day. Esme shared the day's blow-by-blow, things like her most recent crush, her grades on an exam, or her take on her favorite shows.

Months into this daily ritual, Esme had called Maya as usual. But this time, just as she started to share about her day, Maya had interrupted her, saying, "I don't know why you call me all the time. We're not friends."

"All this time, I wondered if Maya had been thinking to herself, *Why is she telling me this? Why is this happening? Why did she choose me? Why won't this bitch shut up?*" Esme shared. The shame that lingered from this memory makes Esme blush to this day.

As Esme reflected on the situation with me, she ricocheted between the raw insecurity of her thirteen-year-old self and the tempered rationality of her now thirty-five-year-old one. She questioned whether she was a universally bad judge of people, but then reminded herself that perhaps she just hadn't been Maya's cup of tea. She felt too fragile to know why Maya hadn't wanted to be her friend but also expressed a wish to know, for closure. She debated if she had been a "freak who stalked and upset this girl" or just a "friend who came on a little too strong." No matter what the truth had been, it was still bothering Esme, deeply, after all this time.

It was this decades-old experience with Maya that drove Esme to approach Jay the way she did. "A lot of years have passed," Esme mused. "Someone can be born and get old enough to drink in the time that happened. But it still nags." When I asked her what it might take for her to overcome that rejection, she half joked, "I've heard on a podcast that people try ketamine infusions for their anxiety. . . . Other than that, it's weird. It's distant, but still there. I can't for some reason quite get over it."

There's a version of Esme's life where Maya never says her cruel words, and Esme doesn't overthink and second-guess her friendships for decades afterward. But this rejection was Esme's social-anxiety origin story, a rupture in her life's trajectory, the fork in the road that brought her to the point where she flips interactions daily, like burgers, inspecting them over and over for the uncooked bits. Esme is an acquaintance of mine, and I worried she might retrospectively cringe at herself about our interview, so I preemptively reassured her that I wasn't judging.

Decades after an event, the past can still live on inside us, haunting our sense of worth and our view of the world. Every time Esme forms a new friendship, she still wonders if they really like her or if she's just misreading it: "Does this person really want to be subjected to me? As long as I'm subjecting myself to them?"

A NEW THEORY OF MEMORY

In the winter of 1999, a scientist named Karim Nader toiled with rats. Every time he played a beep, he shocked them. Soon, the rats associated the beep with the shock—to the point that even the beep alone, without the shock, would make them freeze.

Fourteen days later, Nader played the beep to reactivate the rats' memory of the shock. This time, though, he injected them with a drug that inhibited their brain's fear response, so they didn't freeze. A day later, when they were sober, he exposed them, once again, to the beep. He wanted to know if they would still freeze, like they had initially. Or would their most recent memory of hearing the beep without freezing fundamentally change the way they responded to the beep? Perhaps, he wondered, they would remember their sense of calm on hearing the beep and no longer freak out. What Nader was ultimately trying to figure out was whether early memories—beep, shock—are inalterable. Or do new memories—beep, calm—grasp back in time and rewrite old ones?

Scientists at the time dismissed Nader's experiment as futile. "Don't waste your time. This will never work," Joseph LeDoux, a prominent memory researcher who was Nader's former adviser, told him. LeDoux had argued in a 1989 paper that emotional memory may persist forever. The scientific consensus was aligned with this idea that memories were permanent, a fossilized record of events. We remember them at twenty-two the same way we do at seventy-two. There might be a brief period after the memory formed when our brain's record of the content or emotion associated with the memory could change, like clay, pliable because it has not yet hardened. But after that initial period, it is what it is. This line of thinking suggested that after the rats had registered this memory of beep and shock, that memory would stick. The rats were doomed to freeze whenever they heard the beep.

Except they didn't. Nader found that, a day after the rats had received the drug, when they heard the beep again—they no longer froze. Their memory associating the beep with the shock had transformed, he concluded. Memories are pliable, rebuilt every time we access them, transformed with each remembering.*

Nader's work, and subsequent studies, set the foundation for *memory reconsolidation theory*, the major theory that guides the rest of this book.

---

* It's also possible that instead of the new memory changing the old, the rats formed a separate memory of the beep followed by calm and it became more prominent than the original memory. This is a subject of debate for researchers. If the old memory was still intact and simply less salient, then you'd expect that at some point, the old memory would crop up again, something called "spontaneous recovery," and a fear response like the rats' would return. Studies have found that up to a year after a memory was changed, the fear response associated with the original memory does not return, suggesting the original memory is no longer intact. It's also possible that whereas part of a memory transforms, other parts of it stay the same. The older the memory, and more emotion associated with it, the more difficult it is to transform all of it, researchers think. Transforming these stronger memories may require us to revisit memories repeatedly.

As the theory goes, every time we recall a memory in a context different from the one when it was formed, we change it. Then our brain files away the revised memory. Our memories update so we can use them to better predict the world around us. The rats' memory changed so they didn't have to brace for the shock when it was no longer necessary.

Memories can be transformed because of a striking feature of memory, one explored by a study of epileptic patients about to undergo surgery. In the study, patients were shown short film clips of shows like *The Simpsons* or of celebrities, animals, or landmarks. The researchers recorded which neurons fired as the patients watched. After the patients finished watching, the researchers asked the patients to think about the clips and share whatever came to mind. When they recalled a clip of, say, Tom Cruise in an interview, the same neurons that activated when they watched the clip lit up when they remembered it. "For the Brain, Remembering Is Like Reliving" proclaimed the title of a *New York Times* article about the study.

If we relive memories when we remember them, then we can guide our memories to a new resolution, as revealed by another study where participants came to the lab and wrote about ten negative memories. One group wrote down something positive that occurred because of this negative event, while the other, the control group, didn't. Two months later, when both groups described the original memory, the positivity group described the same memory with more positive details. They updated the initial memory into a patchworked mix of its original elements and newer positive ones.

One person initially remembered how they almost drowned in a pool on a Florida vacation while their parents were distracted at the bar. After finding positive meaning when they later recalled the memory, they added that because their parents felt so guilty, the participant got to choose what the family did the next day. They all went to, ironically enough, the beach.

This change in memory was also apparent in their brains. After they positively reframed the memory, their hippocampus—where memories are stored in the brain—responded differently to its recall. This change didn't occur for memories that were recalled without a positive reframe. At a neural level, the beep-shock link was altered. At the end of this chapter, and all subsequent chapters, I'll share exercises, derived straight from the science, to help us reconsolidate our memories.

We think our worth conveys something about who we are right now, but it actually reveals what happened to us in the past. The more negative emotional memories we have, the more unworthy we feel because, as researchers who study memory put it, "memory is considered to be a database for self-esteem." According to psychoanalyst Heinz Kohut, "the past is reverberating in a person's experience of his identity." Objective truth does not explain why we feel unworthy. It's not because we're simply the worst. We feel unworthy because we have memories of moments that convey we don't matter. In Freud's words, we "suffer mainly from reminiscences." In the previous chapter, we explored how unworthiness is a theory of the self and the world. The pillars of our theory are our memories.

Nader's research offers a way forward. The unworthiness beeps in our lives—the bullying, rejection, neglect—won't inevitably lead us to freeze. Someday, Esme might initiate another friendship. Because no matter how many times the Mayas in our lives have rejected us, we're not doomed. We just need to face our memories.

We don't have to do anything to become worthy—to get a certain job, or sculpt a certain body, or swipe into a certain relationship. Deep below the heft of our memories, we already feel worthy. Feeling worthy isn't about churning out a new self. It's about cleansing the memories that make us forget we were worthy all along.

HOW DOES MEMORY RECONSOLIDATION WORK?

Esme might retort that she "faces" that memory all the time. In fact, she's terrorized by it. It's at the heart of the little voice in her head that wondered if Jay, when she eventually reached out to Esme, was a new friend or just trying to be nice. It's the trigger for her mini breakdown during her bachelorette party planning, when she worried that her friends didn't really love her enough to want to travel to celebrate her, even though, as Jay put it, "I was honored to be on the list of women to be invited. It felt so special." It's the force behind the frantic complements she texted to a coworker who she worried didn't like her. It's the show she watches, sometimes, before bed when she cuddles with insomnia.

This kind of obsessive, repetitive revisitation of our memories is called *rumination.* But rumination is not memory reconsolidation. Whereas reconsolidating distressing memories makes us feel better, unproductive rumination, research finds, makes us *more* likely to become or stay depressed. What makes rumination different from reconsolidation?

Two things. The first is emotion.

To Reconsolidate, First Feel Your Feelings

To reconsolidate a memory, we must access the emotion stored within it, without being overwhelmed by that emotion. This is demonstrated by an assessment called the Adult Attachment Interview. If I was taking you through it, I'd ask you some personal questions about your childhood. *What did your family do for a living? Where did you live? Did you move?*

Now on to juicier questions, because I want the tea. *Describe your relationships with your parents as a young child. What did you do when you were upset as a child? Use five adjectives to describe your relationship with a parent, and add a memory corresponding to each adjective.*

I'd assess your responses to determine your attachment style. As we saw in the introduction, where we discussed the different attachment styles, if you are securely attached, a manifestation of worthiness, you trust others, feel comfortable being vulnerable, and develop healthy relationships. The remaining attachment styles constitute insecure attachments and involve feelings of unworthiness. If you are anxiously attached, you believe you'll be abandoned, so you cling to others. If you are avoidantly attached, you think no one can be trusted, so you distance yourself. Finally, if you have a disorganized attachment style, you might act anxiously *and* avoidantly but in more extreme ways.

You might think I would categorize you based on the content of what you say. If your parents were harsh, I would peg you as avoidant. If they were caring, secure. But that'd be wrong. The Adult Attachment Interview, instead, assesses attachment style by "surprising the unconscious," or assessing attachment not by what you say but by the emotion (or lack thereof) that surfaces when you say it.

If you were avoidant, you'd respond to my questions in a contradictory way by saying something like "My mother was so kind," and then "But when I told her I broke my arm, she yelled at me." You'd be minimizing emotion because you'd describe scary things positively and with limited detail.

If you were anxious, you'd have outbursts, "My father NEVER really cared," or tear up, saying "No one was there for me." You may have an even more intense response, regressing to a younger self, "So I hided [*sic*] from the grown-ups." Your emotion would be so strong, it would be like you were reexperiencing the past.

If you were disorganized, you'd suddenly lapse into silence, which researchers call "micro-dissociative episodes." Your emotions would be so overwhelming that your brain would short-circuit in real time, and you'd suddenly pause, or appear disoriented.

And if you were secure, you'd be up-front, reflecting on the past like an objective third party who understands your experience alongside your parents': "Yeah, my mother could get angry at me. It upset me, but I knew she had a lot going on as a single mom." Even when something troubled you, you'd be honest about the impact while staying emotionally regulated. You could reflect and reason about them, rather than being hijacked into withdrawal (avoidant) or overwhelmed (anxious) when they arise.

The Adult Attachment Interview assesses how worthy you feel, via your attachment style. But it does this by evaluating the degree of emotion cradled in your foundational memories. The insecurely attached possess memories tinged with unprocessed emotions—so they minimize, cry, or disassociate. They have what's called *open* memories, or memories packed with emotion. If you feel sad or angry or ashamed when remembering, the memory is open. If you'd prefer not to talk about it, it's open. If you ruminate on it, it's open.

Studies on open memories identify three qualities of these memories:

1. They elicit significant emotion when you remember them.
2. You do not understand why the memory occurred.
3. You think of the memory as unsettled or not yet behind you. (You still ruminate about it; it still impacts you.)

Secure-ish people's memories are more emotionally processed, meaning they revisit memories without being hit with emotion, without having to deny or break down. In other words, their memories are closed. We can think of an insecure attachment style as a collection of open memories.

Memories only affect worth if they're open (which explains why a meta-analysis found that of all attachment styles, secure people have the highest self-esteem). Evidence of this is in one study in which people were asked to describe a devastating memory, of things like a robbery, death, or fire. Because we have established that our memories affect our self-esteem, we'd assume that recalling these heavy memories would impact our self-esteem. And it does. After recalling the memory, people reported lower self-esteem, but some more so than others.

Although everyone recalled the same tragic memories, self-esteem after recall was lower *only* for people whose memory was open. If they teared up, clenched their jaw, or felt the knob in their throat while remembering, it affected their worth. Open memories still bleed all over our sense of self. As my therapy supervisor once said, "Anything unspeakable to you is still affecting you." I would add, anything unspeakable to you is making you feel unworthy. In contrast, the study also found that people who had experienced devastating events and who had closed these memories had as much self-esteem as people who didn't experience devastating events at all.

This insight frames why therapy doesn't always help intellectualizers. *Intellectualizers* are people who think about their feelings but don't feel them. Because they reflect on their past without feeling it, their open memories stay open. Intellectualizers will ponder, stroking their chins, wondering about the story of their lives. *What explains my trigger around cats? Is it my friend's felonious cat, who drew blood the last time I cat-sat? The one I had to spray with tap water to disorient it enough so it wouldn't swipe again?* They may sound insightful as they spout off theories on their neuroses. But it's all detached, heady, emotionless. They're not clearing any emotion.

According to one study, if we intellectualize, we don't feel any better about ourselves after therapy. That study investigated factors that improve people's self-esteem by the end of therapy. The classic important variable, the quality of the relationship between client and therapist, didn't affect self-esteem. Even the therapist who mirrors our body language, nods affirmingly, and validates our enduring cat ambivalence won't necessarily make their clients feel any more worthy.

So what did predict client worthiness? Emotion. The more deeply the client expressed emotion during therapy, the more they cried and raged and grieved, the more their self-esteem increased by the end. Our unworthiness, then, is a sign we are bogged down by the unexpressed emotion nestled in our memories. To reconsolidate, we must wring out these feelings.

But wringing out the feelings stored in our memories is tricky. To do so, we must access the emotion within the memory but not be overcome by it (like the insecurely attached participants did in the Adult Attachment Interview). Secure-ish people have more closed memories because their foundational attachment memories aren't so stressful as to be overwhelming, but they *are* overwhelming for the remaining attachment styles, triggering outbursts, numbing, or disassociation. If we are flooded with too much emotion, our prefrontal cortex (which allows us to reflect on the memory and, thus, change it) and our hippocampus (which allows us to store a new memory) go offline. This means we can't reconsolidate. As renowned psychiatrist Bessel van der Kolk puts it in his long-standing bestseller *The Body Keeps the Score: Brain, Mind, and Body in the Healing of Trauma*, "As long as people are either hyperaroused or shut down, they cannot learn from experience." This is why accessing these difficult memories with a therapist is helpful. Their supportive presence keeps us from emotional inundation.

Other times, reconsolidation doesn't work, because we don't fully access the emotions associated with our memories. When Esme lies in bed and ruminates on that fateful afternoon, she tries to escape the memory and its linked emotions, as in, *I'm trying to forget what happened.* Our brains replay a memory so we have the opportunity to shrug out its emotion, to close open memories. Open memories lead us to ruminate. Rumination is a glitchy system that doesn't work well, because when we ruminate, we don't access the depth of feelings in the memory but instead stew in the vague negative emotions at the surface of it.

When we reconsolidate, we choose to open ourselves up to the memory and emotion and lean into the feelings, as in, *Yeah, that happened. Now let's feel how I feel about it.* We're not getting dragged into that instant with Maya. We're going willingly. There's also the possibility that we can't reconsolidate because, for complex reasons we'll explore in later chapters, we can't access the emotions buried in our memories at all.

When we remember and feel nothing, we change nothing.

Then Substitute Fresh, New Emotions

For years, Esme didn't tell a soul about what went down with Maya. She was mum for the rest of middle school, even into high school. But although what exactly happened between them was a mystery to everyone, the impact of their fallout was clear. Esme withdrew from others, making only one friend in band class. She coped by focusing on her studies to excess, to the point of having panic attacks if she was worried about a grade or a test. It wasn't until college that she told someone what had happened with Maya. Because if she had done it sooner, she said, "I worried that people would ask Maya's side of the story. And they would learn I'm some weird freak."

Esme's decision not to share what happened kept her from being able to reconsolidate the memory. If she shared, she might have been able to discharge more of the negative emotion in the memory. But reconsolidation involves something else, too. Not only do we discharge the negative emotion; we need to substitute fresh positive emotion in its place. We become emotional archaeologists, digging out the grounds of our psyche, and then we build over them with a new psychological home.

Esme could rewrite her memory by envisioning it ending more happily than it did. Because I put Esme through the wringer by making her relive her pain with Maya, as I interviewed her, I figured I'd ask her a question to help her reconsolidate her memory and hopefully finally gain relief: "If you could go back to that time now and say something to your younger self, what would you tell her?"

My question was inspired by a study involving a similar process. People relived a negative memory, like a death, surgery, or conflict with an abusive partner, but they intervened as their current selves. One participant's partner had lied about committing a crime that he then got arrested for. She told her younger self it wasn't her fault, and she wasn't stupid for believing them. A week later, the participants didn't just report the memory was less distressing and negative; they also reported higher self-esteem.

In the psychology world, this process is sometimes called "reparenting your inner child" and it has been around for decades. John Bradshaw, considered one of the fathers of self-help, explored this technique in his book *Homecoming: Reclaiming and Healing Your Inner Child*, which spent fifty-two weeks as number one on the *New York Times* bestseller list in the 1990s. It explains reparenting as one of the ways he overcame the trauma of growing up with an alcoholic father who abandoned him.

A dramatic example of meeting your inner child comes from the legendary opera singer Enrico Caruso, who suffered from debilitating stage fright. He confided in a letter to another opera singer, Ada Giachetti, in 1904: "Before each performance starts, I get so nervous that I am very nearly beastly with everyone." Before one show, his throat began to constrict as if he was choking. "They will laugh at me. I can't sing." Ready to retreat to the dressing room, he paused to address his younger self, "The Little Me would like to strangle the important Me within! Move out Little Me, the Big Me would like to sing through me! Escape, escape, [so] the important Me could sing!" His throat expanded, and he went on to sing to great applause.

Esme took a softer approach with her inner child: "I'd say 'Don't worry. People will find something special in you. Most of your friendships will be reciprocal.'" Esme was attempting to install joy, safety, and meaning in her original experience. These new emotions are needed to reconsolidate because fresh feelings activate our amygdala, the part of our brain that's switched on when we endure strong emotions, whether positive or negative. The amygdala then triggers our hippocampus to better remember the renovated memory.

So to heal and feel worthy, we must exhume memories, intentionally release the emotions bulging inside them, and inject some positivity in them before they slumber back in our brains. Our goal is to eventually achieve what the English poet William Wordsworth famously described as "emotion recollected in tranquility."

HOW TO RECONSOLIDATE MEMORIES

Even though I walked Esme through the script, carefully following the research on reconsolidation, it was clear in the next moment that asking her adult self to intervene didn't trigger the geyser of relief we both hoped for.

After Esme pep-talked her younger self about her future of reciprocal friendships, she backtracked. "It's only a few blips . . . but they grow so big. How do you make those blips smaller? The rational part of my brain knows they're blips, but the emotional part . . ."

Esme's backtracking reminds us how hard this all is. We learned in the previous chapter just how resolute our negative memories are. When they coalesce into a theory of ourselves as unworthy, we perceive the world as unsafe. We have learned how threatening it is to surrender this theory, even if it makes the world harrowing, because it also makes it comfortingly predictable. Or as Gloria Steinem put it in *Revolution from Within: A Book of Self-Esteem*: "Change, no matter how much for the better, still feels cold and lonely at first . . . because it doesn't feel like home. Old patterns, no matter how negative and painful they may be, have an incredible magnetic power—because they do feel like home."

Reconsolidating foundational memories will occur not in a moment but through regular practice. Steinem herself recommends voyages inward every day for twenty minutes.* She describes her visits with her inner child: In a small room with white walls and sunlight, she envisions her younger self in a worn-out bathing suit, holding a puppy, after returning from catching turtles. When she tries to sit with her, however, her younger self turns away. She doesn't trust the adult Gloria who "left her alone for so long." Soon after that day of catching turtles, Steinem's parents divorced and she became a caretaker for her chronically depressed mother. She'd come to suppress this adventurous little person she labels "Wild Child" to attend to her mom. She'd return, many times, describing the experience as "diving for pearls in

* There's also the possibility that we have a psychological block that impedes us from reconsolidating our memories. In later chapters, we'll explore how to overcome these blocks.

the ocean of the unconscious. Sometimes you come up with a gem, sometimes you don't, but either way, you emerge renewed."

TO BE WORTHY IS TO BECOME NAIVE

Clarifying how worthy people relate to their memories helps us deepen our understanding of worth. To feel worthy is to be unafraid to journey into your internal world, because you can do so without short-circuiting into ruminating, raging, or numbing. You are at liberty to get to know every part of yourself, to befriend even your darkest corners. There's nothing about you that you need to deny to emotionally survive.

To feel worthy is to live in the present. New experiences aren't mangled by the emotion attached to past ones. You respond to them as if they're fresh, happening for the first time. For Esme, finding worthiness would mean operating more like her younger self had, able to take risks without crippling doubt.

When I heard Esme worry about her younger self, I thought about the beauty of that girl who called Maya on her cordless phone every day. She wasn't bullied by an internal voice, suspicious of everyone's intentions. She didn't twirl cringey moments around her brain before bed. She wasn't bracing for the moment someone would tell her, "We're not really friends." Some might call this naive, but I think she was free. Psychologist Abraham Maslow argued that finding our naivete is how we actualize, or grow into the most authentic version of ourselves. Actualizing, he argued, was "unlearned, created, and released rather than acquired . . . if children are naive, then my subjects had attained a 'second naivete.'"*

But part of me also understood why Esme didn't want to be naive again. During my own healing journey, I walked through a local park,

---

* *Second naivete* is a term Maslow borrowed from philosopher George Santayana.

Rock Creek Park, and I gazed at the creek and wanted to cry. A paradox was true: My therapy was working, *and* it was upsetting me. As the tears fell, I realized part of me didn't want to heal. That part of me said that if it did, it would be letting down its guard in a world it wasn't convinced was safe. Healing was, by another name, defenselessness.

To feel worthy is to feel the beauty of being naive without its vulnerability. It allows us to stop bracing, holding our breath, suspecting the benign is the menacing, as if everyone is part themselves and part the ghost of who hurt them. In clearing our memories, we'll be naive in that we won't be adjusting our lives around the fear those past experiences taught us or the conviction that harm is imminent. And yet, fresh hardships won't shatter us like they did the last time we were naive, without negative memories to magnify them. We'll be prepared, not because we're clenching, but because we can trust ourselves to mend from what comes. We'll find the sturdiest version of our innocence.

MEMORY RECONSOLIDATION EXERCISES

Note: If you have a mental health diagnosis, I recommend you only apply these exercises under the supervision of a mental health professional. Even if you don't have a diagnosis, it will be helpful to do these activities with someone you feel safe with. I did them with friends, and we all found the exercises to be powerful, moving us to tears.

REPARENTING

1. **Recall a negative memory** that elicits strong negative emotion. It should be one that still troubles you and impacts how you see yourself.

   Optional: **Reparenting for secure-ish attachment**: To heal from anxious attachment issues, recall a memory of abandonment. To heal from avoidant attachment issues, recall a memory of a time you couldn't trust someone, because if you got too close to them, they would harm you.

2. **Describe** the memory in two sentences.
3. Write down the ways the **memory has impacted you**:
   - What does the memory say about you as a person?
   - What does it say about the world in general?
4. Close your eyes and **focus on the memory**, making it as vivid as possible. While you do, describe it in present tense. To assist in vividly reliving the memory, ask yourself the following questions as you relive it:
   - What do you see?
   - What do you smell?
   - What do you hear?
   - What do you taste?
   - What do you touch?
   - What do you feel?

5. **Picture your current self intervening** in the memory. Your current self should take an action that changes how the events unfolded for your younger self for the better. While you do, describe it in present tense. To assist in vividly changing the memory, ask yourself the following questions:
   - What do you see?
   - What do you smell?
   - What do you hear?
   - What do you taste?
   - What do you touch?
   - What do you feel?
6. **Focus on the new emotions** this action elicits. How do you feel differently? Maybe you feel warmer, your jaw feels less tight, or your chest feels more open.
7. Taking the perspective of your younger self in the memory, **ask for any reassurance or assistance** still needed from your current self. As your current self, **provide that reassurance**.
8. Focus on the **emotions that this assistance or reassurance elicits**. How do you feel differently? Maybe you feel warmer, your jaw feels less tight, or your chest feels more open.
9. Write down the **ways the updated memory impacts you**:
   - What does the memory say about you as a person?
   - What does it say about the world in general?
10. Repeat this practice as needed.

Adapted from Çili et al., "Impact of Imagery Rescripting on Adverse Self-Defining Memories and Post-Recall Working Selves in a Non-Clinical Sample: A Pilot Study."

MEANING MAKING

1. **Recall a negative memory** that elicits strong emotion. It should be one that still troubles you and impacts how you see yourself.
2. **Describe** the memory in two sentences.
3. Write down the ways the **memory has impacted you**:
    - What does the memory say about you as a person?
    - What does it say about the world in general?
4. Close your eyes and **focus on the memory**, making it as vivid as possible. While you do, describe it in present tense. To assist in vividly reliving the memory, ask yourself the following questions as you relive it:
    - What do you see?
    - What do you smell?
    - What do you hear?
    - What do you taste?
    - What do you touch?
    - What do you feel?
5. **Focus on something positive that came** out of the memory. Describe something you learned from the negative event, something good that occurred because of it, or a way it is meaningful to you in some way. Here are some examples:
    - You developed more resilient traits.
    - You uncovered more about yourself, understanding who you are better.
    - You changed or ended a relationship for the better.
    - You understand others more deeply.
    - You found new support.
    - You found a new passion or purpose.
    - You are learning deeper compassion or acceptance of yourself.

6. **Write down** the positives you focused on in step 5.
7. **Focus on the new emotions** that this positive meaning elicits. How do you feel differently? Maybe you feel warmer, your jaw feels less tight, or your chest feels more open.
8. Write down the **ways the updated meaning of the memory impacts you**:
   - What does the memory say about you as a person?
   - What does it say about the world in general?
9. Repeat this practice as needed.

Adapted from Speer et al., "Finding Positive Meaning in Memories of Negative Events Adaptively Updates Memory."

4

Memories We Don't Remember

Ever since he'd turned eighteen, Simon had liked to date women who were fresh out of relationships.

"If you just got a divorce, I love you. If you just broke up with your boyfriend, I'm right there," he told me during our interview. These grieving women needed a good listener, like him, to confess their pain, and his shoulder was always available. In listening but never sharing, he was able to escape the role of boyfriend and assume that of therapist. Perfect, he thought, because no one ever asks a therapist to disclose *their* pain.

But a blossoming relationship with a friend of two years perturbed his usual MO. Liza was as close as anyone had ever gotten to seeing the real Simon. They had met at Bible school, and she was one of the only other Black people there, so they bonded over their struggles of being Black in majority-white environments. They were also both adopted.

Simon's adoption status was also the reason he and I connected. I was referred to him by an organizer for a conference I spoke at on children's services. I was looking to interview people whose worth was impacted by an event they didn't remember, and I figured this would apply to people who were adopted at a young age, like Simon.

At first, Simon didn't like Liza. She was one of those people who always had to be right. But after doing everything together through the program—classes, Bible study, travel all over the country—the two became close because they "were too close not to get close."

Liza had liked Simon for a while, despite having observed his patterns with other girls. His romances would fizzle as fast as they ignited, from zero to a hundred and back down again. There was always a seemingly logical reason Simon ended things. He was an entrepreneur, building a business. He needed to focus on work and had too many demands on his time. He'd end the relationship or, if he could, downgrade it to fling status, diminishing what it was until the other person couldn't take it anymore.

But with Liza, someone he already loved platonically, Simon was committed to not following this pattern. And for an entire month and a half, he didn't. They texted nonstop, told each other they loved each other, and planned their future together. He'd bring out his goofy side, sending her a picture of the waves in his hair and asking if she'd drown in them. In the conservative Christian culture they were steeped in, people started dating in the fall and got married in the spring—and at first, it seemed as if they might be on that trajectory. But Simon's big dreams to enroll in Clark Atlanta University the next year loomed large as a threat to their relationship. At least, that's what Simon claimed.

At the two-month mark, just as he had with all those other girls, and even though he planned for this time to be different, Simon withdrew from Liza.

Now, five years and many therapy sessions later, Simon attributes his behavior with women to a wound he suffered before he was two years old. "I think for me, as an adoptee, I let one relationship define all of my other relationships. And that's my relationship with my birth mother. If my internal belief is *I'm the problem and I make people leave me*, then I just keep reenacting it." Because of this wound, somewhere deep in Simon's psyche, any love, even love with Liza, was a harbinger of abandonment. Liza was going to reject him because his birth mother had, and because his birth mother's abandonment meant, deep down, that he was unlovable. And if that was going to happen, he might as well shut it down first. "You feel that fear [of abandonment]. You instantly detach. Walls start to go up because I have to isolate and protect."

Negative memories, as we've learned, compromise our worth. If we can revisit them and rewrite their endings, we can feel worthy again. But what about people like Simon, whose unworthiness stems from memories that became entrenched before their brain's capacity to remember developed? How do we reconsolidate memories we don't know we have?

If these unworthiness memories aren't conscious ones, it might seem like we can't reconsolidate them. Perhaps Simon just needed to embrace a life as the rebound guy. And the Lizas who love him needed to accept having a therapist who listens instead of a boyfriend who shares. But as we'll find, the fact that we can't access a memory doesn't mean we can't change it. Although the roots of Simon's insecurities were buried below his conscious memory, those roots could still be pulled.

It is possible to heal from what we don't remember.

MEMORIES WE DON'T REMEMBER

By this point in the book, we've come to understand our insecurities as a symptom of our emotionally open memories. In earlier chapters, we've thought of a memory as a scene we can revisit. But the memory of Simon's mother is not a scene. It is a memory stored in his body, an emotional response, manifesting as feelings of abandonment and an urge to withdraw. In other words, the memory is implicit, something he forgot happened, but it is still open, impacting how he feels and thinks of himself. Researchers call implicit memories "a shadow in the brain that can't be consciously accessed."

We know we have implicit memories because even though we don't remember them, they affect how we feel. These kinds of memories trigger what are called emotional flashbacks, which occur when your body recalls something from your past and the subsequent emotional response is stronger than or incongruent with what's warranted for a given situation. You blow up over someone cutting in front of you in line. You cry over canceled plans. You react so strongly because your brain unconsciously links a current event to a past one, so you reexperience the emotion you felt at the first incident. Although these memories evade our conscious mind, they have still needled their way into our nervous system.

Implicit memory means sometimes unprocessed memory manifests not as an image at all, but as a sensation or a feeling. Our heartbeat quickens on the plane because when we were young, we boarded planes alone, shuffled between our divorced parents. Our jaw clenches when a friend brings up a concern because memories are being activated in which conflict meant we had to brace against rage. While open memories are composed of emotion, Northeastern University neuroscientist Lisa Feldman Barrett has found emotions are further composed of bodily sensations. This means remembering a memory activates sensations, just as it does emotion. Understanding how sensations can represent memory can help us reconsolidate at a new level of specificity.

In incarcerated author Jarvis Jay Masters's book *Finding Freedom: Writings from Death Row*, he recounts how in prison, he realized he was abused as a child. In one chapter, "Scars," he shares that he suspected that most of the scars his fellow inmates bore were not from adult altercations but from abusive childhoods. After coming to realize that he, too, was abused, he organized discussion groups for men.

"I spoke to them of the pain I had carried through more than a dozen institutions. And I explained how all these events trapped me in a pattern of lashing out against everything."

In the moment, Masters did not know he was lashing out because his body was replaying abuse memories, memories that caused each new slight to feel like a visceral replay of this early abuse. Yet he still reacted as if it was. Implicit memories replay themselves over and over again in our emotional reactions, regardless of how a new context is different from the original one.

Simon may have been right to fear abandonment by his mother, but he didn't have a clear reason to do so with Liza. We know his implicit memory was at play—that is, open—because he still harbored that fear of abandonment. As Isaac Etter, a speaker on adoption and the founder of Identity, a start-up offering technology to help adoptive parents, puts it, "In order for [adoptees] to be where we are, somebody has to not choose us. It makes us believe that nobody is going to choose us."

HOW IMPLICIT MEMORIES FORM

Imagine I showed you slides of different colors—red, yellow, green, blue. But whenever I showed you the blue one, I sounded a boat horn. Eventually, your nerves would twitch at the blue slide, even if the noise didn't sound, your body electric with anticipation, literally. Even if you didn't want them to, when the blue slide flashed, your nerves would instruct your body to sweat at nearly imperceptible levels, making it better at conducting electricity. This is brought to you by memory. Blue becomes ominous as you remember it paired with a *BURGGGGGGHHHHHHHH.*

Now, what if you damaged your amygdala, the almond-shaped nub in your brain that records the emotional part of a memory? You'd tell me that when the blue slide flashed, you heard a noise. But when the blue cropped up again, you wouldn't get nervous. Your skin wouldn't conduct electricity. Your body wouldn't remember its fear.

What if you instead damaged your hippocampus, the part of your brain that consciously remembers? You would tell me that you didn't know which color triggered the noise. *Was it yellow? Green?* But with your amygdala intact, your body would remember. When the blue slide appeared again, you would feel nervous, and your skin would once again be conducting those electric currents. Your body would register fear, but your mind wouldn't know why.

These findings were revealed in a study of people with brain damage in their amygdala or hippocampus, and it reveals why we're impacted by memories we don't remember. Our brain records the *content* of a memory, a scene of an event, and the *emotion*—the fear, terror, or frustration—in distinct parts of our brains. The hippocampus is the videographer of memory, recording the scene, with the amygdala, the soundtrack of memory, shaping the scene's emotion. Sometimes, as the study revealed, the amygdala's music plays without the hippocampus running its scene. That's when the hairs on our neck stand up and we don't know why.

It's not just brain damage that leaves us with an alert amygdala and powered-down hippocampus. When we are infants, our amygdala develops quicker than our hippocampus, so we start amassing implicit memories early. Also, overwhelming memories and traumas are sealed from our mind but still trapped in our nervous system. One study shockingly found more than a third of women who faced childhood sexual abuse seventeen years earlier didn't recall what they endured. Yet this abuse was explicitly documented in their medical records because they were hospitalized after it. This splitting allows our bodies to alarm us to avoid potential threats, even when these threats are too menacing for us to consciously remember.*

Simon, and the rest of us, are all like the participant who forgot the blue slide but still flinched. Things could have happened while we were still crawling, or during a childhood heaving with so much stress

* This divide between what our minds and bodies know is driven by hormones called glucocorticoids, which we release when stressed. At low levels, they enhance our (explicit) memory, but at high levels, they impair it. For example, one study found that after participants took a glucocorticoid, they showed less brain activity in areas involved in explicit memory.

it settles as a blur. Or the threats to our sense of security may have cropped up in imperceptible ways that only our amygdala noticed—an iciness, a tone, a grimace. Indeed, in one study, angry faces were flashed at people accompanied by a loud noise, and the participants' amygdalas lit up when later exposed to the face alone. This occurred even though the face flashed so quickly that people didn't consciously know it was there. We can deny what happened, but the amygdala always knows. "Reality denied," as the science-fiction author Philip K. Dick has written, "always comes back to haunt."

An event doesn't have to be life-threatening for it to impact our implicit memory. (Studies find this is particularly true for autistic adults, who experience everyday events more intensely.) As children, we are both extremely egocentric and sensitive to our environment. Seemingly everyday events happen to children that lodge themselves into their implicit memory. Let's say we have an important work meeting and can't show up to our daughter's class for parents day. This could explain why, fifteen years later, she is anxious about whether her family will show up for her college graduation.

This is all to say that we can go through a big or a small (at least from our current vantage point) event that devastated our sense of security and forget it even happened, even as our amygdala goes berserk warning our body that it did. If traces of rejection stoop you lower than the soil; if you can't help but shack up with people who hurt you; if your brain welcomes negative feedback at the door but bolts it closed to positive; if, like Simon, you retract like a tortoise when love comes by, you might feel unworthy, even if you don't remember why.

WHEN WHAT WE CAN'T REMEMBER RETURNS

Two things propel implicit memories to the surface: first, stress, which knocks out the hippocampus, allowing implicit memory systems to rise to the forefront; and second, reminders of the original memory.

One place where most of us experience the impact of our implicit memory is in our romantic relationships. In romantic relationships, much of the time we face the *stress* of merging lives, and we find ourselves in a structure that *reminds* us of our families. I was reminded of implicit memory's role in romantic relationships a few days ago when a friend called to tell me she was pregnant.

"That kid doesn't know it yet, but they hit the jackpot!" I told her. For someone like her to become a mother, something must be going right in the world, I thought. She's a nurturer, half mother even in friendship, frying me hash browns when I stayed at her place, gifting me a tote bag from Hawaii for my birthday, and designing and mailing me stickers.

"Thanks," she said in a tone that forked in two, sounding receptive yet sheepish. "I'm just worried I'm going to take out some of my own unprocessed issues on the kid."

I was surprised, I told her, "because when it comes to emotional intelligence, you're goals."

"But that's in friendship," she countered. "In romantic relationships, sometimes I struggle."

Desperation, abandonment, rage, longing, shutdown—romantic relationships stir these intense feelings, which likely have been stirred before, when we were children. Implicit memories of how we attached to a parent in infancy superimpose themselves onto how we attach to a romantic partner. Plus, a meta-analysis found that maternal and passionate love employ the same parts of our brain.

Implicit memory may be acting on our current relationships through our attachment style, which in itself is a kind of implicit memory. According to researchers, early attachment experiences "become part of a person's implicit procedural knowledge and tend to operate automatically and unconsciously." As anxiously attached adults, we don't remember the hot-and-cold love we received as infants that still causes us to fear that everyone will leave us now. And if we're avoidant, we don't remember the times we wept for comfort and our caregiver pulled away. Yet we are still petrified to admit we want love now. We know this past might have happened because we reexperience these triggers, assumptions, and emotions in our current relationships. As evidence of this, one study found that when people saw a picture of their mothers, the more insecurely attached they were, the more areas of their brain associated with implicit memory light up.

Of course, implicit memory can impact much more than our dynamic in romantic relationships. As I alluded to earlier, any disproportionate reaction we have is often provoked by an implicit memory, Dr. Alessio Travaglia, the director of neuroscience at the National Institutes of Health, told me. Therapists use the pithy phrase "If it's hysterical, it's historical" (if we can allow ourselves to reappropriate the term *hysteria* from Freud, who used it to describe women's trauma over not having a penis). As evidence of this, Travaglia's unpublished research involved exposing infant rats to aromas, like cinnamon or cocoa, and shocking them. As adults, they refused to eat the spice associated with the shock.

Some researchers think implicit memories formed in infancy affect us more than explicit ones formed later on. This is because an infant's hippocampus is not fully developed. In recording our memories, our hippocampus also tells us a memory occurred in a distinct context. Without one (or a fully developed one), we're liable to be triggered not just in a similar context, but anywhere. Dr. Lynn Nadel, a professor emeritus at the University of Arizona and a memory researcher, told me he had conducted a study where he found that rats got nervous when reintroduced to a place where they were shocked, but not when introduced to new environments. But if their hippocampus was damaged, they got nervous everywhere. For infantile and traumatic memories, our hippocampus is on the sidelines: for infants, because it hasn't fully matured, and for trauma, because stress has stifled it. These negative infant memories, Dr. Nadel told me, make us feel as vulnerable as traumatic memories do.

Simon has heard people say that adopted children aren't affected by their adoptions because they were too young to remember the loss. And yet Simon, who went up for adoption at age two, felt scared that any woman would abandon him, just as his mother had. What triggered these fears was an incident in the relationship, usually one that might seem minor to others but that he took as rejection. It wasn't minor for him, of course, because in activating his implicit memory, it triggered the same tidal wave of abandonment he'd felt in the past.

Simon remembered how one of his ex-girlfriend's comments on others' impressive clothes or cars made him feel inadequate. It was exactly the kind of thing that would make him flee. "There's always a moment that makes me feel like this person might leave me, and then I just start regressing . . . to a point to where I've already escaped before this person has even realized." He has the image of himself as a two-year-old, on a porch, holding a social worker's hand as his mother left. But in his adult relationships, he lets go of her hand and leaves the porch to go inside before he has a chance to see his mother go.

WE'RE NOT IN CONTROL

When I read this research, I want to shake my fist at nature. *Who designed us like this?* Of course, we struggle to feel worthy when memories spawning our insecurities barricade themselves in our amygdala, or else are imprisoned in memories we can't access . . . unless we experience déjà vu and a sudden gush of stress that makes these memories unleash themselves upon us. We should all meet in the park and protest the nonsensical burden of being human.

The worst part is that if our emotional reactions are often shadows of memories we don't even remember, then we have little control over how we feel. (Of course, we still have control over how we treat others; we just don't have control over how we initially feel in reaction to something.) This unsettles me. If "control" was a band in concert, I'd splurge for front-row VIP tickets so I could meet it backstage and become its groupie. Case in point: I once tried to do the trust fall with an ex-girlfriend, and every time I leaned back, as if lowering my body into a casket, I stumbled back onto the steadiness of a leg before my body tilted past thirty degrees. I wouldn't use the term *control "freak"* per se, because there's nothing freaky about it to me. Harnessing control feels to me more like watching the aurora borealis—*it's so beautiful.*

Maybe we're not all control groupies, but to be human is to crave control, at least a little. It is a fundamental need, one that serves an important evolutionary function. Without some control over our environment, we are vulnerable to all types of threats. I remember a study where people had to do mental exercises while being blasted with a loud noise at random intervals. They were fried afterward—so much so that they made multiple mistakes when proofreading a passage and gave up easily when attempting to solve a puzzle. But some participants were able to press a button to make the noise stop. They made fewer mistakes and didn't give up as easily on the follow-up tasks. They even said the noise was less irritating. This occurred even though none of these participants *actually* pressed the button. It was having control over the pain, rather than exerting it, that soothed them. Why can't implicit memory come with a control button?

The way implicit memory can crop up and hijack our emotions eviscerates any illusion I have of controlling how I feel. But knowing this does alter my philosophy of control. Modern society gives us the illusion that control is attainable. If I want to go to a museum, I call an Uber. If I want the newest Pantene shampoo, I order it on Amazon to arrive tomorrow, or even today if I order early enough. If I'm hungry, I get Chipotle delivered. Convenience culture assures us that if we want something and we have the means, it's ours.

Yet implicit memory debunks the idea that we are entitled to be in control of how we experience others or ourselves. And if we're not in control, we're not defective when emotions overtake us. We're not broken because we feel hurt when we think we shouldn't, or unsafe when everything appears fine, or because we can't make a typo in an email without hating ourselves. We lack control of our emotions because that's how we humans are *designed*, not because there's anything wrong with us. Just understanding this basic fact can be a balm because what is most unsettling about control is often not that we don't have it; it's that we assume we should. There's suffering in this chasm between the control we ache for and the control we lack. There's peace and self-acceptance in surrender, in knowing that there is nothing we should or should not feel. There is only what we *do* feel. And those potent feelings are the historians of our lives, revealing things we've suffered that are often unremembered.

What I'm trying to convey here is how much our feelings of unworthiness aren't our fault. Implicit memory has not tuned into the evolving zeitgeist around consent. It barges in and records threats with abandon (probably for our benefit sometimes, but that doesn't mean we can't complain). Knowing this allows us to practice sensitivity, with even our most frustrating feelings, to acknowledge they exist *and that's okay.* And we can console ourselves with the knowledge that our frustrating feelings of insecurity aren't inexplicable, even if we don't know why they are there. Somewhere in our journey, something happened that made us feel bad about ourselves, and this experience nestled into our implicit memory.

These bodily memories often keep us from being the person we want to be. Simon wanted to be better to the women in his life, particularly Liza, who had been his best friend for years. He wanted to be consistent, considerate, and loving. He could see how much Liza hoped for this, too. "She knew that I wasn't an asshole, and she was never going to let me be an asshole . . . I think that's a sign of commitment to somebody . . . it was like, don't you see that I care about you? Don't you see that? I'm not gonna let this [pattern] define you. There's going to be a path toward something different, a commitment to the best version of yourself."

Now we can understand why Simon felt so trapped in his pattern with women, and why changing destructive behaviors is so difficult when they stem from the memories we don't remember. The deafening noise of Simon's body, the way his heartbeat and blood flow and breathing coalesced to say, *They'll leave you. Leave now. Leave before they do*, was too much to overcome. Liza and Simon spent another year and a half in an agonizing on-and-off-again relationship, with Liza hoping for more but Simon never conceding. It only ended when Liza, like the other women, got fed up enough to leave. Simon describes the status of their relationship now as, "If she saw me on the street, she wouldn't say hello." Reflecting, Simon shared, "I was just a painful person to care about or be in love with. It wasn't in me [to be loved]. Not that I wasn't lovable, but I wasn't able to accept love. So my ability to make sure somebody left me was profound, impressive."

But just because our feelings of insecurity aren't our fault, that doesn't mean we can't change them. Someone who didn't cut down a tree can still plant a flower. Holding this duality propels us to heal while accepting, rather than blaming, ourselves along the way. It allows us to do what author Michael Pollan has learned to do: "Practice being with stillness, being with other people as I find them (imperfect), and being with my own unimproved self. To savor whatever it is at this very moment." We move forward from this bedrock of accepting our out-of-control selves.

In the previous chapter, we learned that to find worth, we should drum up old memories and reflect on the good that came from them or visualize our adult self intervening to make things better. Now, after learning about implicit memory, we must find a way to reconsolidate these memories, too. "People can never get better without knowing what they know and feeling what they feel," the prominent psychiatrist Elvin Semrad once said. But we can't just know what the conscious mind knows. We must figure out what the body knows, too.

HEALING WHAT WE DON'T REMEMBER

One day, I went to see friends for dinner. I had gotten into a car accident a year prior, and for several months after, I'd been getting headaches when I entered a car. At dinner, I mentioned I was trying Emotional Freedom Technique (EFT) to find some relief. EFT involves tapping specific points on the body when experiencing a negative sensation, like my headache. A friend who tends to be particularly skeptical of alternative treatments asked me how EFT works. I wished she hadn't, because I anticipated her internal judgment (although I knew she'd be too nice to say it out loud). Quickly, after I explained, I pivoted the conversation, "So how does everyone like their salad?" I was grateful when she moved on and gave me her thoughts on the balsamic vinaigrette instead.

Although I was nervous that I sounded bonkers when I said tapping points on my body made me feel better, there is evidence that EFT effectively treats both explicit memory and the body-based remnants of implicit memory. When people underwent six workshops on EFT, by the end, it didn't just decrease cortisol (37 percent decrease); it also lowered heart rate (8 percent decrease) and reduced blood pressure (6 to 8 percent decrease). A meta-analysis found that people who underwent EFT decreased their PTSD symptoms much more than people who underwent no treatment . . . and we know trauma often involves implicit memories. And the icing on the cake: Other studies have found that EFT is linked to significant decreases in depression and anxiety rates, too. Although one clear limitation of the research on EFT is that it has been used with people who are consciously recalling memories. More compelling evidence for its impact on implicit memory would involve EFT being successfully applied to treat emotional triggers in the moment they occur.

When clinicians from Sweden, the UK, and the US took five trips to a war-torn village in Kosovo to administer EFT to 105 traumatized people, 103 of them reported total relief. Five months later, not a single one of the 103 relapsed. Relief was described as having no body reactions to negative triggers of memories—in other words, as healing implicit memory.

"Yes, at this moment it is completely gone . . . if the way I feel at this moment becomes all moments, I will be entirely satisfied," one participant said. After the intervention, participants looked up to heaven in gratitude, hugged those beside them, or went home to gather peaches or nuts to give as gifts to the researchers. One woman was so depressed, the researchers had to hold her up to administer EFT to her. Afterward, she jogged to the shed to get a stool for a doctor sitting in the grass.

Yet my eyebrows raised as I read a footnote in this study that said the lead author asked the editor of the academic journal not to send the article to other academics to review because he assumed they'd be too biased, too scathing. The mechanism used to explain EFT didn't allay my skepticism. EFT allegedly works because certain points on the skin send electricity to organs, like the amygdala, to calm the body. They do so through energy highways in the body called *meridians*. When these meridians are blocked, people fall ill. Stimulating the EFT points, because they are supposedly better at conducting electricity to zing along the meridian, should clear the meridian and promote healing. EFT researchers cited a review to imply that their EFT points better conduct electricity than other points do. Yet when I actually read the review, it was inconclusive: "The evidence did not conclusively support the claim that acupoints or meridians were electrically distinguishable [from other points]."

My read of the EFT studies was that it works, but researchers seem to be reaching beyond what's warranted in their explanation as to why. So I was still looking for a reason it worked, one that I could more confidently air at dinner parties without abrupt changes of topic to balsamic dressing.

Francine Shapiro walked around a park, ruminating on disturbing thoughts. During her walk, she started to feel better, so much so that when she revisited those thoughts, she no longer felt distress. Ten years prior, Francine had been diagnosed with cancer, which led her to develop the habit of using her body as a laboratory to discern what soothes her. So she reflected on her relief, realizing that as she thought about the memories, her eyes had darted back and forth. Could the eye movements have had something to do with why she felt better? She pivoted her graduate school research to investigate whether these darting eye movements could help others work through their emotions, too.

Shapiro's hunch led her to develop one of the leading therapies for healing trauma, rapid eye movement desensitization and reprocessing, better known as EMDR, conditionally recommended by the American Psychological Association. In EMDR, people remember a trauma, or its associated sensations for implicit traumatic memories, and rapidly move their eyes back and forth while tracking a moving object, like someone's finger or a digital ball.

EMDR and EFT are uncannily similar: Someone splits their focus between an upsetting memory and something else—eye movements for EMDR and tapping for EFT. Research has even found that the two therapies have similar benefits on negative memories. *Could it be that their success can be explained by the same mechanism?* Maybe splitting your attention while accessing a memory, or the sensations associated with it in the case of implicit memory, somehow improves your body's experience of it? Could memory reconsolidation through straight-up multitasking somehow work? To find out, we'll journey through what's known as *working memory theory.*

Working memory is a form of short-term memory that we apply to meet a goal. So, for example, instead of just registering a red light, you apply this information to tell you to pump the brakes. The memory has to put in a little elbow grease. According to working memory theory, our working memory is like a computer's RAM. We only have so much of it, and if we overwhelm it, it malfunctions. This drawback is an opportunity, though, when it comes to reconsolidating memory. We can conjure up a negative memory, or for implicit memory, a sensation. Then, we can tax our RAM in some way, whether it's eye movements, as with EMDR, or tapping a pattern, like in EFT. In doing so, we won't have enough RAM left to remember the memory as vividly or to relive a sensation as viscerally. The memory or sensation then degrades, becoming less intense the next time we remember it. It's like reconsolidating by carrying grocery bags that are just too full—with emotions, sensations, and tapping—so the sensations tumble out.

Working memory theory may explain why both EMDR and EFT work. Studies find that the more EMDR disrupts our working memory, the better it is at subsequently making our memories less vivid.

Similarly, tapping a complicated pattern of points on the body (not EFT points) while remembering decreased the vividness of a memory. Simply tapping counterclockwise, however, didn't degrade vividness, likely because it was too simple to tax participants' RAM enough.

But if it's just draining working memory that helps memory degrade, perhaps we don't need eye movements or taps at all. Maybe if we perform any task while simultaneously recalling a negative memory or its sensations, then the emotion in the memory shrinks? Indeed, studies find that emotion in a memory decreases when people access it and play Tetris, draw a complicated shape, or even listen to someone say "Ta" repeatedly. A client in a private practice experienced so much relief after recalling a trauma while counting by two that he asked his therapist "Is this magic?"

At the end of this chapter, I'll offer guidance as to how to use EFT* to work through your implicit memories. I'm focusing on EFT instead of EMDR because it's viewed by therapists as safer to administer to yourself. But if you prefer other forms of distraction instead, like playing Tetris while you feel triggered, I will offer an exercise to lead you through that, too. Another reason I recommend EFT is because memories degrade more when you tax the same sense needed to conjure the memory. If the memory manifests as an image, EMDR works well because it is also visual, involving watching an object move back and forth. We need to meet the memory where it lives. And implicit memory lives in the body. It feels like a gut punch, a heat flash of anger, a compulsion to withdraw. With EFT, we use the body to heal the body.

* If working memory theory explains why EFT works, then there must be no special electrical charge at EFT points, as the EFT researchers have argued. One study supports this argument, suggesting that EFT instead works because it involves tapping in a pattern complicated enough to tax working memory. Specifically, a study found that tapping the same EFT points on a doll or on yourself decreased fear equally. Another study, however, found that when students tapped either EFT points or an equally complicated pattern of points elsewhere, the students tapping EFT points felt less stressed after. This study suggests that there may be a mechanism outside of working memory theory that explains why EFT works.

It is unnerving to be so triggered and not know why. It makes you feel like you don't know who you are. It disrupts your fundamental need to understand your story, to have a sense of continuity and identity. But for some of us, the memory we're looking for, the eureka one that explains everything, that offers us control by giving us our story, does not exist. There will be no divine recording that shows what might have happened to us as a child, that will allow us to say, "Now I know how bad it was. Now it makes sense, the way I hate myself."

But a memory doesn't have to be a story for it to be real. If all the proof we'll ever have is in those moments we're hijacked, the raw ways we feel, the fits of rage or fear or self-flagellation, then that's enough. The memories that live mainly in our body are not inferior to the ones living in our mind. They are a different version of real.

Once we take our implicit memories seriously, we can heal even from the things we don't remember, as Simon has begun to do. Simon had gotten into a fight with his current girlfriend, and afterward, he went to work at a coffee shop. There, he spotted an old flame, who laid it on him thick. "My boyfriend just ghosted me," she said. She mentioned their past connection and hinted that she'd be open to rekindling something. There was a past version of Simon who would have said, "Yes, I have a new place, two blocks away. You want to come see it?" His emotional well would be flooded, and he would need this old flame's validation to scoop out the water.

But with his healing, Simon's implicit memories didn't hijack him as much as they did before. The water in the well had settled to manageable levels, so he didn't need short-term validation not to drown. "I think I'm going to go home. I need to make lunch," he said. "Oh great! I can drive you," she responded. "That's okay. It's just two blocks away. I enjoy the walk."

Something Simon and each of us will have to learn as we heal our implicit memories is that if the implicit memory exists within us, then it's *not* outside of us. Maybe we won't get hurt again like we've been hurt before. Although these implicit memories lead our body to tell us that now is a moment of rejection, abandonment, or neglect, just as it was back then, the rejection is not imminent. Even if we feel it is, it's not happening again. It's over.

We're here now.

IMPLICIT MEMORY RECONSOLIDATION EXERCISES (OR WHAT TO DO WHEN YOU'RE TRIGGERED)

Note: If you have a mental health diagnosis, I recommend you apply these exercises only under the supervision of a mental health professional. If any of these techniques increase your distress, stop immediately.

EMOTIONAL FREEDOM TECHNIQUE (EFT)

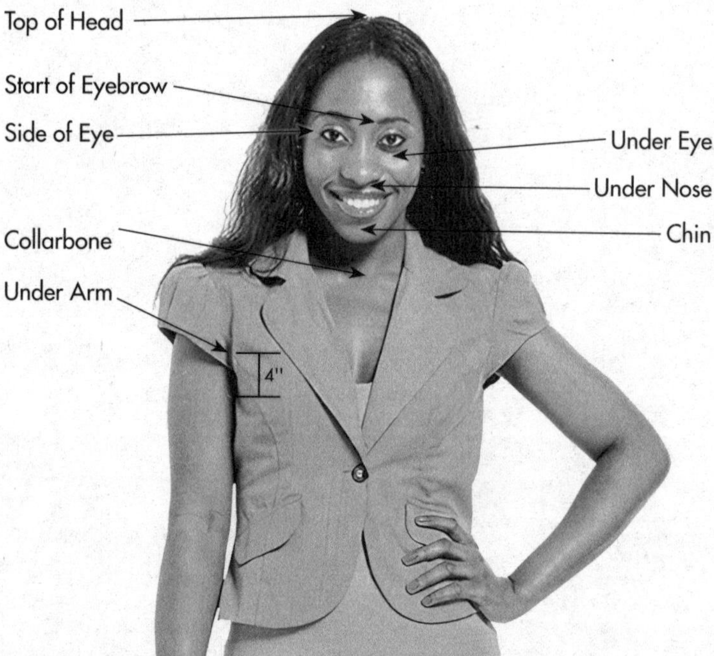

Adapted from the EFT Manual from EFTinternational.org.

1. Think of an **emotion, sensation, or trigger** that's been bothering you. To access implicit memory, you can think of a time when you've felt strong emotion, reactivity, or a need to shut down.

Bring the emotion, sensation, or trigger to mind as **vividly** as possible, as if it was happening right now. To do so, notice where it manifests in your body (tight jaw, lump in throat, etc.).

2. Develop a **phrase** describing the trigger. For Simon, an example is *I feel abandoned, so I want to withdraw.*
3. **Rate** the associated **distress** from 1 (*not at all distressed*) to 10 (*very distressed*).
4. Develop a "**setup statement**" in the form, *Even though I feel (emotion or sensation), I deeply and completely accept myself.*

   You can adjust this setup statement so it feels right for you. (I like to end mine with *I'm on my side.*)
5. **Say** this setup statement three times.
6. **Tap** each of the points in the diagram seven to ten times while naming the emotion or sensation. For example: *This stress, this fear, this tightness.*
7. After you tap through all of the points, pause to **notice** how you **feel**.
8. **Rate** the **distress** associated with this emotion or sensation again from 1 (*not at all distressed*) to 10 (*very distressed*), and note any changes in how you feel.
9. If distress remains, **repeat** this exercise, except when you get to the setup statement in step 4, tweak it to *Even though I* still *feel (emotion or sensation), I deeply and completely accept myself.*

Adapted from the EFT International Free Tapping Manual.

TETRIS

1. Download a Tetris app on your phone or computer.
2. Think of an **emotion, sensation, or trigger** that's been bothering you. To access implicit memory, you can think of a time when you've felt strong emotion, reactivity, or a need to shut down. Bring the emotion, sensation, or trigger to mind as **vividly** as possible, as if it was happening right now. To do so, notice where it manifests in your body (tight jaw, lump in throat, etc.).
3. Develop a **phrase** describing your issue. For Simon, an example is *I feel abandoned, so I want to withdraw.*
4. **Rate** the associated **distress** from 1 (*not at all distressed*) to 10 (*very distressed*).
5. As you reexperience the emotion, sensation, or trigger, play a round of Tetris.
6. After you finish a round, pause to **notice** how you **feel**.
7. **Rate** the **distress** associated with this emotion or sensation again from 1 (*not at all distressed*) to 10 (*very distressed*), and note any changes in how you feel.
8. If distress remains, **repeat** this activity.

Adapted from Engelhard et al., "The Impact of Taxing Working Memory on Negative and Positive Memories."

5

Remember to Feel

"So how did you know you were disconnected from your emotions?" I asked Cynthia, a life coach from Brazil living in Dallas, Texas. Cynthia had responded to a request I put on my Instagram, asking to speak with people who are or had been emotionally numb. If, as we've discussed, we must release emotions stuck in our memories to feel worthy, then being disconnected from our emotions can hinder healing. After all, how can we release old emotions we can't even access?

We often think of people who are numb as human Eeyores, black boxes to themselves and others. Their speech is monotone, their expressions blank, their personality a shade of gray. But Cynthia would reveal that what we preconceive is wrong.

"I think the way that I would suppress my emotions would be . . . by being agreeable."

Although I had never thought of agreeableness as a way to disconnect from emotion, as soon as she said this, it resonated so much I felt gobsmacked. I was flooded with memories of trying to be someone's cultural archetype of good, which as a woman, of course, meant agreeable. All of a sudden there I was in 2016, telling a date in Bangkok who was an hour and a half late, “It’s nice to see you! I’m glad you’re here.” There I was at age six, asking my brother for a kiss because that’s what little girls do, I guessed. There I was in high school, when a friend’s white mom told us about the class on race she took in college, and she turned to me and said, “You know, you would have been a slave . . . back then.” A pause, the oxygen rushing out of the room. “I know. You’re right. I would have been.” The oxygen rushed back in, for everyone else, at least. “You handled that so well,” a friend told me later.

There is something intoxicating about being disconnected from our emotions. On emotional autopilot, most of us will strive to become someone else’s version of good. In place of ourselves, we become a cultural chameleon, transforming into someone else’s definition of what is valuable. As Cynthia put it, “I didn’t have a sense of self. So [I wondered] what was the next thing to do in the track of life that my mom said [was good].” We please our parents; we marry, have 2.5 kids, and a nice house in the ’burbs; our relationships have minimal friction because we’re so chill. Prestige, validation, and status flood in. And yet, we feel empty inside, gnawingly lonely, because we’re estranged from ourselves. The ennui is a symptom revealing a core part of us that regrets: *If only this version of good was my own.*

Healing means we have something to lose. We will no longer be “good,” which will, perhaps, make us better.

THE FACES OF NUMBNESS

And yet, trying to be “good” by suppressing our emotions doesn’t make us truly good. The suppressed emotions, the unprocessed open memories, become the Mr. Hyde to our Dr. Jekyll, hijacking us. The parts of us trapped beneath the ice smash it open. Our numbness will, ironically, manifest in pockets of hyperemotionality because you can’t regulate what you don’t acknowledge. This is true even if we’re only disconnected from a specific emotion, like anger, as Cynthia was, rather than being entirely unfeeling.

We can take out this bombardment of emotion on others or ourselves. Externalizers take out their triggers on others; internalizers, on themselves. Both *-izers* are getting triggered by what is suppressed, but these triggers hit different targets.

I thought about my own triggers, and tendency to internalize, when I was in line at Qdoba. The woman in front of me said to the employee, "I ordered and got my food. They told me to get back in line. I should have went straight to the cashier to pay. Why did y'all tell me that?" Her tone was pointed, her voice elevated. I tensed at the heat behind her words. I wanted to stop bracing, which meant I wanted her to shut up.

But to my surprise, the employee responded kindly. "You're right. You should have gone to the cashier. I don't know why they told you that. You can go now." It was at that moment that I realized how disconnecting from my anger made me shut down at any hint of it in others. When someone was angry, even when their anger was valid, I wanted to flee. And it left me with the urge to control others so they wouldn't expose me to this emotion I avoided.

Yet I wasn't actually cruel to that woman at Qdoba. The lady in line was clueless about the emotional cocktail brewing inside me. I never tried to regulate my own discomfort by yelling at her to calm down, like an externalizer might; I just *wanted* to. As an internalizer, I wouldn't express my triggers, but they'd be roiling me internally, revealing that if you don't know who the victim of your triggers is, perhaps you are.

If I could suspend the horror I feel at causing harm, I'd be jealous of externalizers. They get to release their pain by offloading it onto others, while internalizers white-knuckle it. But perhaps externalizers are jealous of internalizers because, since we don't cause harm to anyone but ourselves, we still get to be "good."

Mike, a scientist in his forties, revealed a severe example of the harm that can be caused by externalizing. He endured cliché male socialization, prompting him to filter out any feelings of weakness. So he pushed away the feelings of unworthiness that originated from his father abandoning him before his first birthday.

One night, Mike's three-year-old son had night terrors and came by for comfort. Mike soothed him. His son returned, still upset. Mike consoled him again. When his son returned the fifth time, still scared, a familiar voice spoke, one Mike had tried to smother: *He thinks I'm not good enough. The things I say are not good enough. The things I do are not good enough.* His son went from being tiny toes and fingers to a tool he could yield to crush these feelings back down. Mike screamed and screamed at his son, in such a rage that he blacked out. He took his son to another room, leaving him in the darkness with the door shut. His son screamed for his dad, banging at the door. It was his wife's shock that he remembers. "It's the worst thing I've ever done," Mike said. After that, his son never called him "Dad" again.

As I listened to Mike's story, I thought about something a fellow internalizer friend said—that internalizing was "the more noble option" because (apparently) no one gets harmed.* I laughed. It felt both absurd and a bit true to think of this relationship with triggers as more noble. But Peter Levine, a trauma specialist we'll get to know more later, wrote in regard to internalizing that although "this approach is more socially acceptable, it is no less violent than acting out."

All of us need a third option to face the emotions we've tried to run from.

HOW WE BECAME DISCONNECTED

Will tells his therapist, Sean, that his alcoholic father would put a "wrench, a stick, and a belt on the table" and ask him to choose. Look-

* Of course, it's debatable whether we can truly internalize. People can pick up on a sudden shift in tone or mood that tends to coincide with internalizing.

ing away beneath his blond bangs, Will says to Sean, "I used to go with the wrench . . . because fuck him, that's why. . . ."

"It's not your fault," Sean says.

"Alright," Will says, opening only the corner of his mouth in his reply.

"It's not your fault."

"Don't fuck with me." Will says, shoving Sean. "Don't fuck with me, Sean, not you!"

"It's not your fault. It's not your fault."

Will buries his head in his hands and weeps.

In the movie *Good Will Hunting*, Will is as emotionally detached as they come. But his breakdown reveals that his cool aloofness isn't because he's just not an emotional person. Studies, in fact, have found that our genes have no bearing on our likelihood of disassociating from our emotions.* If you're numb, Will reminds us, it's not because of who you are. It's because something happened to you.

If you are disconnected from your emotions, sometime in your childhood it was adaptive for you to not feel them. It made your parents like you more or hurt you less. According to structural dissociation theory, babies are natural feelers, and they try to get their caregivers to soothe their emotions. John Bowlby, the father of attachment theory, described how babies separated from their mothers slammed themselves against the floor, cried out in despair, or awoke from sleep shrieking. While the consensus at the time was that babies just needed food and milk to be happy, Bowlby's research revealed that this was not enough. They needed comfort from someone dear.

But if babies don't get the soothing they seek, their next strategy to regulate their emotions is to "alter consciousness"—to suppress the parts of them in distress. This creates what psychologist Janina Fisher calls

* People in the study were only classified as disassociated if they displayed a more severe form of disassociation. Thus, it's possible that people who experience more milder forms of emotional disconnect could be that way because of their genetics.

"fault lines," broken-off parts of their personalities. As psychologist Robert Karen puts it in his article "Becoming Attached":

> A secure child is able to communicate negative feelings like anger, hurt, jealousy, and resentment in a meaningful way. He can cry or shout, fall silent, or say "I hate you," confident of a sensitive response. The insecure child does not have this confidence. His mother, unable to handle her own negative feelings, either becomes dismissive or overreacts. As a result, his negative feelings are either walled off from his consciousness or revved up to the point where they overwhelm him.

When an avoidantly attached baby's mom enters a room, he won't look at her, treating her like a stranger. He has already learned to suppress the part of him that wants love. As Bowlby observed, if this happened too often in their first three years, these babies would stay detached throughout their lives.

Although a meta-analysis found that when we have a history of physical or sexual abuse, we're more likely to be disconnected from our emotions, attachment studies suggest that our parents don't have to be physically violent or sexually abusive to trigger emotional disconnection in us. Perfectly nice parents, who put food on the table and help us with our homework, can still leave us emotionally disconnected. As bell hooks reminds us in *All about Love: New Visions*, care—taking care of our basic needs—does not necessarily equate to love. Love means helping us express all of who we are, including our feelings.

In her memoir *I'm Glad My Mom Died*, Jennette McCurdy reveals a subtle example of how a mother can cause a child to disconnect from herself. Ten-year-old McCurdy ordered cookies-and-cream ice cream instead of her usual nutty coconut at Dairy Queen. "You don't want nutty coconut?" her mom asked. McCurdy froze, waiting to see how her mother would react.

Her mother teared up, "Nutty coconut's been your favorite for eight months. You're changing, growing up."

McCurdy took her mother's hand, "Never mind. I want nutty coconut."

As McCurdy's story illustrates, parents who use their kids to regulate their emotions, instead of regulating their child's, raise kids who are disconnected from themselves. It's the mother who gets angry when her baby cries, telling him "Stop that!" or "I get so upset when you cry. Make Mommy feel better." One study, for example, found that children who experienced this kind of dismissiveness from their moms were more disassociated from their feelings at age nineteen. In another study, mothers reported how much they reject their kid's negative emotions, signified by whether they endorsed statements like "Children act sad to get their way" or "When my child gets angry, my goal is to get him or her to stop." When thinking of an upsetting memory, kids with dismissive mothers said they didn't feel so bad, even when their physiological data confirmed otherwise. Their personality was breaking, fault lines already formed.*

These studies advance our understanding of implicit memory. We've learned it can manifest as sensations and feelings, but our implicit memories can also manifest as the absence of these things. Within the veil of our numbness are memories of attachment figures who told us "Get over it," "You're too sensitive," or "It's all in your head." Numbness, too, is a sign of open memories yet to be closed.

Often, when a parent has failed us in these more nuanced ways, we won't admit it. In fact, studies find that when you ask avoidant children about their parents, they say their parents were great. How can they admit their parents hurt them when their parents taught them to deny their hurt? We rely on these protective narratives of our parents, and

* If you're a parent who is horrified that you may have made some of these mistakes, I hope you know that giving yourself empathy is the way forward. Your self-compassion is not just a gift for yourself, but for everyone. The good and bad twins showed us that beating yourself up won't make you love your kids better, but having compassion for yourself will. You can give yourself the love you may have never had but always deserved; that love will radiate out to the people you love, too. If you're reading this, you're already on your way.

it can feel unsettling to acknowledge anything different. In an interview, McCurdy shared that when a therapist told her that her mother may have been abusive, she ghosted the therapist.

As kids, we learn to deny emotion to escape rejection, ridicule, or abandonment from our parents. For a child, gaining our parents' approval feels as urgent as escaping death; social death, like rejection, feels like physical death. This makes sense for a species that, if abandoned by parents, would not survive.

Mike, the scientist, shut down his yearning for love after his own social death, his father abandoning him. He saw his dad only once, when he was twelve, at his grandmother's funeral. As he stared at the back of his dad's head from five rows back, he remembered not a feeling, but the absence of one. What would love, grief, or yearning do but make his abandonment more gut-wrenching? Shatter his sense of self into even smaller shards?

But then, what does it mean to live a life where your need for love is frozen within you? It means parts of us die so the rest of us can live on, our emotions becoming our martyrs.

THE COSTS OF FAULT LINES

As a child, Cynthia saw half-drunk milk cartons in the fridge. On Monday, Cynthia's father opened a carton of milk. On Tuesday, another. On Wednesday, a third. By Thursday, none of the cartons had been drunk. Still, he opened a fourth. These cartons were supposed to last the family a month, and they couldn't afford extra. Yet her father would open a new one before finishing the last, a votive offering to his power, a reminder that he will do what he wants, and everyone else will adjust, or else. To escape his temper, she'd play quietly with her dollhouse, creating the perfect family with a mother, a kid, and the kind of father who drank a single carton at a time. Growing up with a volatile father taught Cynthia that being "agreeable" was tolerating the intolerable, which required her to bury her anger, her terror, her grief.

What might have traumatized Cynthia is not just her father's behavior, but the fact that she couldn't do anything about it. As evidence of this, a meta-analysis explored why some people exposed to trauma develop PTSD while others don't. As you might suspect, the more life-threatening the event—if the offender was unhinged, billowing with rage, or brandishing a knife—the more traumatized people become. Maybe people who felt the most shame, fear, and horror at the time of the trauma become more traumatized? Yes, the study found this was also true. And yet, there was a certain response to the trauma that even more strongly predicted future PTSD symptoms, and it predicted trauma symptoms more than other classic harbingers of PTSD, like prior traumas experienced, family history of mental illness, or lack of support received.

This response is less of a response and more so the absence of one. The more people disassociated from their emotions at the time of the trauma, the more likely they were to suffer later. The more they felt nothing in one moment, the more likely they were to feel everything later. This study suggests that when we've learned, early on, that our go-to response to stressful events should be to disassociate from our emotions, our mental health becomes vulnerable.

Trauma specialist Peter Levine explains why disassociation makes us so vulnerable. When we go through something traumatic, our bodies surge with energy to help us fight or flee—think an adrenaline rush, Levine argues. And if we fight or flee, we fare better in the long term, because these acts release this energy. In words we're familiar with, fighting or fleeing helps us release the emotion that is liable to get stuck in open memories. Take traumatized rats, for instance. Researchers typically traumatize them by repeatedly shocking them. One study found that when rats could hit a switch to stop the shocks, fleeing the threat successfully, they got less brain damage than rats who couldn't, even though both rats endured the same degree of shock.

In another experiment, rats were exposed to another rat after being shocked. They stood up on their hind legs, slapped, bit, and fought. They could release their energy, rather than it becoming stuck. Fighting rats showed lower levels of stress hormones than rats who were shocked the same amount but were isolated and could not fight.

But sometimes we can't fight or flee because doing so might make things worse, like Cynthia experienced with her father. The horror is too big. The chance of escape is too small. For Cynthia, and for others who have had to disconnect from their emotions, feeling all this energy with no release is like being stuck underwater. You need to come up for air or you'll explode, but you can't. So instead, dissociation sets in, like a circuit breaker, shutting down incapacitating amounts of energy. But the energy—emotions still trapped in our open memories—remains.

Our well of excess energy grows, compounding any energy we've already banished during our childhood to be "good." And then it bombards us. In fact, Levine argues that trauma symptoms, like flashbacks, nightmares, and mood swings, are all ways the energy punches up for release. Triggers are also an example of this energy regurgitation, for those of us who have endured "little *t*" traumas, which psychologists define as everyday traumas, or events that have impacted our nervous system that weren't necessarily life-threatening.

Energy bombardment feels like an intrusion that creates rapid shifts in how we see others or ourselves, making us suddenly aggressive, withdrawn, or self-critical, like thinking that making a typo means I'm a fuckup. What is suppressed makes us possessed. The purpose of this bombardment, trauma researchers think, is to heal us. It arouses us to finally fight or flee, but now in the wrong circumstance. When Cynthia's son was thrashing about to keep her from changing his clothes, his defiance activated her own dormant energy. She pinned him to the bed to force him to change. She reflected, "When I'm with my kids, [now] I have authority . . . I was big enough to fight."

We are one person when this energy is dormant, and another someone, foreign to our regular self, when it blasts out, like Mike was that night with his son. We become suddenly more aggressive toward others, if we're externalizers, or if we're internalizers, toward ourselves. In Cynthia's case, she was a star student, getting all A's, turned star professional, getting promoted ad infinitum. She eventually worked in one of Brazil's biggest companies, Telecom. She paid for an apartment alone, while sending money to her family. When it came to her children, though, she'd falter.

Her son would cry, tantruming in the back seat of the car. Her banished terror returned. "It was really hard for me to deal with that. I wanted it to stop." She'd raise the volume on the radio so loud he'd get scared, so loud he'd quit crying to make it stop.

Tears falling, she told me, "I can't believe I did that to my kid."

HOW TO FEEL AGAIN

Against a backdrop of thirsty grass on an African savannah, a cheetah hugs an impala close. The embrace looks kind of romantic, as if the cheetah wants to smooch him. But it's also deceptive foreplay when your true goal is massacre. This is why it's so hard to trust love. *Sigh.*

The impala's expression is unsettling. He is lifeless, his eyes black and rolled back. When the cheetah's arm shifts from beside his head, it rolls to the ground with a thud. If he's not dead already, he seems doomed to be soon.

The cheetah hears something, veering her neck toward the noise. A potential threat? The cheetah tries to grab the impala's neck in her mouth to foist him elsewhere. But he's too bulky. She drops him. The cheetah gives up and runs away.

I'm watching a video of this interaction at a café. Why? To encourage myself to order the lemon tartine, so I, too, can be too bulky to be carried away by life's cheetahs. Really, though, I'm watching because if the impala can revive from freezing, from numbness, perhaps we can, too.

The video zooms in on the impala, lying on the ground, his body motionless. He still looks dead. And even with the cheetah retreating, he hasn't moved. I burn with the same righteous anger that smacks me when I watch protagonists in a horror movie walk down the bloodied stairs toward the shrieks. *You fool! You need to get out of there!*

But then, his stomach inflates. He breathes. The rest of his body stays frozen, as if only his stomach resurrected from death. *You might want to wake yourself up a little faster,* I think. As if on command, his stomach pumps more quickly. He shoots up, sitting on his legs.

Now the impala is shaking, erratically, like he's been electrocuted. He trembles and trembles and trembles, long enough to make me wonder if he'll ever stop. But then he shoots up again, this time on his legs. He trots away so merrily that I want to shake him even more: *Do you realize you almost just died!!??? Now you're acting like nothing happened???* But more than just baffling, what the impala did was also incredible.

He has shown us it's possible to break free of numbness, to return to life.

When trauma specialist Peter Levine watched the cheetah-impala interaction, he hypothesized that the impala's shaking released the energy mobilized during the trauma so he wouldn't be bombarded by it later. The energy release inherent to the shaking explains why impalas and other wild animals can endure regular violence and not get traumatized. Perhaps if humans could learn their own version of shaking, he thought, they could free up the trapped fear and panic lurking beneath their disassociation, evading later energy bombardment. They may even use this method to release emotions long frozen from childhood. To put it in words we've used before, they could close their implicit memories, the kinds that manifested in sensations in their bodies.

For animals to teach us how we can heal ourselves, we must overcome what Melanie Challenger, in her book *How to Be Animal: A New History of What It Means to Be Human*, calls "human exceptionalism," the idea that we as humans are completely distinct from animals. After all, humans share their lower brain structures with animals. And Levine writes, it's our most human part, our neocortex, that keeps us traumatized, since with it, we override the energy release. The neocortex gets us to ignore our nature, which he describes as "animals with an instinctual power to heal." In recognizing the continuity between animal and human experience, Levine created a form of therapy called Somatic Experiencing. Somatic Experiencing involves paying attention to what you sense in your body to heal.

Levine developed a method of healing (at the end of the chapter, I'll share this Somatic Experiencing exercise in more detail) that mirrors the impala's behavior. It involves tracking sensations in your body as they evolve. This sensation is thought to comprise the excess emotional energy still locked within. It's important to not analyze why it's there or what it means, because this pulls you out of your body. Instead, as Levine advises, we should let our body speak its mind. This means that you don't have to remember the memory where the trigger originated to heal it, which is helpful because it could have developed when you were an infant.

As we track the sensation, our body may feel urges to do spontaneous movements, things we allow our body to do rather than command it to. These spontaneous movements are akin to the impala's trembling. When it shook, it released the whirlpool of energy within. When we focus on sensations we feel, we may experience the urge to gulp, pout, shake, or even kick or punch, like we're in a kickboxing class. We should follow our body's lead, doing what it wants, without judging or suppressing its journey.

Spontaneous movements can help us stimulate and complete a fight-or-flight response, even one contained from long ago. And just by stimulating fighting, another rat study suggests, we can diminish the impact of trauma. In that study, rats were shocked. They were then exposed to another rat, so they would get on their hind legs to prepare to fight them. Except the other rat was behind plexiglass, so they could never make physical contact. But even assuming the fight position led these rats to get fewer ulcers than rats who did not.

After reading Levine's work, I showed up freshly in therapy. When we processed memories, my head would want to spin to the right. I'd let it. I'd sway. I'd shake. As I followed a sensation, I'd let my body glide, like a quarter circling a drain. I felt self-conscious at first, but eventually I didn't. Judging meant I was in my head and not my body. Living in my body meant there was nothing to judge myself with; when the editor becomes the writer, she stops correcting and starts expressing.

Levine's work was inspired by the work of philosopher Eugene Gendlin. When Gendlin studied humans in therapy, he came to the same conclusion about the importance of the body for healing. Gendlin observed thousands of therapy sessions and noticed that the most successful ones involved clients attuning to the ways a problem manifested in sensations in their bodies.

Based on his observations, Gendlin developed a concept called body trust. I used to think "trusting your body" meant that if you suddenly felt like withdrawing from someone, you were picking up on something bad about that person. Yet your body may be reacting because you are reliving a memory of something threatening. For example, avoidantly attached people often feel like withdrawing because they're reliving an implicit memory of intimacy being tied to threat. How our body reacts does not necessarily indicate some sort of truth about the person in front of us. It can suggest something about our own history instead.

As I read Gendlin's work, I realized that his concept of body trust means that we should trust our body to know what it needs to do to heal itself if we give it the chance, as the impala did intuitively. As Gendlin puts it, "Every bad feeling is potential energy toward a more right way of being if you give it space to move toward its rightness." Even if we tend to override our body, it's always showing its wisdom. It leads us to the first burst of air in our lungs when we break through water, to the coolness of liquid when our mouths dry, or to jerk our hand back at the scorch of a flame. Our bodies continuously monitor and adjust to maintain our well-being; if we can trust our body to achieve our physical homeostasis, Gendlin argues, then why not emotional? To leverage body trust, Gendlin developed an exercise involving observing these sensations, labeling them, and asking what they mean. I share this exercise at the end of the chapter as another method to release emotion within implicit memory.

When I felt anxious about not being as productive as I hoped to be, I tried Gendlin's exercise. I lay on my couch, closed my eyes, and tracked the sense of this anxious energy in my body. I felt the shallow breathing, and drive to act, that accompanied my anxiety. I asked why it was there. *Fear of death,* I heard. At first, this was surprising. But then, I thought it made sense. Anxiety is there to keep us from dying. At some point, my nervous system learned to equate not completing tasks with dying, a social death of disappointing myself and others, conflated with a physical one. Exploring the sensation eased the panic. Understanding my body's signals also allowed me to reassure myself that failing at my work would not kill me.

In revisiting the body-based residue of my memories, I was learning not to abandon my insides: not to perpetrate on my muscles and my heart and my lungs that same harm—of dismissal—that someone once perpetrated on me. If we are to treat ourselves as if we are worthy, I realized, we must treat our heaving chest, our rattling foot, or our stiff neck as if they are also worthy of our tender attention. It's not just that we are worthy of care as a whole body but within every tissue, every artery, every cell. We return to moments of harm and settle in beside the sensations left over from them, as if to say, *From my memory, down to my emotion, farther inward to the atom of my sensation, I am here. I am here. I am here.*

And once we trust our bodies, we can return to the memories where energy is trapped and finally release it. We can let our bodies complete their emotions, giving our feet, our hands, or our throat a way out of a place only they knew we were trapped in. We reanimate the emotions cordoned off along our fault lines. When we've been so numb to certain feelings, for so much of the landscape of our lives, that anything different has seemed impossible, we can finally feel possibility. It's like oxygen rushing in after a lifetime of holding your breath, thinking, all along, that you knew what it meant to breathe.

WHAT IT MEANS TO BE GOOD

Cynthia's fifteen-year-old daughter stomped into the house, furious about how a friend had treated her. She ran to her room and slammed the door so forcefully that Cynthia was afraid she'd break things. The Cynthia of ten years ago would have yelled at her daughter to get the anger to stop. Once, when her daughter was three and upset, Cynthia locked her in the backyard. She told her daughter she could come in when she knew how to control herself.

But Cynthia had since been doing Somatic Experiencing therapy. There, she learned to ease her body into tolerating anger. In one session, her therapist held a punching bag in front of her and asked her to hit it, to discharge her stored anger. At first, Cynthia couldn't get herself to do it, telling her therapist, "I'm going to hurt you."

"I'll be okay," the practitioner reassured her. He had to move the bag to the sofa so she'd be comfortable punching it. In another session, her therapist stood in the kitchen while she was standing on the sofa in the living room, flanked by blankets and heating pads. He'd slowly walk closer to her, inviting her to tell him when to stop. As he inched, she tracked the feelings coming up in her body and named them, understanding what her discomfort felt like. It took five tries until her body was ready for him to come within five feet of her.

As her daughter surged with anger, Cynthia approached and asked, "You seem upset. Do you need some help?" Her daughter told her about a disagreement with her friend. Cynthia was still triggered by her daughter's anger. She worried something bad was going to happen to her. Her therapy did not cleanse all the emotion inflaming her nervous system; it can take years and years to wring out all the emotions trapped there. But in getting to know the pain she'd locked away for so long, she could sense where it lived and soothe it so it didn't possess her. She leaned her body against the wardrobe behind her. She felt grounded as it held her weight, and she reminded herself, *This is not about me. This is not your emotion. This is* her *emotion.*

"Do you want to express [your anger] in a way that doesn't hurt you?" Cynthia asked her daughter, as she watched her pace around the room. When her daughter said yes, Cynthia gave her a pillow, and her daughter repeatedly slammed it against the bed.

Minutes later, her daughter, calm, hugged her. "Thank you, Mom. I know what to do now."

Later Cynthia's husband asked her, "You didn't say anything to her? You didn't give any advice, any words of wisdom?"

"No, not a single word," Cynthia replied.

Cynthia learned from her family that to be good meant to be "agreeable," which really meant collapsing herself to accept the unacceptable. But she is teaching her daughter a definition of good that's different from what she learned, a version we could all use. The definition of good she imparted meant to "turn into their internal compass and connect with their body and emotions to guide [them]."

This kind of goodness is predicated not on the parts of us we ignore, but on the parts we express. Goodness becomes authenticity. Goodness becomes wholeness, requiring us to be all of ourselves. It means welcoming back the parts of us trapped beyond our fault lines. It means bearing the truth of all we've been through and feeling in our bodies the ways it bleeds into now.

In finding this wholeness, we don't expect ourselves to be someone else's version of good anymore, a version of good that means constricting the latitude of feelings we allow ourselves, disconnecting from our body's communication. To become truly good, we'll sometimes be bitter, weak, ungenerous, upset, or desperate, because the only way to become anything different is to inhabit the bad things more deeply.

SOMATIC EXERCISES

TRACKING EXERCISE

The purpose of this exercise is to help you access and release sensations stored in your body. These sensations are thought to be a byproduct of open memories within you that are not yet processed (and thus are affecting your sense of worth). To work through these memories, in this exercise you will track a sensation as it moves through your body. It may be overwhelming to confront the sensations in your body so directly. If so, stay at step 1, focusing on what comfort looks like in your body, before moving on to the remaining steps.

1. **Notice comfort.** First, get comfortable in a chair. Pause to notice what comfort feels like in your body. Notice what relaxation feels like to you. Where do you feel opening, release, ease? Take note of how your body registers the experience of comfort.
2. **Close your eyes and scan your body.** Start at your head and move to your chest, your stomach, your thighs, your knees, your ankles, and your feet.
3. **Find tightness.** As you scan, find a spot in your body where you feel the most tightness or tension.
4. **Observe tightness.** Observe the tightness or tension. Allow it to be as it is without interpreting or analyzing it.
5. **Track changes in sensation.** As you observe the tightness, track how the sensation wants to move or change. Allow it to. Focus on the new sensation that arises.
    - If the sensation doesn't shift automatically, you can ask the sensation, *What would be a right next step here?*
    - To get the sensation to move, you can also try **pendulating**: Switch between noticing the tightness of the sensation

and the feelings of comfort in your body that you identified in step 1. Bring that feeling of comfort back to the tightness of the sensation. Register what the sensation feels like when you mix it with feelings of comfort and safety.

6. **Allow spontaneous movement.** As you track, your body might want to move in certain ways. You may shake, your head may shift, you may kick, or you may raise your arms. Allow these spontaneous movements.
7. **Return from your thoughts.** If thoughts arise, return to focusing on your sensations by saying, *Now I'm aware that I sense [insert sensation].*
8. Take a moment to **appreciate the sensation in your body**, as it is now, after the work you've done with it. Focus on it, but at a distance, remembering the sensation isn't all of you.

This exercise was developed based on suggested exercises from Peter Levine's In an Unspoken Voice, *and from his and his colleague's article: Payne, et al., "Somatic Experiencing: Using Interception and Proprioception as Core Elements of Trauma Therapy."*

BODY TRUST EXERCISE: FOCUSING

This exercise is based on the idea of body trust, that your body knows how to heal if you allow it to. It involves you feeling and labeling an uncomfortable sensation in your body and understanding what it is communicating.

1. Sit comfortably and close your eyes.
2. Ask yourself, ***What's been upsetting me lately?*** Picture all the problems that come up, laid out in front of you.
3. **Pick the problem that feels the biggest.** Stand back from it and notice what this problem feels like when you locate its presence in your body. If you find your mind chattering or ruminating on the problem, try to go down past the thoughts into the sensation in your body.
4. **Pick a word or words to describe how the problem feels** in your body, such as *blocked*, *vile*, *heavy*, or *ashamed*. This shouldn't be a word that you force onto the feeling, but one that naturally arises from what you sense in your body. You know the word is right when it leads you to feel a slight shift in what you sense in your body.
5. **Compare your sensation with the word you chose.** Ask yourself if the word is right. If it is, you'll feel the sensation change. If you don't feel the change, you can choose a new word that better reflects what you feel. When you feel a match between the feeling and word, take a moment to notice how this alignment feels in your body.
6. While noticing your body's sense of the problem, **ask your sensation what it is about the problem that makes you feel [insert word chosen from step 4 or step 5]**. The answer shouldn't arise from your thoughts, but it should flow out of what you sense in your body.

7. Take a moment to **appreciate the sensation in your body**, as it is now, after the work you've done with it. Focus on it, but at a distance, remembering the sensation isn't all of you.
8. **Return to step 1** as needed. You may have to practice this activity a few times to feel the release.

Adapted from the focusing exercise in Eugene T. Gendlin's book Focusing.

6

The Parts Who Own Our Memories

As I listened to Rose, a twenty-six-year-old operations analyst, tell me the things her mom said to her, I wanted to hurl the pillow I was cradling against the wall.

"'No one actually cares about you. People just hang around because they pity you. . . . You're ugly, and I'm the only one who loves you enough to tell you,'" Rose recounted. Hot waves of anger crescendoed in me and then receded as I tried to part ways with my own vicarious anger so I could orient to our interview.

But to be angry around Rose is lonesome. Because she *wasn't* angry. In fact, I got the sense that, at least initially, it was a surprise to her that her mother's comments warranted anger. Yet she *could* get angry at other parents who acted like her mother did. Rose told me about a friend from college with an abusive father. This friend spent hours crafting an intricate bracelet as a gift for her mother. Then her father destroyed it, its pieces raining down like candy from a busted piñata.

"What?" Rose said. "Your dad intentionally broke a bracelet to make a child mad? That's ridiculous!" In an if-A-then-B kind of way, Rose deduced that if she was angry at this shitty father, then perhaps she should be angry at her own parent, too. It was intriguing to me to see Rose rebrand anger as an equation. Using the principle of extrapolation, she could understand, at least intellectually, that anger at her mother's behavior was called for.

Yet Rose's anger wasn't gone. As we've learned in previous chapters, the emotions we suppress don't disappear. They get distorted. When we mute them, they're bound to hijack us, leading us to act out in extreme ways. Or else these emotions leak out and express themselves indirectly, anger simmering into passive-aggression. For Rose, both occurred. While most of the time anger eluded her, in some moments, her anger would catapult into rage, like when her boyfriend, James, accidentally dropped some noodles down the sink while trying to strain them, and when he rushed Rose to get on a roller coaster as its doors opened, and when he placed her umbrella on a dirty floor.

"[I was] just feeling how harsh her reaction was to innocent mistakes I made," James said. Rose's rage sprung forth so explosively that it was as if it was protecting her from being killed. And yet, "I'm not a murderer," James said.

Most of the time, however, her anger simmered into passive-aggression. I heard once that passive-aggression is how you express anger when you think your anger is invalid (and then I promptly decided against leaving sticky notes for my roommates, reminding them to take out the garbage). When Rose was miffed with James, she would walk forty feet in front of him, avert her eyes, or *harrumph-I'm-fine* him.

James has a hunch about why Rose's anger is not forthright, why it has become a species that wavers between teetering on extinction and then violently reasserting life. He thinks Rose's shame has gobbled up her anger. Shame allows Rose to stay close to her mother, despite her vitriol. It hisses in her ear *You deserve this*, a thought that keeps Rose locked in the role of doting daughter like a straitjacket. Rose's anger might annihilate their relationship, and compel Rose to leave, when the little girl inside her still needs her to stay. Rose added that she thought a fearful part of her also muffled her anger. Rose's mom would transform into an "animal" if Rose spoke back, sometimes reaching for the nearest cup to heave at her.

"I'm afraid to point fingers toward her because she's literally going to chop off my finger," Rose said.

But Rose's mom, who is from China, lives there now for eleven months of the year—too far away to pollute Rose's air. So why did Rose's anger mostly file itself down into nubs of passive-aggression, even with James, when her mother could only seethe from seven thousand miles away?

Rose's mom was never *really* far away, psychologically speaking. According to a theory called Internal Family Systems (IFS), we all have a family of selves inside us that are each called parts. As we'll learn, these parts are stuck in a loop of our horrible memories, transposing their emotional bite onto what we experience now. This explains why, when James and Rose were on vacation and he beat her at Connect 4, she scribbled in her journal that she felt hopeless, worthless, pathetic, and inferior. *I'm not good enough. I can't get anything right. What am I useful for?* she thought. It was as if James had humiliated her the same way her mother would have.

James looked on, concerned and surprised, he recounted to me as I interviewed him in his apartment. "Highlighting the absurdity of it," he shared in his salmon-colored plaid button-down, "it was this idyllic location, on this tiny island, off the coast of Belize. Food was being made for us. Our days consisted of reading books, eating food, going for a swim . . . and those [shameful] parts [were] very loud for Rose." Another part of him felt lonely and unseen, and he set aside time to process what he dubbed her "false accusations"—of him as a humiliator, a violent punisher. "Do you even know me?" James said in response.

When Rose reflected on that Connect 4 story, she could see the ways her parts weren't *seeing* James. *Not good enough*, *useless* . . . these were words her mother would trample her with, not James. "'I might as well just raise a dog. At least a dog comes to their host. You don't do anything for me,'" Rose remembered her mother saying. And I was back to wanting to hurl my pillow and free Rose, psychologically, from her mom's clutches.

I wanted to free the young part of her still trapped in those memories, making her hear her mother's words echo even in silence. Free her legs so they could stretch long enough to walk her away. Free her eyes so they could see, not objects flying toward her head, but the presence of a person who loves her, playing games with her and making noodles for dinner. Free her shame so it doesn't convince her that abuse is her doing and her destiny. Once those were free, I was sure her anger would be, too.

But as long as Rose's shame part reigned, it would banish her anger to the psychological depths of her psyche. As I alluded to in the last chapter, researchers theorize that if our emotions are too overwhelming, we regulate them by literally altering our consciousness, suppressing the parts of us containing these feelings. Yet we *need* all of our emotions, like Rose needed her anger, to become whole. In my own journey with anger, I've learned that it is a wellspring of vitality that affords us the ability to defend ourselves when threatened and, thus, is necessary to make us feel worthy. And freeing our anger keeps it from metastasizing into rage.

Up to now, I've emphasized the importance of reconsolidating memories, both implicit and explicit, to regain our own sense of worth. But Rose's story reveals that sometimes the memories we need to reconsolidate are inaccessible. Our memories are embedded in parts. And our parts are layered on top of each other, blocking memories from other parts from surfacing. We need to heal certain parts before we can access, and heal, others. Rose needed to express her anger to heal, yet she could only do so if she confronted the part of her that held shame first.

And if shame could suppress her anger, it could suppress other parts of her, too, memories—implicit or explicit—that she needed to reconsolidate. Sometimes, healing doesn't just happen horizontally, as we face our dispersed network of memories, but vertically, as each memory reveals another layer of sediment underneath, another part that needs healing, one we couldn't access until we tilled the layer above it.

What do we do with these top layers, the parts of us, like Rose's shame, that guard us from our own healing? How do we navigate these parts of us so hell-bent on keeping us a secret from ourselves, like their life depends on it, because at one point, it did?

PSYCHIC MULTIPLICITY

Therapist Richard C. Schwartz approaches the guards that block our own healing with reverence. He created IFS, the theory based on the idea that we are not one self, but a family of selves, or, as he calls them, parts. He has seen, firsthand, how parts of us tamp down other parts to protect all of us from the consequences. Of course, these consequences may no longer exist, as was the case with Rose and James, yet our open memories convince us they do.

If you haven't heard of IFS, you might think only people with dissociative identity disorder (formerly known as multiple personality disorder) possess parts. But Schwartz argues that we *all* harbor a mosaic of parts. Each part can have a different age, temperament, desire, and even gender. Kate Sloan, a thirty-two-year-old sex writer and IFS client described her parts as "two different consciousnesses active in my body, such that it almost felt like flickering back and forth." One of Schwartz's clients with bulimia shared, "In the course of ten minutes I go from being a professional who has it all together, to a scared, insecure child, to a raging bitch, to an unfeeling, single-minded eating machine."

Schwartz wasn't the first to suspect that we are we. As far back as the fifth century, Plato philosophized that the soul flourishes when its different parts work in communion. The psychology world has pre-Schwartz precedent for psychic multiplicity. In the twentieth century, Roberto Assagioli, an Italian Freudian psychoanalyst, called selves "subpersonalities" that he aimed to unify. Other psychoanalysts have said that the point of therapy is to allow the "sometimes smooth but thin casing around the self to dissolve" so that each self can speak. Renowned psychiatrist Harry Stack Sullivan called the idea that we have one self "the very mother of illusions." Parts have even been depicted on the big screen, where we've seen the warring emotional selves of an eleven-year-old girl try to find harmony in the 2015 Pixar knockout *Inside Out*.

I've undergone IFS therapy, and it has expanded my sense of reality. The identity of a single "self" disconnected me from all my parts. Thinking of myself as parts helps me access emotions (implicit memories) that would have been elbowed out if I painted my emotional multitudes with the broad brush of a single self. *No, I'm not annoyed* becomes *Yes, a part of me is.* This greater precision on what we feel is called emotional granularity, and researchers call it an "emotional expertise." People with it are less likely to self-medicate with alcohol or get aggressive when provoked, and they experience less depression. (The study that examined granularity and depression was called "Feeling Blue or Turquoise?") The more we can be aware of how we feel, the more we can regulate how we feel.

IFS also helps me be less attached to suppressing my vulnerabilities, as they become mere parts of me and do not define all of me. It helps me make sense of people who seem to have become their opposite, like when the people who have made me feel the most safe hurt me. Instead of seeing them as villains in pretty masks all along, I can trust the ways that parts of them, at least, were safe.

If we allow for multiple selves, our sense of reality exceeds its keyhole, and we notice the plurality of realities happening within us. Each part experiences reality alongside us—the three-month-old shrieking to apathetic ears, the five-year-old whose parents tossed them to the nanny, and the ten-year-old bullied into a shell of themselves. The psychological timeline is not linear but simultaneous.

Alan Lightman, American physicist and writer, shares a vivid example of how our younger parts shape our reality now in his novel *Einstein's Dreams*. A middle-aged man has dinner with his wife, goes to bed after, and gardens on Sundays. On Tuesdays, when he delivers stones to the masonry in town, he turns meek. When he offers his stone to the chatty mason, he is unable to meet the mason's eyes, staring at the wall while responding. As the rocks are weighed, he plants himself in the corner. As people in town pass him during his trip and say hello, he fastens his eyes to the ground.

Forty years ago, on a March afternoon, the man peed on himself in class. Kids saw the puddle dripping from his chair. They made him walk around and around. They pointed at his pants and hooted. A clock with big red hands read 2:15 p.m. As he walked, more boys caught on and howled, chasing him and laughing, chasing and laughing. "That memory has become his life," Lightman describes in *Einstein's Dreams.* As people pass him on the street in town, his eyes affix to the ground because he feels as if they see his shame on his pants. When his children visit, he talks to them through the shield of the door so they can't see his wet circle.

"He is the boy who could not hold it in," Lightman writes.

We don't go to therapy to deal with what happened to us, psychoanalyst Philip M. Bromberg argues, but to deal with what is happening now, and what we are sure will happen again. Our parts are not experiencing reality as it is, but as it was, whipping out hunches about what's happening now so it matches what happened then, and then reacting and coping as if it did. The man carrying rocks goes into town and is also the humiliated little boy forced to scuttle around class with a wet spot. Rose, now a high-powered analyst, plays Connect 4 as a little girl clinging to her mother by haranguing herself. No wonder a single experience from decades ago still affects us. That experience is not a moment in time; to a part of us, it is every moment since.

TALKING TO PARTS

Schwartz calls the parts of us that block us from accessing other parts "protectors," and the vulnerable, often desperate and overwhelmed parts they hide are "exiles." Someone might have to confront a sixteen-year-old overachiever protector, white-knuckling through piles of assignments that suppresses their six-year-old exile and their feelings of powerlessness. These feelings originated when the six-year-old blended into the wallpaper as their depressed mother dozed for seventeen hours a day. We can only access the exiles and their memories if we know how to navigate the fortress of the protectors.

The irony is that, deep down, we are often the opposite of who we profess to be (or in parts lingo, the part we show the world acts in the opposite way of the part it protects): The overachiever has a part that whimpers in a well of powerlessness, the people-pleaser burns with rage, a puffed-out chest encases a fragile heart. The avoidantly attached person has protectors that are unfeeling to mask an exile that feels terrified that love equates to harm. The anxiously attached person has protectors that are preoccupied with connecting to distract from their fear that connection means abandonment.

Schwartz's original approach was to get these protectors to lower the drawbridge to their exiles by being stern with them, roleplaying a finger-wagging father. With Roxanne, a client who self-harmed, he spent a two-hour session badgering the part that cut her, enlisting Roxanne to hassle that part of herself, too. Eventually, it relented, agreeing to stop. Schwartz left feeling like "we had won the battle."

Roxanne arrived for the next session with a deep gash across her face. Schwartz gasped. "I come from this 'first, do no harm' background with my medical father and family, and I could just see that I was doing harm to her, and that was a horrible feeling for me," Schwartz reflected.

"I give up. I can't beat you at this," Schwartz told Roxanne.

"I don't want to beat *you*," Roxanne's part said.

Finally, Schwartz stopped steamrolling the part and started listening to it. Roxanne had been sexually abused and would cut herself to distract her from her rage—a rage that, similar to Rose's, if expressed, might have intensified the abuse. Now, whenever Roxanne was afraid or angry, this same part intruded to protect her from the danger it thought would come if it didn't stifle her rage.

"I could, in my own mind, shift my view of the [self-harming] part from some kind of enemy or antagonist to a hero. It was a hero in her life, but it was also stuck in time," Schwartz recounted.

Ironically, it was one of Schwartz's parts that was initially keeping him from treating Roxanne effectively. Schwartz learned how to wag his finger from his father. A prominent physician researcher who expected academic excellence from his children, Schwartz's father had branded him a "good-for-nothing" because of his son's lackluster report cards, words that haunted Schwartz even as he became the visionary therapist who created IFS. "I had an underlying sense that I was fooling people, and I was driven to achieve in order to counter that suspicion." Yet when he saw Roxanne, he was overtaken by the part that had learned to use criticism to compel growth, despite the way it backfired for him.

Now Schwartz has a deep respect for our top layers, the parts of us that resist our own healing; in fact, he reminds us that we have "no bad parts" via the title of one of his books. He labels the relationships between parts a "delicate ecology" that must be navigated with care. Similarly, therapists reframe clients' mental health issues as not a problem but a solution. These symptoms are ways of coping with distressing memories held in parts. For instance, as I've alluded to, if an insecure part of you expects rejection, based on past memories, confidence would be a bad idea because your self-esteem would plunge more precipitously when you're inevitably rejected again—so insecurity is the solution.

If we destroy our solutions, we won't feel cured. We'll feel defenseless. "What if, the more we lectured, drugged, and tried to banish or control parts like this one, the harder they would fight to protect [us]?" Schwartz asked. What if instead of trying to stomp out, go to bat with, or disguise our insecure parts in a pantsuit of security, we tried to understand them instead? We can ask them how old they are, what their greatest fears are, why they act the way they do, and what they are afraid might happen if they don't. Then maybe they'd be willing to listen when we told them that the problem they are fighting has long since passed.

When we stop treating the parts of us we struggle with—our depression, anxiety, or insecurities—as flies to be swatted, and start appreciating them as misguided helpers, we free ourselves from internal conflict. We stop judging ourselves when we're in pain and start realizing that even our pain is trying to help us. The secondary feelings, feelings *about* our feelings—of shame because we're so sensitive, for example—begin to clear. We bring tenderness instead of scorn to our most hurt parts. We defined a sense of worth in chapter 1, not as the absence of insecurities, but as the ability to acknowledge and regulate them; IFS provides us with a vital tool to get there.

When we talk to a part with fresh curiosity and understanding, we become new actors in the memory that part lives in. A moment of suffering rebirths itself into a moment of care. We, in being caring and curious, are reconsolidating the part's memories of being mistreated. When Kate Sloan, the sex writer, noticed an anxious part popping up during her improv class, she put her hand on her stomach and breathed, asking that part, *What's bothering you? What are you worried about?* The part replied, *People are going to think I'm weird and not want to be my friend*, and then it showed her memories of her sitting alone at summer camp or at school. *What do you need to feel even 5 percent better?* Kate asked the part. The part asked Kate to put on pink lipstick to feel confident. It's interventions like these that help Kate stop feeling like "three kids in a trench coat," as her therapist calls it, and more like an adult, with a kid peeking out from behind her dress. At the end of this chapter, I'll share some reflection questions to help you get to know your parts and other exercises to help you work with them.

The more we get curious about our protector parts, the more likely they are to give us access to the next layer, the memories they conceal, that we can then reconsolidate. To help Rose access concealed parts, she went to a therapist-led wellness retreat in Olympia, Washington. The retreat had all the typical wellness accoutrements: yoga, hiking, and meditation. But at night was the entrée, an activity called sculpting. It involved her getting other people to act out her parts.

"Who do you want to play your shame?" the therapist asked. Rose picked a woman named Lee, who grew up on a resort, spending her younger years people-pleasing its guests. Lee also underwent a slew of surgeries that left her hot with shame when she looked at her body.

"I am bad. I can't do anything right," Lee said, embodying shame. The shame she was demonstrating was too watered-down, not vicious enough.

To prompt Lee to personify the real deal, the therapist played Rose's mom. "I sacrificed so much for you. I'm so disappointed. You don't do anything for me. I love you so much, and you don't do anything for me. You're such a failure. You're just like your dad, from the same blood, lazy pigs," the therapist, acting as Rose's mom, said.

"I don't want to make Mom mad. I'm bad. I'm bad. I'm bad," Rose's shame responded.

Rose chose people to play other parts of her, too. Disassociation came online, responding to the commotion by asking for her childhood comfort foods, like spicy noodle soups. Fear was there, keeping Rose atop a staircase, unable to get any closer to her "mother," who shouted from the bottom of it. Even a part called "manipulative anger" started to put on a show of anger to gain sympathy: "I'm going to kill myself so people can know how much pain I'm in."

"Let's pause," the therapist said, playing herself, now. "Do you realize how loud these parts are? There's no way to find your exile. What do you need to say to each of these parts so they can trust you?"

"You can trust me. I'm grown now. I need to step in to protect young Rose," Rose said to her parts, trying to help them realize that she's no longer a child, trapped at home with her mother.

"No, I'm protecting young Rose. I know how to do that. I have been doing it my entire life," Rose's shame said, refusing to relent.

"I know how much you've tried to protect me, and you've worked so hard. You've worked too hard, but I am strong now. I am there to protect young Rose. If you can just give me one chance to . . . do this a little differently," Rose said.

Shame finally relented.

Rose approached young Rose, her exile, who was hiding under the stairs. She was timid and sweet. "I'm so scared. I don't know what to do. I just want to be loved. Why am I not loved?" her exile said.

All of her parts watched quietly. Rose held her hand and gave her a hug.

LOVING THE PARTS YOU HATE

If we love a woman but stop caring for her as soon as we notice her flaws, then we didn't love her at all, psychologist Erich Fromm asserts. How, then, can we love ourselves if our love ceases as soon as we have an imperfection? And if our faults are just parts bearing our pain, then damning these parts is like punishing ourselves when we need us the most.

"Let no aspect of the human experience become alien to you," one of my professors told me in graduate school. This, according to him, was the seat of empathy. Now I think of it as the seat of security. Some of my parts are terrified; some egotistical; some fragile; some superior. I've fought the losing battle of trying to shut them away. Now I try to give them the love they've starved for.

When people close to me tell me about their parts, they feel ashamed that their feelings are so irrational and out of control. After learning about IFS and being a client of it, I understand why they're irrational—because they are not staked in the present, but stuck in a time warp of past hurts. This is why an offhand comment from a colleague made them want to strike. The kind words their wife exchanged with a waiter made them surge with jealousy. They yearn for a turbulent relationship after they've finally found a stable one. They add that they know they need to ignore these menacing urges, that they don't like themselves for what they feel, and that they're even a bit scared of themselves, each disclaimer a wince bracing for my disapproval. At one time in my life, that disapproval would have come. But now, having learned to be present with my own parts so their fears don't masquerade as judgments, I say to them, "Hey. It's okay that you feel that way. It's a part of you that needs your attention. You've been fighting it for so long. Why not get to know it instead?"

When Schwartz encourages us to love all of our parts, even the parts we struggle with the most, the advice sounds well-worn enough to be cliché, the power of love to transform people, or parts of people. But it is revolutionary against popular advice to think positively (and simply ignore the parts of yourself that are hurting). It's revolutionary against mindfulness exercises that require watching your negative thoughts float by like a river (instead of treating them like manifestations of legitimate parts of you that need help). And it's revolutionary against self-help advice to treat your ego like the enemy, the name of a book that has sold more than a million copies (rather than understand what pain your ego is engorged with to keep it so inflated). It's revolutionary against the backdrop of how we've treated ourselves our entire lives. Because for us to come this far and for parts of us to still be so prickly, critical, or downright suicidal, they must have never known our love.

Loving the most difficult parts of ourselves is revolutionary because it involves us offering ourselves a certain type of love that's not what is typically sold to us, to get high on or obsess over or seek to be made complete through. It's not the kind of self-love that involves pasting sticky notes of affirmations on your walls. It's a love that requires awe, seeing a part of yourself as vaster than just its pain. It's a love that requires humility, recognizing that we don't truly know a person, even when that person is ourselves, so we offer up curiosity. And it's a love that requires the trust that even the parts of us that torture us are doing their doggone best.

To become the kind of person who can love our most insecure parts, the ones that make us feel lower than dirt, we must become the highest version of ourselves. For Schwartz, though, finding this highest self doesn't require evolution. Deep down, below the angst of our parts, our highest self has always been there, waiting.

WHY YOU'RE ALREADY SECURE-ISH

According to attachment theory, you can become secure by surrounding yourself with securely attached people (if those people exist . . .). Their sumptuously unflappable nervous systems, clockwork reliability, and earnest goodness will eventually dislodge your negative assumptions about others. Perhaps, then, you've looked for securely attached people under the bed, between the couch cushions, and in the dusty crawlspace, but you haven't found them. Disappointed, you realized that many of these securely attached people aren't on the market. Their charms have left them with an already full relationship Rolodex.

Here's where IFS comes in.

According to IFS, you do not have to find another secure person to heal. You *are* the secure person. Even if you have insecurities, they comprise only a part of you. Schwartz would go as far as to say there are no criminals, alcoholics, or schizophrenics, that these are mere parts of a greater whole. I find this claim to be a nice thought but overblown, given that many disorders, like schizophrenia, have a strong genetic component and cannot be reduced to a traumatized part. Yet I agree with psychologist Patricia Deegan that it's critical that we realize that our suffering isn't all of us: "Once a person comes to believe that he or she is an illness, there is no one left inside to take a stand toward the illness. Once you and the illness become one, then there is no one left inside of you to take on the work of recovering, of healing, of rebuilding the life you want to live." Plus, when we recognize that whatever part of us we're struggling with is just that, a part, it brings us hope that we can become more than our pain, because we already are. As one IFS client, Nancy-Lee Mauger, an artist and French horn player in Boston, put it, "For me, the most amazing thing was learning about a part of me that was suicidal and knowing that that was just a single part of me. It wasn't my entire being. That changed my world."

And the secure part of you, which Schwartz calls the "Self," is vaster than any of your parts. This Self is who you would be if you grew up with people who attuned to you perfectly. It has eight qualities, which Schwartz calls the eight C's: connectedness, clarity, compassion, courage, confidence, curiosity, creativity, and calmness. If, when speaking to a part, you feel critical of it, you aren't speaking to it from the Self but from another part. You can ask that part, and any other subsequent parts, to step aside until you feel compassion for the activated part. When Schwartz's clients suddenly became compassionate toward a part, he'd ask them which part was speaking. They'd say, "That's not a part like those others, that's more myself," or, "That's who I really am." The Self is our truest self and is always there, even if other parts often bury it.

Finding the Self within is a far better option than finding it elsewhere. After all, the longest relationship you'll have is not with the secure person you've fantasized about who will love you at your worst. The longest relationship you'll have is with yourself.

The Self, in being greater than the parts, can be wielded to help the parts. An oft-used metaphor when it comes to IFS is of the parts as members of an unruly band. The trumpet is off-key, the drums are deafening, and the flute is drowned out until the conductor brings the musicians in harmony with one another. This is the role of the Self. It compassionately listens to parts so they don't act out in extreme ways, so they flow in harmony with the other parts rather than trying to destroy them.

Here's where Schwartz's thinking pivots from what we've learned in earlier chapters. We've thought about our sense of self as a product of our memories; memories are the database of self-esteem. Our parts, Schwartz would agree, often function as products of our memory, defending us against the horror—or shame or sadness or hurt—in our history happening again. But Schwartz argues that parts aren't just a reflection of memories. They have personalities outside of them, too, ones that appear only once their memories are reconsolidated. Once your inner child processes their fears of being abandoned, for example, you may become more playful as that part's true personality has more space to flourish. And even if we haven't worked through any of our traumas, the Self always exists, unblemished by whatever we've been through.

If you're a science person and this Self stuff is all beginning to sound a bit "woo" to you, then one IFS therapist, Rachel McDavid, whom I interviewed, imparted that your "skeptical parts need to be celebrated because they're the parts that have kept [you] safe consistently and ongoingly. They are discerners. They are guides."

Your skeptical parts are justified in their skepticism because research on the Self, and IFS more generally, is limited. While Schwartz's book on IFS, *No Bad Parts: Healing Trauma and Restoring Wholeness with the Internal Family Systems Model*, has become popular enough to be published in more than twenty countries, and over twelve thousand clinicians are trained in IFS, studies examining the impact of IFS are few, and most contain small samples. The studies that do exist have found that IFS therapy decreases PTSD, depression, internet addiction, and arthritis. (But it didn't reduce anxiety or improve confidence in people's abilities.) I did not find any studies examining the impact of IFS on self-esteem or secure attachment, although studies have found that it impacts related concepts: One study suggested that it decreased shame and guilt, and another found that it increased self-compassion. Schwartz also conducts trainings on healing attachment wounds through IFS.

Despite the limited IFS research, many prominent academics have theorized on the existence of the Self. Bessel van der Kolk wrote about something similar to the Self in *The Body Keeps the Score*: "Beneath the surface of the protective parts of trauma survivors there exists an undamaged essence, a Self that is confident, curious, and calm, a self that has been sheltered from destruction by the various protectors that have emerged in their efforts to ensure survival." Psychologist Carl Rogers has emphasized that the empathy of the therapist should help the client become "a more effective therapist, for himself." Academics have called something like the Self "impathy." The more people are led by the Self, one study found, the better their sleep, mental health, and relationships. The Self can enhance acts of memory reconsolidation. It can anchor us and unleash our compassion as we face our most ornery protectors, or the exiles they protect. I'll share an activity at the end of this chapter that helps you access the Self to better reconsolidate memories in your parts.

If even a part of you is open to embracing a spiritual side of healing, then you'll be in the company of Schwartz. He calls the Self the "divine within." He also finds inspiration for the Self in other religions. For Quakers, it's called Inner Light. For Buddhists, it's rigpa (Buddha mind). For Hindus, it is Atman of the Self. For Sufis, it is the Beloved or God Within.

What would it mean to go back to the kinds of memories where you were paraded around the class after peeing yourself, like that man from *Einstein's Dreams* who averted his eyes while he delivered rocks to the quarry? But this time, your Self would be beside you to tell you that to always be in control of your body is to be nonhuman, and that to lose control is to be deeply human. Your Self would say that you do not have to circle the class if you don't want to, but that if you did, they'd be there, behind you, to cover you. As everyone cackled, they'd say that not an atom of your worth is defined by the volume of the howls, and to listen to their voice instead, as they said nothing you could do would ever make them love you less. Maybe, after all these years, you'd finally look up.

HOW ROSE FOUND HER ANGER

When I showed James a rough draft of this chapter, after reading it he looked out into the distance, tears welling up behind the wide rims of his glasses. "I think [Rose has] been letting in [my love]. It's still hard for her. I'm just so proud of her. In the background of my own family and people not really changing . . . it's just so wild to see. If you work really, really hard at something, [you] will actually change."

Rose has put a lot of elbow grease into her healing. She read up more on IFS, mapped the universe of her parts, and regularly met with an accountability partner to discuss her parts. But what really helped was that after doing all these things, she was struck with the idea that her mother had parts, too. Her mother's hands grasped so tightly to control, she speculated, because a young part of her feared Rose might leave her.

I wondered if this insight was unsettling. To see a parent as a powerful, vengeful God is to believe, amid their wrath, that a strongman was in control. There was a divine plan. To realize that a parent was more child than God is to admit that what you endured was not calculation but chaos. Violent parents were ruled by an inner humiliated eight-year-old with the teeth of a grown-up. That parent was never truly there—brutal and omnipotent and all-knowing—as you made them out to be. It was a mirage that broke you.

But this was not Rose's take. Her fearful and shameful parts lapped up the thought of her mother as a child. It soothed their fears and created an opening for her exiled anger. When you reimagine your greatest threat as a child, whose temper is trying but not lethal, whose screams are rattling but not deadening, whose power is somewhat but not boundless, then who is left to fear? "Seeing my mom as a child . . . It's just kind of cute," Rose reflected.

While much of Rose's anger still remains vaulted, trickles of it have seeped out. She's noted the times she's felt it. Annoyance came at her mom's foreboding look when Rose volunteered her phone charger to an unhoused person. She saw a "glimpse" of anger when her mother tried to convince her to give her a special ringtone so Rose would never miss her calls. Anger became her when her mother got disgruntled toward her grandmother for lumbering around too slowly.

One day, James spilled his drink on Rose's couch while playing video games. She could default to her typical reaction and lurch a curt "It's fine" at him while she sprayed and wiped the couch with a pace, at least, that was furious. But the fearful part of her had started to believe that danger *might* not be sure to follow if her anger uncinched. "I think I'm mad at you for spilling that on my couch. Is that okay to tell you?" Rose asked. "Yeah. That's okay. I'm sorry. Thanks for telling me. I'd always much rather you tell me when you're mad," James replied. For a part of Rose, that was a revolutionary thought.

IFS EXERCISES

IFS EXERCISE 1: ACCESSING THE SELF

This exercise will help you access the Self to heal your parts. You can also access the Self and return to memory reconsolidation activities in earlier chapters to amplify the impact of those previous exercises.

1. **Ground yourself:** Close your eyes, take a deep breath, and feel the weight of your feet on the floor.
2. **Scan your body:** Notice any sensations of tightness, tension, or excess energy. These sensations represent your parts.
3. **Separate:** Picture yourself separating from these sensations to a place of expansiveness. You know you've found the separate space if you feel the eight C's: connectedness, clarity, compassion, courage, confidence, curiosity, creativity, and calmness.

   If you have trouble finding this place, say something reassuring to your parts, like telling them that you'll be back or that you want to separate from them so you can understand them.
4. **Notice:** Pause and notice what it's like to feel the Self. Note where you feel the Self energy in your body. Notice the increased openness, positive emotion, or calm that you may feel.
5. **Access parts from the Self:** Turn and notice your parts and thank them for allowing you to access the place of the Self.
6. **Extend self-energy:** Picture yourself extending the energy of your Self to your parts, so you're accessing their feelings and sensations from an anchored place.
7. **Ground:** Take a deep breath, open your eyes, and shift your focus back to what's around you.

IFS EXERCISE 2: SPEAKING TO PARTS

This exercise will help you get to know your parts so that they are less likely to overwhelm you.

1. **Access the part:** Choose one way to access a part:
    - Scan your body and notice where there is tension.
    - Think back to a time when the way you felt didn't fit the situation. Perhaps you felt the opposite of what you expected, particularly strong, or not at all.
    - Think back to something you've ruminated about, a thought that has been playing on a loop.
2. **Access the Self:** As you access this sensation, feeling, or thought, close your eyes and envision the part that holds it.

    Ask yourself how you feel toward this part.

    If you feel anything but the eight C's (connectedness, clarity, compassion, courage, confidence, curiosity, creativity, and calmness), you're speaking from another part rather than from the Self. Ask the part to step back and give you space, or go into a waiting room, until you feel compassion toward this part. (If it's helpful, return to IFS exercise 1 to access the Self.)
3. **Dialogue between part and Self:** Now dialogue with this part from the Self. As you ask the part the following questions, don't answer for it. Make sure you are connecting with the part and letting it tell you its answers.
    - How old are you?
    - How old do you think I am?
    - What do you feel?
    - What tends to trigger these feelings?
    - Where are you located in my body?
    - What do you fear?
    - What makes you act the way you do?
    - What do you fear will happen if you stop acting the way you do?

- What memories do you hold?
- What other parts are in conflict with you? What do you need from one another?
- What are you trying to protect me from?
- How do you interpret my current problems?
- What kind of support can I offer you?
- What would you rather be doing?

If, during this reflection, you suddenly feel emotionally overwhelmed, foggy, shutdown, or distracted, you may be going too fast. Return to exercise 1.

Richard Schwartz does not recommend that we heal our exiles without the help of a trained therapist. You can find one through the IFS directory at ifs-institute.com/practitioners.

IFS EXERCISE 3: SOOTHING A PART

This exercise should help you soothe the feelings (implicit memories) that are stuck within your parts.

1. **Think of an emotion** you've been struggling with, such as anger, resentment, fear, burdensomeness, abandonment, distrust, unworthiness, sadness, etc.
2. **Scan your body to notice where this emotion manifests**, perhaps as tightness in your jaw, a blockage in your throat, or anxious energy in your stomach.
3. **Picture this tension in your body as a part.** Notice what it looks like, what emotions it feels, what age it is, and what it wants to say to you.
4. **Place a hand on the area of your body where this part manifests** to see if that provides comfort or relief. If so, leave your hand there while you move to the next step.
5. **Ask this part what affirmation it needs to hear from you to feel safer.** Here are some examples:
    a. For anxious parts:
        - I'm here.
        - You are inherently worthy.
        - Other people's actions do not reflect your worth.
        - I'll never leave you.
        - No matter who you become, I will love you.
        - No matter what happens, you'll be okay.
        - You're safe.

    b. For avoidant parts:
        - I won't let you down.
        - It's okay to need people.
        - However you feel is okay.
        - I will respect your needs.

- It's okay to feel vulnerable.
- I feel what you feel with you.
- I will show up however you need.

6. **Repeat the affirmation to your part.** The affirmation should produce a change in how you feel. Translate the words into a felt sensation in your body. What happens when you do? Let the positive sensation accompanying the affirmation impact the negative feelings the part holds.
7. **Notice how the affirmation affects the part** as you finish the exercise. Observe how the part feels differently, and let that part express any messages to you in reaction to the affirmation.

7

Memories of Stigma

Most people would describe a cane as tall, thin, or sturdy. Yet to Catarina Rivera, a cane—the white one people with vision impairment use—meant furtive stares, crude assumptions, or snide remarks. Rivera was born deaf, and she started going blind at seventeen. Before that, she thought you could tell if someone was blind by their cloudy corneas. Yet after her vision degraded, her coffee-colored eyes looked the same as they did when she was fully sighted. It was the white cane that would mark her.

For many years, Catarina tried to downplay her blindness. She still had some vision, as do many people with vision impairment. So she kept her blindness a secret and stammered to explain herself when she knocked over glasses at dinner.

The first time Catarina cried about her blindness was when she was diagnosed. She sat in the doctor's office with her family, awaiting the results. She suspected something was wrong with her eyesight during summer camp, when she was playing outside at night with her friends and couldn't see a thing.

The doctor told her she had Usher's syndrome, the most common cause of blind-deafness, and would progressively lose her vision. There was no treatment, no cure, and all they could do was monitor the condition.

Catarina's tears fell in that office, not just because of what the doctor said, but because of what he didn't. He didn't say that with the help of assistive technology, she could navigate the world just fine. He did not tell her stories of other vision-impaired people who were living rich, fulfilling lives—people like Haben Girma, a blind and deaf Harvard Law School graduate whom Catarina would later meet. Haben tried rock climbing, kayaking, and even skiing. The doctor didn't tell her that a disability can be an ability in a certain context. If there was a power outage and people needed to evacuate, for example, she'd be most adept at navigating the darkness.

As she remembers it, the doctor didn't give Catarina a reason to believe that she could still have a good life. So Catarina felt as if her life was now passing like grains of sand through an hourglass. When the last grain fell—when she was completely blind—with it would fall the last grain of her worth. No one would date or marry her. She'd be isolated. *My life has been too good up to now*, Catarina thought to herself. *It was always bound to get worse.*

Or perhaps, it was not.

Much of what Catarina assumed about her future as a vision-impaired person was based on stigma. Blind people as depicted in media and pop culture are not main characters, love interests, or even very complex. Their defining feature is not their sense of humor, boundless kindness, or pizzazz. It is their blindness. And that, in our society, often makes them objects of pity or butts of jokes. This is what stigma does. Stigmatizing an aspect of a person—whether it's their ability, sexuality, neurodivergence, race, class, body size, criminal history, or anything else—whittles down their vastness. Not only does stigma collapse their full, complex humanity into one thing; that thing also becomes bad.

To overcome stigma is to reclaim that vastness. We'll do this through *identity stretching*; it's a process of expanding our sense of our identity beyond the malnourished story we've been told. Memory work will help us do this. Reconsolidating negative memories of stigma is part of this process, along with a new strategy that brings positive memories to the forefront.

Catarina felt her identity stretching when she read *Not Fade Away: A Memoir of Senses Lost and Found*, a book written by Rebecca Alexander, a public advocate with Usher's syndrome. It also stretched when she watched videos from YouTuber Molly Burke, who talks about her blindness but also makeup and fashion. It stretched when she attended a social group for blind people, where she became mesmerized as people folded up their white canes and placed them on the table. "But it was the way they did it, like it wasn't anything out of the ordinary . . . for the cane to exist. That really struck me," Catarina told me.

A white cane *could* mean more than jeers and judgments, Catarina learned. She just had to stretch to make it so.

WHY STIGMA IS WORTH STRETCHING

It made me sad to hear about how ashamed Jai Stephenson, now twenty-nine, felt about their sexuality when they were in college. But it made me sadder that Jai thought they *should* feel ashamed of their sexuality. At their church, they were open about their attraction to women. (At that time, Jai identified as a woman but now identifies as non-binary.) "I referred to my sexuality as a spiritual stronghold, my battle with the flesh. People who knew were proud of me, proud that I boldly took a stand in the face of the devil for the cause of Christ." When we have internalized stigma deeply enough, we resist our liberation from it.

Jai made me realize that we must first *want* to relinquish stigma before we can explore the mechanics of how to cleanse ourselves from it. To do so, we have to buy into the idea that stigma represents something wrong in society rather than in us.

Some think of stigma not as culturally manufactured but as an inherent quality of some identities, like Jai did, making it, therefore, useless to resist. What is shameful is thought to be universally shameful, an absolute reality, rather than one model of it.* Philosopher J. David Velleman points out that Adam and Eve realized they were naked and covered themselves with fig leaves. They didn't need to learn about culture, or for fire ants to invade their crotches, for them to realize the shame of their nudity, so the story suggests that what is shameful is not constructed; it is inherent.

Another reason we might see stigma as factual is because when most people see a thing a certain way—a stigmatized identity, in this case—we assume they're right. "Ten million people can't be wrong," the popular marketing phrase goes. But public consensus has never been a reliable barometer of truth. If we peek back at history, we see the majority can be and often has been wrong. Social progress has been driven by a group once in the numerical minority. Abolitionists were outnumbered in opinion in 1837, a year when proslavery mobs attacked a warehouse full of their press materials and shot the newspaper editor. ACT UP organized for research and treatment for people dying of AIDS, and gay men in particular, at a time when the government didn't, their languishing a reflection of the homophobic zeitgeist. "If I'm dying from anything, I'm dying from the President of the United States," Vito Russo, an ACT UP organizer dying of AIDS, famously said.

Dr. Martin Luther King Jr. recognized the value of being maladjusted to injustice, even when it is branded as normal, when he said in his speech at Southern Methodist University in 1969, "There are some things in our nation and the world to which I am proud to be maladjusted and wish all men of goodwill would be maladjusted until the good society is realized." The healthiest people, psychologist Erich

* This line was inspired by a quote from anthropologist Wade Davis: "The world into which you were born does not exist in an absolute sense but is just one model of reality."

Fromm reminds us, are often considered the most neurotic because they're sensitive to dysfunction, even when it is disguised as normal.

But what drives so many to reject people with a certain identity, even if those people aren't causing any harm? It's not because who they are is wrong. It is because who they are threatens the social order. For example, the neoliberal idea of a leaner government that skimpily supports its citizens led to a deified hyper-responsible self-sufficient "self" that further stigmatizes people with disabilities or those in poverty who depend on assistance. In *Born Losers: A History of Failure in America*, author Scott A. Sandage cites that words like *first-rate* and *good-for-nothing*, for example, first cropped up to express one's credit worthiness, and later, their general worthiness. Under capitalism, you must become credit worthy to be broadly worthy.

When people violate our concepts of what is normal, we shame them. Yet if we realize these concepts are human-made and not absolute truth, then these identities we stigmatize become an invitation and not a violation. They teach us where we need to stretch our concepts to grow as a society to better serve everyone. But instead, what often happens, as Jean Baker Miller alludes to in *Toward a New Psychology of Women*, is that disabled people, people of color, or poor people internalize that they are to blame for their own mistreatment. Then there's no reason to shine a light on holes in social services, institutional racism, or policies that enshrine income inequality. When systemic problems are morphed into or treated as personal failings, existing systems breathe easy.*

This is all to say that we would do well to not trust the opinions of those who make us feel inferior for existing as we are. If Jai had known this, perhaps they wouldn't have experienced months of daily tears, endured sermons on protecting children from homosexuals, or re-

* And in a way, we might breathe easier, too, when we don't challenge systems, according to Miller, because "blaming the person(s) [or system] who hurt us so can seem much harder than continuing the masochistic circle of self-condemnation. This is especially and tragically true if one believes that the other person [system] is absolutely necessary to one's very existence."

marked, "I don't know, I just think there's something wrong with it," when they visited the gynecologist.

Questioning the validity of stigma is necessary but not sufficient for shedding it. As we'll soon find, even if we believe the stigma is wrong, it can weasel its way into our psyches so that ridding ourselves of it is easier said than done.

HOW STIGMA MAKES US FEEL UNWORTHY

The cost of stigma is not just that it causes us to see a part of ourselves negatively. The greater cost, I'm convinced, is that we are stuck chronically evaluating ourselves, measuring ourselves against an ideal decreed by our stigmatizers. After eating yams with other Black people, for example, Ralph Ellison reflected in *Invisible Man*, "What a group of people we were, I thought. Why, you could cause us the greatest humiliation simply by confronting us with something we liked." He continued, "This is all very wild and childish, I thought, but to hell with being ashamed of what you liked. No more of that for me. I am what I am!" You become, to yourself, something to judge, to behold, an artifact, rather than a reality to experience, a being unfolding.

Sasha, a forty-three-year-old woman who works in communications, gained eighty pounds after being diagnosed with multiple disabilities that left her bedridden for months. She spends what she estimates to be four hours a day thinking about how she should work out so won't hate herself, how she shouldn't eat the food in front of her, how she should go for a walk, but how when she stands up it will be a spectacle. "I can't believe I'm a human being on planet Earth who has spent this much time thinking about their body instead of just being in their body. . . . How horrifying to look back on my life, on my deathbed, and go, 'You spent a hundred thousand hours thinking about how much you hated your body.'"

When we internalize stigma, our perspective is replaced by that of our stigmatizers. We wonder first what will appease them, and in doing so, we become secondary to ourselves. We lose touch with what we enjoy, what makes us come alive, what expresses who we are. Before Sasha gained weight, "working out was fun," she said. "Riding my bike was fun. Going to dance class was fun. It was a big part of my life. It was something that was part of my identity." Now, movement is something she feels she must do to be a worthwhile person. And the stakes of moving—her entire sense of worth—often overwhelm her into staying in bed.

Stigma can cause the self to split in two, as people create a persona that is less vulnerable to stigma. There's the identity laced with the shame we try to suppress, and then there's the counter-identity we create to prove we're worthy, the grueling mask we try to fuse onto our face. The "best little boy in the world" hypothesis describes how gay men hyper-achieve, or become the best little boy, to compensate for feelings of inferiority. A study found that gay men are more likely than heterosexual men to say that their worth depends on what they achieve, as if their worth required proof. The longer they concealed their sexuality, the more they felt they had to achieve to prove their worth. Adam D. Chandler was a closeted gay man who saw himself in the hypothesis, coming out in a *New York Times* article, where he recollected that he wrecked exam curves, petitioned the dean to overload his schedule, and ran to be the president of clubs he'd just joined. As the stigma stubbornly persists, the mask does, too.

Deprivation causes obsession. When we are deprived of acceptance, the journey to find it becomes all-consuming: hypervigilance for negative reactions, chronic self-policing, assuming a false but more "legitimate" persona. Toni Morrison intuited this obsessiveness when she said,

> The function, the very serious function of racism is distraction. It keeps you from doing your work. It keeps you explaining, over and over again, your reason for being. Somebody says you have no language and you spend twenty years proving that you do. Somebody says your head isn't shaped properly so you have scientists

working on the fact that it is. Somebody says you have no art, so you dredge that up. Somebody says you have no kingdoms, so you dredge that up. None of this is necessary. There will always be one more thing.

Feeling worthy means you stop being obsessed with pleasing people who stigmatize you. You're no longer beholden to acting in ways that will escape their disapproval, and instead you do what is most important to you. Sasha shared an example of what secure-ish would look like regarding her body: kids playing in a puddle. She was hiking in the rain to burn calories, and she saw a boy about to step into a huge puddle. "Watch out for the puddle there. It's really deep," Sasha told the boy. "Where?" he said, right before he leapt into it.

These kids are fantastic, Sasha thought to herself. *They are, of course, burning calories. They don't know it. They don't care. They're just little kids who are physical, who are in their bodies, who are doing what they're supposed to be doing as human beings. . . . How do I live in a way that I can be them and remember what it was like to be active because I just loved it, and not because it's tied to my value as a human being?*

To be free is to cease to think of freedom.*

IDENTITY STRETCHING

To make someone a criminal doesn't just require finding them guilty. It requires engaging them in a certain kind of pomp and circumstance. They are stripped, searched, and dressed in a jumpsuit. From then on, they live in a cell, sleep on a mattress that some might call a mat, and eat food they did not choose from a cold plastic tray. It is not just the

* This line was inspired by a quote from poet Khalil Gibran: "For you can only be free when even the desire of seeking freedom becomes a harness to you, and when you cease to speak of freedom as a goal and a fulfilment."

judges' verdict, but the culmination of these rituals that compels them to think of themselves as criminals.

Shadd Maruna, a criminologist at University of Liverpool, argues that the accrued impact of all these markers is deadly. When ex-convicts come to see themselves as criminals, Maruna found in his groundbreaking study of male ex-convicts in Liverpool, England, they continued to commit crimes after they were released. It was not just their relationships, job prospects, or social programs that determined rates of recidivism. How ex-convicts saw themselves, as inherently bad or as worthy of redemption, was key.

Some criminals wanted to leave prison, stop offending, and pursue other goals in life. They failed, however, because criminality had become baked into their identity. They felt, in Maruna's words, "doomed to deviance." As one twenty-eight-year-old male said, "I'm a thief, but if there was some other way, I'd do that. I guess I'm just a thief—no more, no less." Another thirty-three-year-old said, "I'm at the stage now where I'm resigned to the fact that I'm an addict and I'm going to be an addict to the day I die, and nothing's going to change that."

One twenty-seven-year-old male was released from prison and soon after, he injected heroin for what was in his mind the last time. His face turned blue. He woke up in the hospital. The doctor asked him if he tried to kill himself, and he told the doctor he was just trying to get a hit. "Smackheads, they deserve what they get," the doctor replied. "I just got straight back into it then, and I was going out, I was robbing, shoplifting, scheming, borrowing, begging, and I wasn't getting anywhere fast. I knew what I was doing, getting back into the old routine, and I didn't want to, because I knew exactly what would happen, you know. I'd end up dead somewhere," the man reflected.

How does Maruna propose we help ex-convicts see themselves as more than a thief or an addict? A graduation ceremony. I must admit, I hate graduation ceremonies. This seems like something to be embarrassed of, like hating puppies or summertime or bouquets (which I also hate; can't we celebrate without killing something?). But Maruna's graduation ceremonies intrigued me. The same sentimental music would play that marked the passage of one season of life to another. Someone lofty would say a few words, perhaps try to squeeze in a joke that would get a few dutiful chuckles. There'd be certificates with names written in calligraphy. The graduate, however, would not be celebrated for the papers they churned through or the exams they crammed for. They would be celebrated for ending their prison sentence. These "status elevation ceremonies" would involve a formal moment of collective forgiveness, when ex-convicts would be acknowledged for regaining their standing in society. Just like rituals helped criminals see themselves as such, a ritual could help them see themselves as more than that.

Affirming rituals are one way to stretch ex-convicts' identity beyond that of a criminal. Another way is for an authority figure to acknowledge their goodness. Ben Walter sat in juvenile court with his father, who consistently made him feel insignificant and stupid. The judge said, "What's happened to Benjamin is a complete travesty. No, we're not looking at a hardened criminal that has made a decision to be a bad person. We're looking at a kid." In Ben's mind, up until that point, he wasn't a kid. He was a danger to society. But that moment stretched his identity and changed his life. Ben Walter is now the CEO of Chase for Business Banking.

Another poignant story of an authority figure stretching someone's identity came from a mom whose son was murdered. A fourteen-year-old boy killed her son to prove himself to his gang. At his trial, the mother of the slain boy told the fourteen-year-old boy who had ended her son's life, "I'm going to kill you." She had a funny way of acting on it, though. She started visiting the boy in jail, left him money for snacks, and brought him small gifts. He didn't have anyone else. When the boy was about to leave the detention center, the mother asked him where he'd go and what he'd do. The boy didn't know. The mother offered to connect him to an employer. She told him he could stay in her extra room.

After he was living in her home for eight months, she called the boy into the living room to talk. "Do you remember that time in the courtroom when I told you I was going to kill you? I did. I didn't want that boy who could kill my son for no reason to remain alive, which is why I started to visit you and bring you things. That's why I got you the job and let you live here in my house. That's how I set about changing you. And that old boy, he's gone. So now I want to ask you, since my son is gone and that killer is gone, if you'll stay here. I've got a room and I'd like to adopt you if you'd let me."

Not all of us have a criminal history, but Maruna's ideas about identity stretching can help anyone relinquish stigma. Some, like the ex-convicts in Maruna's research, do this by seeing themselves as more than their stigmatized identity: *I'm not just a criminal.* Others choose to stretch their stigmatized identity to mean something good, or at least not so bad. One of the most effective interventions for shrinking the gap in grades between white and Black students involves the latter kind of identity stretching. Black students on predominately white college campuses intuit that their race marks them, that no matter what they do, they'll be judged. This sense of vulnerability can make hardships like struggling to make friends seem insurmountable, like an inevitable result of their differences rather than something that can be overcome. The researchers cooked up an ingenious way to stretch this belief about their identity. They had participants read accounts from other students who struggled with belonging and eventually found community. The participants even wrote an essay to a future student about some of their own initial struggles with belonging that they had already overcome. Over the years, the GPA of Black students participating in the study shot up, and by their final year, the GPA gap between Black and white students was cut by 79 percent. The happiness gap between Black and white students also disappeared. The power of the intervention is that it subtly stretched their Black identity so it did not mean they were doomed.

RETRIEVAL COMPETITION THEORY

As we've learned, stigma internalized metastasizes into internal dialogue, you yapping to you about yourself, an opinionated, and uninvited, guest who won't leave. Like, get out of here, auntie internalized ageism, and leave me at peace in my wrinkles. To be powerless against the happenings of your own mind, for a part of you to become a henchman serving what is against you, is demoralizing. Yet as twenty-eight-year-old Marc Almodovar discovered after years of these internal lashings, you're not powerless. The mind does not just happen to you; you happen to it.

"You're so lazy. You have no ambitions. What's the point of trying?" is a glimpse into what Marc's internal dialogue looked like. This was the product of him enduring years of failing report cards and disappointed family members, topped off by a guidance counselor who told him he wasn't going anywhere in life. The counselor even called his mother to tell her he might be held back a grade. When Marc's mother confronted him for being unmotivated, he broke down. "I need help. I'm not doing okay. I think so poorly of myself. I speak very badly of myself. And I just, I don't have this confidence. I'm really struggling and just not okay."

The ADHD diagnosis that came after might have saved Marc's life, as it helped him dare to suppose he wasn't doomed nor defective, just different. Therapy, his success as a speaker, and leading an online community for men with ADHD all helped him, too. After Marc spoke on a popular podcast, *Translating ADHD*, a sixteen-year-old Puerto Rican kid reached out to him to say that after listening to Marc, he could finally relate to someone. Marc, who is Puerto Rican and Cuban, felt as if he was saving his younger self. But Marc also needed another medicine, something to tête-à-tête with the aggressive voice inside his head.

Enter the pep talk. Marc discovered that whenever the aggressive internal voice barged in, he could actively tell himself something kind. He's been doing his pep talks regularly for years. Often, when he doubts himself, residual self-doubt from years of being seen as a failure because of his ADHD, he drums up the memory of that sixteen-year-old kid whose life he changed and reminds himself of his impact. Days before our interview, he forgot to complete his daily exercise of one hundred squats and pushups. Before the critical voice started yapping, Marc told himself, *You missed this thing. The good news is that you're not defined by that, because you have a lot of wins. This doesn't have to be something that impacts your confidence, and tomorrow is a thing.* After all his practice, Marc finally sounds like the adult that younger him needed.

We've learned that you can identity-stretch through rituals or affirmation from others. Through his pep talks, Marc stumbled onto a way to identity-stretch using the science of memory. According to retrieval competition theory, our worth depends not just on our negative memories, but on how accessible our negative memories are relative to our positive ones. While memory reconsolidation involves transforming negative memories to positive, retrieval competition involves focusing more on positive ones, or even generating more good memories. Then, as new negative experiences arise (as they inevitably will if you have a stigmatized identity), we'll be less vulnerable to them, our store of positive memories acting as a buffer. At the end of this chapter, I share exercises to make positive memories of your identity more accessible or even develop new positive associations with it, like through developing your own pep talks or doing visualizations.

Applying retrieval competition theory, according to a meta-analysis, improves people's self-esteem more than standard therapy. Marc has had much success in focusing on the positive, intentionally reminding himself of the sixteen-year-old-boy he inspired so that memories like the guidance counselor who lost faith in him have faded into the distance. Yet I still felt a bit sheepish about retrieval competition theory. Sure, it might help to focus on the positive, but the stigma memories would still lurk. I liked memory reconsolidation because it transforms pain so it doesn't exist.

But after getting deeper into writing this, I've realized that to be healed doesn't mean to be perfect, not a crumb of trauma residing in your nervous system. Healing is more about becoming more okay with being imperfect. Sasha was not only terrorized by the voice inside her telling her to exercise and count calories, but also by the counter-voice expecting her to be perfectly okay with her body. "You're not supposed to say you don't like yourself, and you're not supposed to associate working out with losing weight. You're supposed to just do it because it's good for your mental health and it's good for your heart, it's good for your body, and the results will come. So it's like this constant battle in my head that leads to paralysis," Sasha told me.

Simultaneously, the idea of feeling perfectly okay with her body as it is seemed unobtainable to Sasha. "What am I, some kind of spiritual guru? What kind of mental obstacle course have you accomplished to go against everything that society and your lived experience tells you to actually overcome that and move on with your life?" Retrieval competition theory leaves room for Sasha's body image to be imperfect. She doesn't have to achieve guru status to reconsolidate the memories of every article on weight loss she's ever read. The negative messages are going to exist. But finding worth means that the negative messages don't comprise the only voice that tells you who you are.

Merlin Sheldrake, author of *Entangled Life: How Fungi Make Our Worlds, Change Our Minds and Shape Our Futures*, would agree with Sasha that we are inevitably impacted by our environment; in fact, he argues, we are environments. We're teaming with microbes that do many of the things we think our body does for us, like digesting food or protecting us from disease. We're ecologies, not individuals, he concludes, a network of relationships, and there are no clear lines demarcating where our bodies end and microbes begin.

To be impacted by substances outside our selves (if we even have a self, but bear with me here . . .) is not a personal failure. It is the very nature of our existence. Our survival depends on being subject to outside influence. Instead of trying to steel ourselves against ecology, which is impossible, we can remix our ecology, and not just the one outside us—the guidance counselors we avoid, the career we choose, or the media we consume—but the ecology inside us, too, one science-backed pep talk at a time.

Changing our internal ecology means that if our negative self-talk is persistent, then our ability to interrupt it needs to be just as persistent. On autopilot, we will continue to put ourselves down, compare ourselves, and zoom in to our perceived flaws. We can't control where our rumination goes, but we can control our response to it. Instead of the chatter being the end of our conversation with ourselves, it needs to be the start of a talk that ends in compassion. Every blast of negativity is an opportunity, an alarm bell alerting us to a wound that requires our kindness to heal, to say, *This body does so much to keep me alive. I need a beating heart, and breathing lungs to love like I do, so thank you for being the material that allows me every love I've ever had*, or *My brain works differently, and that's what makes me creative, unique, and vital in this tapestry of human beings*, or *I may not be who I used to be, but no one was meant to stay the same in this life. I am a part of nature, growing, changing, transforming, in concert with the rhythm of all things.*

Our self-talk won't change from one or even a couple of compassionate responses, but it will change after a regular practice of this. Marc is living proof. He is now a successful speaker on ADHD and leads an online men's ADHD support group with twenty-three thousand members. As he put it, "I'm thinking of [younger] Marc [and] I'm like, wow. That was me at one point. That's crazy. On the internal battle, I've come such a long way. I am an example of how working toward a shift in the self-dialogue can help an individual start to blossom."

IDENTITY STRETCHING

When we reject the idea that we are inferior, we have space to create our own idea of what our identity means. Writing this chapter has led me to stretch my own view, to make new meaning of stigmatized identities. I marvel at the way these identities persist, despite the stigma. Others have tried to destroy them, but they have proven themselves indestructible. There are still blind, queer, transgender, fat, and Indigenous people, and on and on. These identities that live represent the sometimes quiet, sometimes even shame-addled, revelation of our individuality. They are rebellious, disobedient, and self-affirming, objects of awe, these parts of us that survive even the gravest approbation. They are signs that people don't all acquiesce to the demands of their circumstances—which might dictate that identities like theirs should be eradicated or else pushed to the margins—but possess an essence beyond those demands, a willingness to make the dictates of circumstance confront its own limits. They shine a light on the edges where we can grow as a society so as to become a better container for the authenticity of everyone.

I'm also moved when I hear the meaning-making of others with stigmatized identities who have worked to shed the propaganda of their stigma. To Andrew Solomon, who wrote *The Noonday Demon: An Atlas of Depression* about his battle with depression, disability means that dependency is normal and that it "has its own particular poetry. It is a fundamental aspect of intimacy, a defining quality of love." Disability is also about "how we seek meaning in who we are rather than in who we might have wished to be." To Cyndi Jones, a vicar at Atonement Lutheran Church, her disability, combined with her faith, helped her realize that "you, exactly as you are, are essential to all of creation in a way that we cannot understand, that without you creation would be incomplete."

Sabrina, an artist in her mid-thirties, views her pansexuality as a bridge to better love. Even if she's been taught to only love men, she can look at "the soul of anyone and be like, 'Oh, there's so much beauty here. I can love you.' This is what will save the world, the ability to look at people you're not supposed to love and love them." Wil, who is polyamorous and has built a platonic and romantic chosen family, says of polyamory, "Being able to look at my family and say we broke all the rules and we're happy and healthy and functioning shows me that in all other aspects of life, that could be true, too. Things don't have to be better through the systems that currently exist. There's more out there for us. We could be living better. We really could. We just have to try."

Catarina now stretches other people's views about what it means to be blind. She is a public speaker who launched a disability empowerment retreat and is a leading voice on making travel accessible for people with disabilities. Powerful stories from other people living with disabilities have helped her stretch into finding pride in being blind. One story that has stuck with her occurred at a disability rights protest in March 1990, the Capitol Crawl, where more than sixty wheelchair users got out of their chairs to crawl up the steps of the Capitol building, poignantly portraying the urgency of their need for accommodations. A young girl crawled up the steps while her nondisabled mom crawled beside her, telling her, "You don't have to do this. You can stop at any time." "No. I want to. I'm doing this," the girl told her mom.

Stigma has always come with duality. Wherever it exists, stigmatized people also exist, identity stretching, painting stories of themselves as fully dignified, fully human, and worthy of celebration over denigration. And the pride that comes after stigma is a force majeure. I could be proud of my sneakers, cooking skills, or hairdo, but pride is a more boundless force when its seeds are planted against a backdrop of hate that has made its existence not just nice to have, but vital. It was only here, against the grisly backdrop of a society where that little girl had to leave her wheelchair and crawl up those steps, that her self-affirmation, her sureness of her own right to fully inhabit the world, her pride in herself, could move Catarina and me so much. As Catarina finished the little girl's story, we both teared up. I thought of the tears back in the doctor's office when she found out she was going blind. Except, if her tears could speak, this time I imagine they'd utter something different from shame.

RETRIEVAL COMPETITION THEORY EXERCISE

The purpose of this exercise is to help you identity-stretch a stigmatized identity. You will be drawing up positive associations with the identity that will eventually become more accessible than negative ones.

1. Choose an identity that you have been stigmatized for. This can be your age, body type, class, sexuality, race, disability, etc. What have you learned to believe is negative about this identity?
2. Do you believe that your identity is 100 percent negative? If not, what are some positive aspects of this identity that might contradict the negative ones? Write down as many as possible.
3. Write a story about a specific instance when a positive aspect of your identity was demonstrated. This can be something that actually happened or something you imagine happening.
4. Visualize yourself in the positive story related to this identity in step 3.
5. Based on the story, develop a positive statement about this identity.
6. To make the positive story of your identity (step 3) more vivid, visualize it while:
    - Playing a song that aligns with its positive aspects
    - Assuming a posture and facial expression that reflect the positive feelings you have toward the identity
    - Reciting your positive identity statement
7. For the next week, repeat step 6 every day, three times a day (three minutes each time). Write down the following:
    - Time of exercise

- Success in reliving from 0 (not at all) to 100 (totally)
- How believable the reliving experience is from 0 (not at all) to 100 (totally)
- If success or believability is low, think about ways you can improve on reliving the memory or making it more believable for next time

8. During the same week, whenever you tell yourself something negative about your identity, remind yourself of any of the positive aspects you've discovered about it so far. This can take the form of:
   - A pep talk where you tell yourself exactly what you'd want to hear to feel better about your identity
   - Remembering or visualizing your positive story of your identity
   - Playing the song that aligns with the positive aspects of your identity
   - Reciting your positive statement about your identity
9. After the week is over, think back to a time when your identity was perceived more negatively. So you can feel more confident in the threatening situation, now think of the positives of your identity by:
   - A pep talk where you tell yourself exactly what you'd want to hear to feel better about your identity
   - Remembering or visualizing your positive story of your identity
   - Playing the song that aligns with the positive aspects of your identity
   - Reciting your positive statement about your identity

This exercise was developed based on Korrelboom et al., "Competitive Memory Training (COMET) for Low Self-Esteem in Patients with Personality Disorders: A Randomized Effectiveness Study"; and van der Gaag et al., "Initial Evaluation of the Effects of Competitive Memory Training (COMET) on Depression in Schizophrenia-Spectrum Patients with Persistent Auditory Verbal Hallucinations: A Randomized Controlled Trial."

8

Psychedelic Memories

"Freshman year, I was shy and insecure. Now I'm a senior and I know who I am," one of my students shared with the rest of the psychology class triumphantly. I noticed that "knowing herself" was an accomplishment, a marker of prestige, as some students nodded in admiration, others agreed, and some, who could not compete, shriveled into silence.

Internally, I had my doubts that this student knew herself at twenty-one, but bubble-bursting isn't my teaching style. Looking back, I have more reflections. Does "knowing yourself" have an end point where the story of who you are is officially "known"? And if so, how could you ever evolve?

By claiming to know herself, I imagine this student wanted to convey that she was secure in herself, something we are all searching for. But did that mean knowing herself? In fact, some researchers think knowing one's self may be a sign of insecurity more than it is one of security. The insecure, after all, know themselves, if we define it as remaining steady in the story of themselves despite any information to the contrary. People with low self-esteem, we learned in chapter 2, are so sure that they're unlovable that they deflect compliments and affirmations. To be anxiously attached is to know with certainty that you're discardable despite how many people treasure you. *It's only a matter of time before they get some sense and leave*, you're sure. To be avoidantly attached is to know your vulnerability is so intertwined with shame that every person who has tried to love what's behind the curtain of you has been viewed more as a threat than a friend. Insecure attachment means the self is a little too known.

Perhaps, then, our greatest danger comes from knowing ourselves, from having this fixed story as to who we are. It was believed that Buddha first thought so. He advised us to strive for "no self," or anatta, lest we suffer as we toil to protect this self and are torn up when we fail. Robin Carhart-Harris, a professor in the Department of Neurology at the University of California, San Francisco, would agree that a too-fixed story of self can spur suffering, but for a different reason. When we are harmed, he theorized, we stop seeing life as predictable—*anything bad can happen anytime*—which is its own kind of pain. To find certainty, our brain cements a story of ourselves (like *I'm bad*) and the world (*You can't trust anyone*). Some semblance of certainty returns to us. But this coping mechanism preserves our struggle, like freezing your credit at your lowest score. Sure, it won't descend from here, but it *will* stay bad.

Being stuck in one unchanging story of self is something that people with many different mental health issues share. Depression's sense of inadequacy will coerce you to ignore a hundred compliments and bathe yourself in that niggling criticism. Anxiety's story of omnipresent danger will rewrite safety into mere prequel for threat. Addiction will leave you neglecting yourself altogether to hyper-fixate on a substance. Suffering can come not just from disorder, but also from a different kind of order, as one researcher put it. The more locked our brain is in one mode, the more fixed our sense of self, Carhart-Harris argues, the worse our mental health. Even a fixed positive story of ourselves—*I'm a musical prodigy*—can leave us reeling when our skills and abilities inevitably change.

Having a too-fixed story of self also disrupts memory reconsolidation. How do we inject love into our memories if we see ourselves as fundamentally unlovable? How can we reassure our younger selves of their worth when we feel irrefutably inferior? Memory reconsolidation requires us to provide ourselves with fresh perspective. Yet when we do, a fixed sense of self might offer its rejoinder.

Remember Esme from chapter 3? She tried to reassure herself after being rejected by a friend, "It's only a few blips [of rejection]," but her optimism wavered. "The rational part of my brain knows they're blips, but the emotional part . . ." Because of her negative sense of self, grains of self-acceptance slipped through her fingers. Her self acted as what German professor and philosopher Thomas Metzinger calls an "ego tunnel," filtering out information that didn't corroborate its negative self-perception, even if that information was key to her healing. To reconsolidate, we need to crawl out of this tunnel.

We need to lose ourselves so we can find ourselves.

HOW TO LOSE YOURSELF

The Johns Hopkins Bayview Medical Center campus is an unassuming place to house some of the most noteworthy research in the mental health field. The window of the building to my right was boarded up with a wooden plank. In front of me was the building I was visiting, which looked at least a decade older than me, with layers of glass pool tile above the entry door. After I entered, I chatted up the security guard while waiting in the lobby. He had no idea about the kind of research happening in the building.

Dr. Albert Garcia-Romeu, or Al as he told me to call him, arrived to escort me to his lab. He had kind eyes, a salt-and-pepper beard, and a broad, teddy bear–like build. On our initial Zoom call, the formal air of his role, as a principal investigator at Johns Hopkins Center for Psychedelic and Consciousness Research, was punctured by the electric guitars lined up against his wall and the gold plastic Mardi Gras beads hanging from his doorknob. He told me about a colleague I should interview and then warned me that the guy was a jerk. I appreciated that, to him, academic accolades could not render a shoddy character irrelevant. This is all to say, Al struck me as a nice guy who broke the mold of a stuffy academic.

I visited Johns Hopkins to understand what environment might be conducive to people losing themselves. I became convinced, after reading the research on psychedelics, that if anything will help you lose yourself, it's psilocybin (also known as shrooms), LSD, ayahuasca, MDMA (ecstasy), or the other members of their trippy family. Of course, for many decades, these substances triggered panic for this same reason. Sensational reports of people lunging out of windows, scrambling their brains, and being propelled into psychosis halted the science of psychedelics for decades. One *Life* magazine article described LSD as "a one-way trip to an asylum, a prison or a grave." Forging a sense of self is ultimately an attempt to build a line of defense, making us less susceptible to influences that don't uphold our worldview. Lower the self's guardrails, and you're more defenseless, for better or worse. Contemporary psychedelic researchers are trying to figure out how to lower these rails for the better.

Psychedelics help us lose ourselves because they disrupt the normal rhythm of the seat of the self in the brain, known as the default mode network. This allows us to escape a dictatorial story imposed by our sense of self. As Michael Pollan puts it in *How to Change Your Mind: What the New Science of Psychedelics Teaches Us about Consciousness, Dying, Addiction, Depression, and Transcendence*, "These compounds can loosen the ego's grip on the machinery of the mind, 'lubricating' cognition where before it had been rusted stuck." The desire for self-verification (to reaffirm what we think we know of ourselves, as we explored in chapter 2) recedes as preexisting beliefs about ourselves become malleable.

People taking psychedelics describe the process as a brain reboot or as "a holiday away from the prison of my brain."

Their potential to relax our beliefs about ourselves is the leading theory for why psychedelics successfully treat so many mental health issues (although *how* they do this is not fully understood, Al said). In one randomized controlled study, people with treatment-resistant depression received two rounds of psilocybin. These were folks who had tried everything, but nothing worked. Despite the intractability of their depression, it receded immediately after they took psilocybin: 71 percent decreased depressive symptoms by at least half, and 58 percent were no longer depressed at all. In comparison, depressive scores for people in the control group slightly increased during the study. Patients in another study described their experience as "therapy on steroids," and "ten years of therapy in one day." Psilocybin has been found to be two and a half times more effective than traditional therapy and four times more effective than antidepressants.

After reading this research, I showed up at the lab composed of 75 percent serious writer and 25 percent fangirl. When Al asked a colleague which room was free so I could tour it, his colleague mentioned that participants were taking part in studies in some of the rooms. Wow, I marveled: People were changing their lives right then, all around us.

We arrived at a nondescript room with a beige couch that I stretched myself across to mimic the participants. On other days, people had lain there with eye masks and headphones on as they underwent their psychedelic journey. The eye masks made their hallucinations reflect whatever went on inside them, their psyche personified, rather than outside. The music intensified their emotions while they confronted their psyche. Two therapists watched, typically not doing much but telling participants to "Go with it" if they were freaked out. They were meant to trust the participants to heal themselves.

Al hired an interior designer to choose décor that sent his participants the message: *Relax, you're safe here.* They adorned the walls with decorative straw plates and nature paintings: a panorama view of a valley, six feathers standing up as if they were waiting for the bus, and a fern with long, thin fronds. The designer had previously decorated rooms at Spring Grove Hospital Center, where researchers conducted early studies on psychedelics. There, participants successfully healed from alcoholism and existential distress, Al told me. "But in other [locations], they would put you in a hospital room, and they would strap you to the bed [with a] really high dose. And those folks weren't getting better."

Décor, typically ancillary in research labs, is a priority in a psychedelic research lab because it can determine the nature of the experience of losing yourself, whether it is blissful or bleak. Aside from setting, the other determining factor, research finds, is your mindset when taking the drugs, known as "set." This idea of set and setting builds off wisdom from Indigenous communities, who have been using psychedelics for more than fifteen thousand years. In Indigenous healing ceremonies, instead of therapists, there are shamans or curanderos (healers). Instead of music played through headphones, there are drummers, singers, and prayers.

The emotional and visual processing centers of your brain speak to each other while you're on psychedelics, so how you feel about yourself and your environment when entering the experience affects what you hallucinate. To nurture the right set in participants,* Al paired them with therapists for multiple sessions before they took psychedelics, and these therapists were the same ones supporting them the day they took the psychedelics.

Set and setting are so important because psychedelics reinstate the critical periods we experience as kids, when we were far more vulnerable to our environment. Because psychedelics make your brain less

* People who have bipolar, psychotic, or personality disorders (or whose direct family members do) are typically screened out of psychedelic studies. This isn't typically spoken about as a way to encourage the right "set," even though it seems as if it would be. They're excluded because psychedelics can elevate the risk of psychotic breaks and manic episodes, particularly for people with a genetic predisposition to these ailments.

rigid than a sober adult's brain and more malleable, like a child's, what happens when you're on them can imprint itself on you long afterward, much like how a child is treated determines how they see themselves, sometimes for the rest of their lives. This is why researchers emphasize the risks of taking psychedelics without proper precautions. In Johns Hopkins's sixteen-page consent form, they list risks like strong feelings of fear and anxiety, paranoia, intense crying, and even changes to your personality. One study found that of the people experiencing bad trips, 39 percent rated it among the top five most challenging experiences of their lifetime. A therapist shared that his patient, a woman in her fifties, took psilocybin with a friend. She was flooded with memories of her emotionally abusive father, who had an alcohol addiction. After the trip, memories kept emerging, propelling her into a depression.

As I chatted with Al, I chewed on this idea that losing the self on psychedelics transformed his participants into something like children. Like a child, they didn't have a fixed story of self to butt in and protect them in its janky way. This meant that at no other time in their lives, aside from their childhoods, would they be as psychologically vulnerable as they were when they were on the couch I was currently on. It also meant that even if they didn't have the right set and setting during their childhood, it wasn't too late. Here, in a way, was a second chance at childhood.

Everything about this set and setting at Johns Hopkins University was a kind of bet for what would make a child feel safe. Because to lose yourself and find yourself again while on psychedelics, you need to be surrounded by the right people and in a safe place. The books on the shelves, on topics like puppies and the cosmos, and the comfy couch I sunk into took on this new meaning. The psychedelic guides would help steady you, trusting you to work yourself out of your pain, but offering solace if it gets to be too much, like the parents of secure-ish children do. I didn't know if Al had kids, but it struck me that he and his therapists, as they accompanied people through their psychedelic journeys, through losing and finding themselves, became parents.

MEMORY RECONSOLIDATION ON PSYCHEDELICS

On October 26, 2006, Jonathan Lubecky was returning from his tour of Iraq and looking forward to four things: hugging his wife, playing with his dog, riding his motorcycle, and eating a dish called shrimp ducky at Copeland's, a local restaurant.

None of these would come to pass.

As he deboarded the plane, he watched everyone else in his unit reunite with someone—a girlfriend, wife, parent, or child. No one came to welcome him. He had asked his parents to be there since he hadn't heard back from his wife for the last few weeks. "Well, we came when you left. Do we have to be there when you arrive?" they asked, turning down his request. As he would soon learn, his wife ran off with a lieutenant colonel, took the dog, and sold the motorcycle. Copeland's had also gone out of business, so a steaming plate of shrimp ducky was not in the cards. It was all like "a bad country song," Jonathan described.

His next few months were unbearable. Stripped of people who had anchored him, whether from his unit or within his own household, he was alone with himself, a self that had become knitted with the horrors of his tour in Iraq. He had nightmares that would leave him shooting up, stick straight, in the middle of the night, soaked in sweat; panic attacks that left him to imprison himself in his closet at the first pop of fireworks; and a deluge of fear, misery, and terror. When Jonathan would eventually go to the VA, he'd find out he had the highest tier of PTSD severity measurable.

And then there was the record that played on loop in his head: *I'm worthless. I have zero value in society. The world would be a better place without me in it.* This sense of worthlessness could easily be attributed to his PTSD, but if he was honest with himself, it was a record that played long before his tour in Iraq, its lyrics forming during a childhood he hardly remembered. Scenes he could pull together were of an erratic mother screaming, a brother taking drugs, and people getting beaten up, himself included. One of the reasons he joined the military was to take the needle off record, to finally prove that he was worthy.

On Christmas Eve 2006, Jonathan went to a bar in Raleigh, North Carolina, and had a few drinks to take the edge off it all. While there, he heard church bells. *I don't need to be in a bar on Christmas. I need to go there*, he thought to himself. But the church was full. "By this time, I've got tears streaming down my face. I'm like, 'I just got back from Iraq. I really just need to go in there. I'll stand in the back.'" They turned him away, citing the fire code.

Jonathan took his tears to the war memorial in downtown Raleigh and thought about how to end his life. As he did, he remembered that in the briefings he received after he returned from Iraq, he was told that he should go to the hospital if he had thoughts of ending his life. So he drove to Womack Army Medical Center at Fort Bragg, and he told the psychiatrist, "I'm going to kill myself."

"Do you have guns?" the psychiatrist asked.

"Yes, a lot."

"Do you have ammo for these guns?"

"Yes, a lot."

"Okay, here are six Xanax. Don't take them all at the same time because it'll kill you. When you get home, give your guns to a neighbor and come back after the holiday."

When Jonathan went home, he put a gun to his temple and pulled the trigger, feeling "[the] most peace I had felt in my whole life." Yet the bullet never came. The gun malfunctioned.

Later Jonathan would interpret the defective gun as a sign of a higher power, but at the time he thought, "I felt like I was such a failure that I couldn't even kill myself."

In the years after that first suicide attempt, Jonathan tried established treatments for PTSD, cognitive behavioral therapy, exposure therapy. Nothing worked. To manage his symptoms, along with the symptoms of a traumatic brain injury, he was taking forty-two pills a day. He attempted suicide four more times.

Eight years after his first attempt, he was in regular therapy, even attending classes to get a degree, although his symptoms persisted. One week, his psychiatrist had an emergency and couldn't see him, so he saw her intern instead. She slid him a piece of paper. "I want you to open that when you leave the VA. I'm not supposed to tell you about that, so just stick it in your pocket." The paper read, "Google MDMA PTSD."

Jonathan's googling revealed that a nearby trial was taking place to examine whether MDMA could treat veterans' PTSD, led by Michael Mithoefer, a psychotherapist and clinical researcher at the Medical University of South Carolina, and his wife, Ann Mithoefer, a nurse. They were supposed to cap the study at twenty-five participants, but they let Jonathan enroll as their twenty-sixth. I asked Jonathan whether he had hope that the treatment could work. "I fully expected this shit not to work. I pretty much did this because this seemed like something fun to do before I ended up inevitably killing myself."

In a house converted into a research lab, Jonathan was offered a green pill on a green dish. "I kind of was hoping that, like, they'd have a red pill and a blue pill, like *The Matrix*, and that one was placebo and one was active, but it wasn't it," he said. After he took the pill, the psychologists asked him softball questions about Iraq. "What was the weather like? What was the food like?" It didn't take long before Jonathan's mind led him to the memories that still troubled him.

One was of another man in his unit, a twenty-year-old named Nick. Jonathan had been assigned to help trucks navigate the road so they didn't detonate any bombs. He was removed from the position and someone else took his place. The truck he used to command drove over a bomb that shattered the bones in Nick's leg. It was later amputated. Jonathan blamed himself, because he thought he should have been the one commanding the truck.

The meaning he made—that it was his fault, that he was to blame—was drawn from a familiar script. While he was on MDMA, more memories arose with this same script, ones originating in his abusive childhood.

Early LSD researcher Stanislav Grof theorized that memories of the same emotional charge are grouped together in our minds in what he called a COEX, a system of condensed experience. I think of it as a cone of memories that triggers the same kind of emotion, like a worthlessness COEX.

The COEX starts accumulating its memories very early, and it gathers more memories throughout our lives. The fuller it becomes, the more it impacts our sense of self and mental health, suggesting that things that get to us now have precursors in our childhoods. The COEX explains the nature of triggers, why seemingly small events can send us reeling, because they unleash the cumulative emotion captured in the COEX. It also explains why earlier events can take a while to impact us. It is only when additional memories/emotions are planted into the COEX that the size of the COEX gets big enough to manifest in psychological symptoms, Grof theorized. Grof thought that LSD helped people clear out the emotions in their COEX by guiding them to unlock and work through memories—some long-buried—lodged within it. If Grof was right, then it would mean that for Jonathan, healing from PTSD was not just about reconsolidating his memories of what happened in Iraq but his connected memories from throughout his entire life.

Psychedelics provide us with unique access to the memories in our COEX. Loosening the grip of the self, researchers speculate, allows memories and emotions to bubble up that have been disavowed. They lead us to experience hypermnesia, or enhanced memory for past events that are "central to character formation." In fact, the term *psychedelic* means to show one's "soul" or "mind." Early psychedelic researchers reported, "Frequently whole sequences unroll before the patient's eyes as though they had been stored on microfilm." Memories might have been repressed because these emotions and memories were buried, too overwhelming for our psyches to confront. Alternatively, our emotions or memories may have been repressed. As I mentioned in the last chapter, if our parents don't regulate our emotions, we alter our consciousness—suppressing the parts of us in distress. Experiences or emotions that violate what our parents wanted are blasted into the purgatory of our unconscious. On the neural level, this looks like the seat of the self—default mode network—repressing the activity of the part of the brain associated with memory and emotion, the limbic region. David Nutt, a professor of neuropsychopharmacology at Imperial College London, described the default mode network as "the neural correlate for repression."

A tsunami of memories? A lifetime of emotion suddenly unleashed? This may sound incapacitating. But psychedelics don't just offer us all of our buried pain; they also offer us a life jacket to stay afloat amid it. They deactivate the amygdala, the part of the brain that makes us feel threatened, allowing us to return to our traumas with neural bumpers on. People taking psilocybin in a study reported that when revisiting memories, something like an inner therapist sprung up to anchor them. One psilocybin study participant described, "The feeling of being in the presence of something divine, something holy. It is real and within you," and another said, "[I] feel like I've ingested my own psychotherapist."

MDMA (ecstasy) is unique in that it doesn't make you hallucinate like other psychedelics. But it's similar to the others in that it disrupts your sense of self while deactivating your amygdala, allowing you to create a new positive meaning of past experience. While other psychedelics, like ayahuasca and psilocybin, have been shown to have promise for memory reconsolidation, their potential to produce hallucinations makes it difficult to determine whether people taking them are accessing memories or are hallucinating. MDMA, thus far, has the most support as a psychedelic that can help people reconsolidate memories. Much of the research on it has been to treat people with PTSD, a disorder of memory. A meta-analysis found that people with PTSD who took MDMA were 2.6 times more likely to go into remission than those who took a placebo.

When Jonathan was on MDMA, his amygdala finally calmed, and it was the first time he could revisit his memories, like the one with Nick, without spinning into a panic attack. With the seat of his sense of self deactivated, his script for himself—as at fault, to blame, unworthy—changed. This allowed him to look at old memories without the same sense of culpability and self-blame. When he thought about Nick and his lost leg, he realized, "It's not my fault," and that "Even though I couldn't be there for him when he got hit, I can still be there and help him today." Now, Jonathan regularly calls Nick to check in on him and help him get access to services he needs.

It might be apt to say that psychedelics saved Jonathan's life. Since taking MDMA, his PTSD symptoms were cut in half and his suicidal ideation was eliminated. But as I reflected on his story, I realized that it wasn't just that psychedelics saved him. The *idea* of something like psychedelics would have saved him. He would not have attempted to end his life if he had had hope that his life would become what it is now, he told me. (He's a political consultant lobbying the government to expand safe access to psychedelics.) People in the military, he said, could embrace the suck as long as they knew there was an out, a day ahead, when it would all be over. This is the power of the stories we have of ourselves. The panic attacks and fear and nightmares wouldn't have been enough to kill Jonathan. But the story that he'd be battling these terrors forever would have. When determining whether to live, the story of what his life could be mattered even more than what it was. Loosening the vise grip of a story, and allowing yourself to not know yourself, was lifesaving work. It is the heartbeat of hope.

A FRESH TAKE ON WORTH

Elizabeth Richwine, a fifty-seven-year-old woman, wanted to be more like who she was before she contracted Lyme disease. Her story of herself was that she had a certain "flair," a gesticulator who magnetized her listener, italicizing words by emphasizing certain syllables. It's not amazing; it's *amaaazing.* Her words were tools to persuade and inspire. In her job, bringing innovation to the food industry, she once convinced beverage company employees that they needed to visit a habitat for naked mole rats. They wanted to manufacture a new drink that screamed community, and apparently, naked mole rats have a unique take.

But since she contracted Lyme disease eight years prior, Elizabeth had been living in a mental fog, stumbling over and even losing certain words, often too fatigued to keep searching for them. She had been relentless about finding a cure. But the medical field had nothing more to offer her. Maybe try Pilates and sleep hygiene, her doctors said. She tried a clinical trial out of Columbia University that given her temporary relief. All the while, she was "scraping, clawing, struggling, biting to maintain some level of performance and functionality that I could be proud of."

Elizabeth had been signed up for the Johns Hopkins Lyme Disease Research Center database for many years before she saw the recruitment ad for a psilocybin study. Al would be one of her therapists. He told her that, yes, psychedelics could have some promising physical effects, like reducing inflammation. But it could have powerful mental effects, giving her new ways to cope with the stresses of Lyme disease. Elizabeth gave a dismissive "Yeah, yeah, yeah" to all the mental health impacts Al described. What she really needed, she thought, was physical relief.

But the mental relief helped her get her life back. On psilocybin, she realized that finding herself again didn't mean returning to who she was. It meant being okay with who*ever* she was, which changed in each moment. She had been skipping First Fridays, a mix and mingle among twenty or so of her friends at someone's house, because she felt anxious about her struggles with expressing herself. Yet after psilocybin, she realized, "I'm just gonna bring what I have. I'm gonna be who I am."

This more fluid identity—relinquishing the need to have a fixed story as to who you are—is one of many changes in the self that occur after psychedelics. As I combed through these changes, I realized that the sense of self induced by psychedelics synched up with the characteristics of a more evolved sense of self, as theorized by developmental psychologist Robert Kegan, among many others. For example, psychedelics have been found to lead to long-term changes in psychological flexibility, a kind of agility in regards to self and emotions that allows us to accept our feelings, stay present, and shift our view of ourselves as needed. (In fact, studies find that the more psychedelics improve our psychological flexibility, the more they improve our mental health, too.)

Although not all of us will take psychedelics, the research on them and their impact can give us a better idea of the worthy sense of self we aim for by doing all of this memory work. It is characterized by four qualities that reinforce one another:

- **Regard:** No matter what you feel, do, think, or measure up to (or don't), you are worthy.
- **Acceptance of emotion:** You accept, rather than run from or deny, difficult feelings.
    - Because you have high regard, your feelings don't mean anything about your worth. You're not better or stronger if you feel less.
- **Fluid identity:** You allow yourself a new experience of your identity in each moment.
    - Because you accept your emotions, as new feelings arise that you accept, they stretch and reshape your experience of your identity.
- **Mindfulness:** You are present, experiencing the uniqueness of each moment.
    - Because you have a fluid identity, you don't impose a story as to who you are or what is happening. You're present, experiencing what is.

Our self, when it's not so rigid—because it's bracing for threat, defending against perceived slights or hell-bent on its own glory—becomes something less predetermined, a more *fluid identity*, arising in reaction to what occurs in the present. British writer Alan Watts shares the metaphor of a fist. Open your hand and it disappears! That's because a fist was never an entity and always a process (the closing of one's hand).

Instead of observing how we experience something, whether we like or dislike it, we often use an identity as a shortcut to tell us if we should. With a more fluid identity, we register emotions, preferences, and experiences that we would otherwise dismiss. While mulling over my own fluid self, I got a flyer from a meal prep company. It offered me 60 percent off for a few boxes of their fresh, healthy meals. I threw it out. When I thought about why, I realized that ordering single-person meals didn't jive with the identity I have of myself as a connector. Eating single-person meals at home seemed lonely; I should be cooking a big batch of stew with an open-door policy for anyone who's hungry. But actually, I hate cooking. And no matter how much I connect with others, there will inevitably, and mercifully, be nights that I am home alone, having dinner with myself. I plucked the flyer out of the garbage.

As I was writing this chapter, a friend mentioned that she often meets people she feels sexually attracted to and would have more one-night stands but didn't want to be that kind of woman. My self-antennas were tingling, as I saw in real time the way our stories about ourselves can limit us from *being* ourselves. As a participant in a psilocybin study shared, their concept of their personality excluded parts of them they repressed. They became aware of "an existence of 'repressed' personalities that are 'in me' and yet separate from [my] ordinary conscious mind." As another participant described, "Ordinary personality is an intentional configuration (something 'I chose') that is separate from the true self or 'soul,' but which ideally 'allows the soul to shine through it.'"

With a more fluid self, we stop imposing our dog-eared autobiographies onto the present and instead experience it more fully; we become more *mindful.* Each moment is more unique, vibrant, and alive, because it's not a child of the past. And you, yourself, a reaction to each crisp moment, are more awake, versatile, and sprawling. Being more mindful might require us to ask ourselves, as Erich Fromm suggests, if we drink soda or if we drink a label. Instead of relying on our story of our love of Pepsi, and chugging a can without even questioning whether we like it, we start to actually taste it, to fall in love again in each moment, or perhaps out of it.

We're not just more mindful of our emotions, but also more *accepting of our emotions.* We stop rejecting emotions because they threaten our sense of self. One man taking part in a psilocybin study described himself as unemotional, repelled by others' emotions, and seeing emotions as weakness. Psilocybin helped a memory materialize that drove these beliefs: "I became myself at age seven after my [grandparent] had died. I totally was back there, so vivid, so real, I had the emotions that I would have felt at the time: fearful, why did this happen, the naivety, the shock and confusion. I was getting overly upset and my parents were saying 'Boys don't cry.'" He had the breakthrough that it is "not [a] weakness to be emotional, that's an unhealthy attitude."

Sometimes, we don't let ourselves feel because we think these feelings say something bad about who we are. *I don't want to cry during this movie, because I'll be a wimp. I don't want to still be grieving this relationship, because that means I'm pathetic. I don't want to admit I'm attracted to this person, because they aren't the type of person someone like me should be interested in.* But when we don't need our feelings to adhere to the simulacrum that represents our identity, we are free to admit all of who we are to ourselves.

It's so difficult to accept our evolving identity, experience, and emotions in each moment because doing so makes everything newer and, thus, more unpredictable. As Carhart-Harris mentioned, an insecure sense of self is, ironically, a way to provide us security as we (think we) know what is happening, and it becomes something we're familiar with. To feel worthy is to find security not by imposing a familiar story of who you and others are, but by having high *regard* for whoever it is you are in a given moment. Even when you don't look how you want to, or have the job you want, you know you're still worthy. To have high regard for yourself means that there is a part of you that, no matter what you do, loves, approves of, and understands you. (Think of the

Self in our Internal Family Systems chapter.) It doesn't need you to be anything different from who you are—no matter how anxious, spiteful, petty, or weak you feel—to love you. As Elizabeth realized, "The same value I bring to a day when I am not sick is the value I bring to a day when I am sick, even though it might look a little different."

What an acceptance of one's feelings, identity, and experience culminates in is an acceptance of reality. We resist reality because we don't feel our self can bear life as it is. So we ask, "Why me?" and "What if it were different . . . ?" But in a secure-ish state, our self feels strong-ish enough to handle what *is*. We tolerate whatever twists life takes. Erin, a cancer patient taking psilocybin, stated, "One of the really vivid images that I had was a sketch of a dinner table—it was almost this round circle that represented a dinner table—and at the table was cancer, but it was supposed to be at the table. And the feeling I had was cancer is a part of everything. It isn't this bad separate thing; it's something that's part of everything, and that everything is part of everything. And that's really beautiful. [An] acceptance of the human experience."

What I hope you don't take away from this is that feeling worthy means coercing yourself to be okay with what you're not. Surely, anyone who gets cancer will rage, grieve, and resist, and that doesn't mean they're simply not evolved enough. As we learned in chapter 1, we only get to secure-ish by having high regard for our insecure parts. So scream, pout, or weep, and all the while tell yourself that your feelings are valid, that there's space for them, too, and that you love those parts unconditionally. You come to accept things as they are by being there for the parts of you that don't.

Psychologist Hillevi Ruumet, drawing from Hinduism and Tantric traditions, imparts that self-growth is shaped like a spiral. Moving forward involves moving back to where we were, but stronger this time. This means that to evolve is to return to our insecurities, with more regard. To feel worthy, more generally, requires spiraling back to our fluid, childlike sense of self. Yet this time, instead of us needing regard from our parents, we have regard-ish within.

The spiral metaphor also reveals that "worth" isn't a fixed state. New circumstances will arise that shift us out of our sense of secure-ishness. What's important is that we don't cling to our identity of worth so much that we don't recognize that we've returned to a state of vulnerability. Descending the ladder of the self is okay. All we can do is try to have high regard for ourselves as we descend.

Having worth means not having to experience oneself the same stale way. It means going along with what is, rather than being haunted by what you think should be. This means sprinkling humility into your life plans, permitting yourself feelings and urges that violate what you *should* feel, ceasing to measure life by whether it meets the metrics of the self's prediction, and more generally, experiencing life more than predicting it.

For me, it meant reassurance. As I stared down my next few years as a thirty-three-year-old woman who had to make far-reaching decisions about kids and marriage, I was reassured that whatever path I moseyed down would be okay. I felt less susceptible to grief spurred by life not going as planned. I felt more liberated from the toss and turn of regret that comes from seeing your life as deviating from what you wanted so much so that you don't realize all you *do* want in this life you have. With a more fluid identity, wherever I ended up, that was my destiny.

As I hiked and thought about this idea of the fluid self, a voice inside me said, *Whoever you are, I will love you.* It may seem peculiar to think of yourself as a "whoever," as if you don't know yourself or control who you are, but I was starting to realize that maybe I didn't, at least not fully. And maybe I didn't know others as much as I thought either, so I could let them evolve. This was all, somehow, okay. *Whoever you are, I will love you*: The phrase lit a lantern inside me that glowed throughout my body.

HEALING BEYOND WHAT WE IMAGINED

Psychedelics illustrate how losing ourselves can facilitate a profound level of healing. To convey the gravitas of this work, Al told me about his father's kidney cancer. If his father had had the cancer fifteen years prior, he would have died. But with the development of new therapies, he survived and went on to have a good life. To Al, psychedelics were the mental health equivalent of these lifesaving medical treatments, something the mental health world had long lacked before psychedelics.

As I listened to Al, a feeling leapt in me, a feeling I was familiar with but only in that moment could articulate as grief. It was the grief of loving someone whose sense of self kept them from seeing your love. Sitting with a client who had been sexually assaulted, who was gentle and tender, and who told me that she was damaged. She thought no one would ever love her for anything but her body. A friendship disintegrated because I made a comment that triggered a script of them being a monster. A guy I had liked who was convinced that my genuine feelings for him were simply threats because they would inevitably be yanked away.

I wasn't immune to interrupting love bestowed upon me with my story of self either. In my younger years, it looked like me dumping people who I was *sure* would dump me so I could do it first and retain some control. And then, to their confusion, I'd get upset when they accepted being dumped and didn't fight for the relationship. Now it was more subtle. I often take jokes as barbs. Friends, or even my therapist, tried to warm up to me by gentle teasing. Instead of joining them in the reverie, I sulked.

It is isolating to love people who don't accept love. All the backed-up love, without release, mutates into grief. Grief, I realized, wasn't just about loving and losing. It was also about not being able to love fully, like a limb hungry to stretch stuck crunched at your side.

Yet Al was raising the possibility that psychedelics could heal the self so that backed-up love—for both ourselves and others—could be freed. Entrenched pain could break loose. Where there was once stagnancy, there was now hope because the self on psychedelics, like Al's father's kidney cancer, was no longer terminal.

Al walked me to his office, where he showed me talismans embodying this hope, gifts from his research participants: a mushroom figurine composed of seashells; a gilded rock with a painting of red mushrooms on its face; a wooden placard, this one from Elizabeth, that read "Psilocybin therapy: The most intimate thing three people can do with their clothes on." The most pronounced symbol of hope stood erect on his shelf, beside his books. It was a glass vase filled with dozens of lighters gifted to him from longtime smokers who quit after taking part in Al's psilocybin studies.

As obsessed as I am about healing (y'know, writing a whole book on it), I'm not always Pollyanna about it. I want to believe that there's healing beyond what our selves imagined. Now that idea makes more sense to me because I know the projections of the self are less reality and more of a safety mechanism. Yet our world teems with suffering, and there are moments when I falter into resignation. Perhaps the gorgeousness in a person will never grow bigger than their pain. Perhaps we will never get to love people, or ourselves, as much as we aspire to. Perhaps we will never fully relinquish these shrunken, armored-up stories we define ourselves by.

Yet perhaps, I thought to myself, eyeing the vase full of lighters, we will.

And perhaps, even if we don't, it will be okay.

TAKEAWAYS

At the time of this writing (February 17, 2026), psychedelics are illegal, federally, and classified as Schedule 1 drugs: dangerous and addictive, with no recognized medical use. Some states, however, have decriminalized the usage of the drugs (meaning resources will not be dedicated to arresting people who use them), and Oregon, Colorado, and New Mexico have even allowed for supervised administration of psilocybin at licensed centers. To track the legality of psychedelics by state, visit psychedelicalpha.com.

Although psychedelics are a powerful tool for memory reconsolidation—which could, when used safely and under the guidance of a professional, help us feel worthy—they remain inaccessible. Still, the science of psychedelics and the self offers us takeaways whether we access these substances or not. These takeaways aim to help us feel worthy by loosening up our fixed story of self.

REGARD

1. When you are rejected, ask yourself, ***What if I don't take their reaction to me as a reflection of my worth?*** *How would I feel differently?* Pause to acknowledge this new feeling.
2. When you're at a low point, remind yourself that this is an opportunity for you to practice loving yourself no matter who you are, how you feel, or who you've become. Tell yourself, ***Still now, I am here on my own side.***

MINDFULNESS

1. Treat people with **habitual open-mindedness**. You don't know them because you know their race, gender, or sexual orientation. Instead of imposing a story, be present for how you actually feel around them.

2. You have a story about what will happen to you. People will abandon you, betray you, hurt you. Have humility around this story. Instead, pay attention to what's actually happened. Has this person given you any evidence that they will harm you? Abandon you? **Proceed in relationships based on what's happening rather than what you're assuming.**

ACCEPTANCE OF EMOTION

1. Notice when you have feelings that violate your sense of who you are. You thought you'd love being a doctor, but you dread it every day. You want to cry, but you've learned vulnerability means weakness. It's okay to be different from who you thought you were. (You never were that thing in the first place, as you defined it.) **Get curious about feelings you have that break your mold of "self." They aren't threats but revelations** that'll help you know who you are.

2. Your pain has information about who you are, what you don't like, what you are challenged by, or what still impacts you from your past. **Reframe negative emotions** not as pure pain, but as **opportunities to know who you are more deeply**. This will help you turn toward and accept your feelings.

FLUID IDENTITY

1. You have a story of what you like and don't like. It may or may not be true. **Stop predicting life, and start experiencing it.** Try the thing you thought you wouldn't like, and see how you actually feel about it.

2. Things will happen to you that you don't expect. Your health will decline, you'll lose your job, you'll lose people you thought you'd keep forever. It may feel as if this all "shouldn't be happening." **But there are no shoulds. There is only what is. You can bear this version of reality, too.**

9

Conclusion

Despite the fact that we have more resources than ever to become secure, rates of secure attachment have been dropping. This is a moment in which therapy is heralded as an ultimate cure for social ills . . . and yet the words *therapy speak* have become synonymous with manipulative gobbledygook. This is a time when self-care has become more prioritized than ever . . . and yet it has led to burning bridges with community. We earnestly want to become better, healthier, and more secure . . . yet somehow getting there has meant becoming more stilted, inauthentic, and disconnected from others.

Something has gone terribly wrong with healing.

What we've gotten wrong is that healing was never about learning to regurgitate the same therapy-speak-ridden language, but rather learning to listen to our own internal language. It was never about disconnecting from others to take care of the self, but connecting to ourselves in order to connect, truly, with others. It was never about learning to say the "right" thing, but about learning to say the true thing. It was never about becoming perfect—secure, self-cared, therapy-fluent—but always about becoming real.

After I told a friend about some of these revelations, she began to apply them in her life. When her girlfriend left for the night, she would start to feel despair, shake, and sometimes even get feverish. For so long, she ignored her body and tried to numb out by distracting herself. She thought she was secure, but, she said, "I realized I was just ignoring the part of me that was anxious, and I didn't want to treat a hurt part of me like that anymore." When she explored her pain instead of ignoring it, she thought back to when she was seven. Her parents sent her to live with a physically and emotionally abusive aunt. After her mom visited her, her body underwent those same intense intrusions that it did when her girlfriend left. Back then, she coped by cradling a cup her mother had drunk from and left on the table.

"I used to think I'm someone who is strong," my friend said. "I have a higher threshold for pain than other people. You can dump it on me and I can take it. I literally told myself I like pain. But then I realized it was my trauma speaking and trying to normalize itself. As much as I say I love other people and I protect them and nurture them, I need to do that for myself as well. Now I see myself as someone who deserved to be loved, to be spoken up for, to be cared for." Healing did not mean forcing herself to act "strong" by turning her back on her trembling seven-year-old self. As she learned, sometimes healing means finally being able to admit how much pain we are in so we can do something about it.

This book isn't about becoming secure, but secure-*ish*, because I believe that becoming real means relinquishing categories for ourselves. When we categorize something, we feel safe. Categories allow us to predict behavior: We know how the anxious, avoidant, or secure person will act. Yet in categorizing what is ultimately uncategorizable, we're also imperiled. Parts of ourselves that we break off to become a thing, one thing, take on a mind of their own. The need for love, broken off in the avoidant-ish, mutates into a need to be superior, an indirect wish to gain love. If matter cannot be created or destroyed, then the pain we turn away from just changes form. It becomes our triggers, our rage, our withdrawal, our preoccupations, our chronic pain, our chaos, our cruelty—unless we face these emotions instead.

Sometimes, in categorizing ourselves, we also end up breaking off our greatest strengths. When we categorize ourselves as anxious, for example, we break from the secure-ish self inside, leaving us to acquiesce to painful relationship dynamics when our secure-ish self would demand more. There is no virtue in making ourselves simple. Liberating ourselves from categories helps us become real.

When we disrobe ourselves of categories, we are no longer defined by how we *should* feel and instead admit to how we actually *do* feel. This occurred for my friend when she shed the need to be "secure" so that she could attune herself to her anxiety. But facing our feelings alone is not enough. Sometimes doing so can make them bigger, make us wallow, or overwhelm us all together.

We must offer something new to our pain, the rootedness of a Self, the wisdom of an adult updating the child's it's-all-my-fault logic, the drum of a mantra, *I'm here, I'm here, I'm here.* I think of becoming secure-ish as an act of internal collaboration. We cannot forget our multitudes—that we are never *all* pain, that the fact that we still exist means more is going right with us than wrong—and when we remember this, we become our own keeper.

THE IMPACT OF BECOMING REAL

When we become real, we find greater freedom, possibility, and connection. We've learned that to do so, we must confront our memories. Memories have much more gravity than most people think. They are not just videos that our brains play when we want. These videos play at all hours, in a dimension simultaneous with the one happening now. They shape the way we feel, see ourselves, and even behave in the present.

Jerry was afraid of taking a book deal, because, since his father left, he was convinced that all good things would end in disaster. Esme never initiated another friendship because of her hunch that people didn't really like her, ever since her seventh-grade friend didn't. Rose couldn't express her anger to her boyfriend, because in her childhood, if she pointed her finger at her mother, it would get chopped right off.

For all of them, what happened then was still happening now. We cannot be truly free if our free will is being exercised in a context that happened decades ago. Only when we confront the past so we can return to the present can we be truly free.

In this question mark that is the present, we cannot be sure what will happen next. But we can trust that if scary things happen, we'll be ready to feel our way through them, to allow the scariness to touch us and blow through us. Yet with our memories finally closed, we can step out from their cages and into a world where scary things aren't inevitable; all that is inevitable is possibility.

As we become more free in this way, we free others, too. Just like some spirits are said to need to possess a human to act, trauma is the same. It does not hang in the air like viral particles or cling to surfaces like germs. Much of trauma is dispersed through a human host, possessing a body to transmit itself to another body. When someone degrades another, the trauma spreads from one host to another. This means that the more we heal, the less we act as hosts and, thus, agents of transmission. Our healing is an act of collective care, for ourselves and everyone who comes after.

Psychologist Abraham Maslow, in his private journals, also emphasized that the end of the self's journey is to benefit the collective. Toward the end of his life, he described his misgivings with his initial idea of self-actualization: "All sorts of insights. One big one about SA [self-actualization] stuff, brought on, I think, mostly by my deep uneasiness over [popular press] articles [on the topic] . . . I realized I'd rather leave it behind me." It wasn't that self-actualization, the need at the top of his hierarchy, wasn't important, but it just wasn't the end goal. He was set to share this idea in his 1967 address as president of the American Psychological Association. Yet shortly before the speech, he suffered a heart attack and went into intensive care. He died three years later.

The "something beyond" self-actualization was self-transcendence. To Maslow, this meant committing to a cause greater than one's self and being more generous, helpful, and driven to make the world better. In his journals, Maslow wrote, "As he gets to be more purely and singly himself he is more able to fuse with the world. . . . That is, the greatest attainment of identity, autonomy, or selfhood is itself simultaneously a transcending of itself, a going beyond and above selfhood. The person can then become relatively egoless."

Losing yourself is both the first and last stage of evolution. We are faced again with the spiral of growth, that moving forward means returning to where we were, but in a different way. Putting transcendence at the end of self-actualization is aligned with thinking from some Indigenous communities who, according to Yuria Celidwen, a senior academic of Nahua and Mayan descent at the University of California, Berkeley, consumed psilocybin to "restore balance with that [the natural] world. So the context is never individual wellbeing or mental health, but the collective wellbeing of the environment as a whole." Self-actualization is a mere stepping stone to transcendence.

I'm spiraling back to before I started writing this book. Reading the research taught me that I could give people the tools to develop healthy relationships, but without also reckoning with themselves, they wouldn't *feel* connected. Even if they were swaddled in safe relationships, they would still feel unsafe, their insecurities stamping their past challenges atop the contours of the present.

Without the walls erected by our pain, we breathe in the plight of other human beings more deeply and are more moved by the tragedy of their hurt, stomping our feet along to the rhythm of their triumphs. Feeling worthy means living in such a state of unity that care for one another becomes not a fringe feature of human existence but an inevitability of it. This work on ourselves has been a long but necessary digression to return us to each other.

Acknowledgments

I wasn't sure I felt worthy enough to write a book on worth, but you taught me that to be worthy wasn't to be boundlessly confident and void of all insecurity but was to tenderly tell the truth of my insecurities first, to myself, and then to those who love me. You taught me that worth means being nothing different than who I am; that my imperfections are perfection; that to be flawed and to struggle and to not know and to regress and doubt and get bruised and bruise—all of that, and yet we are worthy. To my therapist, Alyssa Duda, thank you.

Writing *Worth* has taught me that how loved we think we are is only a crumb of how loved we are. And yet, there are people who've given me glimpses of this kind of unimaginable love (in no particular order): Lauri Ng, Stephanie Shih, Heather McQueen, Fiona McQueen Kapner, Leah Fuller, Mikelann Scerbo, Jason Rhee, Mark Santana, Kana Felix, Jarrett Stroman, Krizia Gupiteo, Harbani Ahuja, Zaria Qadafi, Vanessa Battiste, Loraine Brown, Michael Abdullah, Rabia Wickboldt, Ohvia Muraleetharan, and Sarah Magid—for that love and for being my companions through the exercises in *Worth* as we cried, faced ourselves, and admitted our most secret corners to each other.

One way that I experience the inherent unity of us all is when I share an idea with a person, and they with me, our thoughts weaving into each other's so that it's no longer clear where their mind stops and mine begins. To the people who thought with me while I wrote *Worth*: Steven Roberts, Nolan Krueger, Alex Harlig, Olamide Gòkè-Paríolá, Kyle Moore, my writing critique group Emily Tamkin, Brandon Tensley Julie Beck, Atima Omara, Rhaina Cohen, and all the members of my author support group, and to all the researchers whose science contributed to this book. (Check them out in the notes!) And thanks to the authors I do not know personally but whose breathtaking writing and thinking gave me a compass when I was stuck: Safiya Sinclair and Merlin Sheldrake.

Thanks to the people who showed me I was never alone while writing *Worth*: the team at Putnam who edited, improved upon, formatted, and envisioned. My editors, Ashley Di Dio, Michelle Howry, and Melanie Fried; Maija Baldauf, managing editor; Almudena Rincón, managing editorial assistant; Gaelyn Galbreath, production manager; Janice Barral, production editor; Lorie Pagnozzi, interior designer; Christy Wagner, copyeditor; M. P. Klier and Jane Herman, proofreaders; Molly Pieper, associate director of marketing; Ashley Hewlett, assistant director of publicity; and Sanny Chiu, cover designer. Thanks to the team at Calligraph Agency. Thanks to Victoria Gillison, Sophia Thompson, and Ethan Lac for their help with organizing content for this book. Rabia Wickboldt gave me feedback on the original cover and offered up some mock-ups she made. Those mock-ups spoke to me, and now my beloved friend's art is on the cover of this book. It was always fate to have you with me here, Rabia.

Worth starts in the home, and I had a mom who always saw the best in me and told me so, Gina Franco; a father who would encourage deep thoughts around the dinner table, Stefano Franco; a brother who doubles as a confidant, soothing my most vulnerable moments with his empathy, Stephen Franco; and a sister who always makes sure I have a place to call home, Tania Vazquez. To my nieces, who are the loves and joys of my life, Natasha and Angelica Vasquez, please know that wherever you go and whatever you do, I am with you. You may feel alone in this life, but you never ever are.

I'd like to also acknowledge you, the readers. When I think of people who've been harmed yet who refuse to bleed onto the next person, who put their foot down and declare "This ends with me," I want to tear up. I can only imagine the kind of world we'd live in if more people were like you. You are my hope.

Notes

Introduction

xiv **childhood and adult attachment:** R. Chris Fraley et al., "Interpersonal and Genetic Origins of Adult Attachment Styles: A Longitudinal Study from Infancy to Early Adulthood," *Journal of Personality and Social Psychology* 104, no. 5 (May 2014): 817–38, https://doi.org/10.1037/a0031435.

xiv **"not even past":** William Faulkner, *Requiem for a Nun* (Vintage Books, 1975), 73.

xv **"An Anxious Person Tries to Be Chill":** Coco Mellors, "An Anxious Person Tries to Be Chill," *The New York Times*, September 2021, https://www.nytimes.com/2021/09/10/style/modern-love-an-anxious-person-tries-to-be-chill.html.

xvi **"better than you are":** Marion Woodman, "Addiction to Perfection: The Still Unravished Bride; A Psychological Study," in *Studies in Jungian Psychology by Jungian Analysts*, 12, edited by Daryl Sharp (Inner City Books, 1982), 61.

xviii **A 2022 report:** Sapien Labs, *The Deteriorating Social Self in Younger Generations*, May 2022, https://sapienlabs.org/wp-content/uploads/2022/05/Rapid-Report-The-Deteriorating-Social-Self-in-Younger-Generations.pdf.

xviii **Number of high school students:** Sherry Everett Jones, "Mental Health, Suicidality, and Connectedness among High School Students during the COVID-19 Pandemic—Adolescent Behaviors and Experiences Survey, United States, January–June 2021," Morbidity and Mortality Weekly Report, *Supplement* 71 (April 2022), https://doi.org/10.15585/mmwr.su7103a3.

xix **depressed at age forty-five:** Andrea E. Steiger et al., "Testing the Vulnerability and Scar Models of Self-Esteem and Depressive Symptoms from Adolescence to Middle Adulthood and across Generations," *Developmental Psychology* 51, no. 2 (February 2015): 236–47, https://doi.org/10.1037/a0038478.

xix **Compared with secure babies:** Jennifer Puig et al., "Predicting Adult Physical Illness from Infant Attachment: A Prospective Longitudinal Study," *Health Psychology* 32, no. 4 (April 2013): 409–17, https://doi.org/10.1037/a0028889.

xix **Underestimate how much others love us:** S. L. Murray et al., "Self-Esteem and the Quest for Felt Security: How Perceived Regard Regulates Attachment Processes," *Journal of Personality and Social Psychology* 78, no. 3 (March 2000): 478–98, https://doi.org/10.1037//0022-3514.78.3.478.

xix **Ignore blatant signs of acceptance:** Jessica J. Cameron et al., "Acceptance Is in the Eye of the Beholder: Self-Esteem and Motivated Perceptions of Acceptance from the Opposite Sex," *Journal of Personality and Social Psychology* 99, no. 3 (September 2010): 513–29, https://doi.org/10.1037/a0018558.

xix **misremember past experiences:** Tamlin Conner Christensen et al., "Remembering Everyday Experience through the Prism of Self-Esteem," *Personality and Social Psychology Bulletin* 29, no. 1 (January 2003): 51–62.

xix **higher-quality relationships, a meta-analysis found:** Benjamin W. Hadden et al., "Relationship Duration Moderates Associations between Attachment and Relationship Quality: Meta-Analytic Support for the Temporal Adult Romantic Attachment Model," *Personality and Social Psychology Review* 18, no. 1 (February 2014): 42–58, https://doi.org/10.1177/1088868313501885.

xx **transcend, rather than:** Jamie Arndt et al., "The Intrinsic Self and Defensiveness: Evidence That Activating the Intrinsic Self Reduces Self-Handicapping and Conformity," *Personality and Social Psychology Bulletin* 28, no. 5 (May 2002): 671–83, https://doi.org/10.1177/0146167202288011.

xx **be compassionate and altruistic:** Mario Mikulincer and Phillip R. Shaver, "Attachment Security, Compassion, and Altruism," *Current Directions in Psychological Science* 14, no. 1 (February 2005): 34–38, https://doi.org/10.1111/j.0963-7214.2005.00330.x.

xx **regression in the service of the ego:** Ernst Kris, *Psychoanalytic Explorations in Art* (International University Press, 1952), 171, http://archive.org/details/dli.ernet.29026.

xxi **"our collective struggle":** bell hooks, *Sisters of the Yam: Black Women and Self-Recovery*, 3rd ed. (Routledge, 2014), xi.

xxii **"recommend you gather others":** G. Shteynberg et al., "Feeling More Together: Group Attention Intensifies Emotion," *Emotion* 14, no. 6 (August 2014): 1102–14, https://doi.org/10.1037/a0037697.

xxii **not temporarily affected:** Johanna Hedva, "Sick Woman Theory," 2020 (italics in original), https://www.kunstverein-hildesheim.de/assets/bilder/caring-structures-ausstellung-digital/Johanna-Hedva/cb6ec5c75f/AUSSTELLUNG_1110_Hedva_SWT_e.pdf.

Chapter 1: Defining Worth

4 **someone else's fault:** Michael H. Kernis et al., "Secure versus Fragile High Self-Esteem as a Predictor of Verbal Defensiveness: Converging Findings across Three Different Markers," *Journal of Personality* 76, no. 3 (June 2008): 477–512, https://doi.org/10.1111/j.1467-6494.2008.00493.x.

4 **in something important:** Michael H. Kernis, "Measuring Self-Esteem in

Context: The Importance of Stability of Self-Esteem in Psychological Functioning," *Journal of Personality* 73, no. 6 (December 2005): 1569–605, https://doi.org/10.1111/j.1467-6494.2005.00359.x.

4 **more hostile than:** Michael H. Kernis et al., "Stability and Level of Self-Esteem as Predictors of Anger Arousal and Hostility," *Journal of Personality and Social Psychology* 56, no. 6 (June 1989): 1013–22, https://doi.org/10.1037//0022-3514.56.6.1013.

4 **smoothest and most intimate relationships:** Michael H. Kernis, "Measuring Self-Esteem in Context."

5 **critiqued his ideas:** Michael H. Kernis, "Optimal Self-Esteem and Authenticity: Separating Fantasy from Reality," *Psychological Inquiry* 14, no. 1 (2003): 83–89, http://www.jstor.org/stable/1449049.

6 **"lack of fear":** Abraham H. Maslow, *Toward a Psychology of Being* (Start Publishing, 2013), 169.

6 **"real self with":** Carl R. Rogers, "The Processes of Therapy," *Journal of Consulting Psychology* 4, no. 5 (1940): 161–64, https://doi.org/10.1037/h0062536.

6 **"we cannot move away":** Carl R. Rogers, *On Becoming a Person: A Therapist's View of Psychotherapy*, 1st ed. (HarperCollins, 1995), 17.

7 **were *more* depressed:** Sean M. Barnes and Steven Jay Lynn, "Mindfulness Skills and Depressive Symptoms: A Longitudinal Study," *Imagination, Cognition and Personality* 30, no. 1 (September 2010): 77–91, https://doi.org/10.2190/IC.30.1.e.

7 **anxiety and panic:** Anke Ehlers and Peter Breuer, "How Good Are Patients with Panic Disorder at Perceiving Their Heartbeats?," *Biological Psychology* 42, nos. 1–2 (January 1996): 165–82, https://doi.org/10.1016/0301-0511(95)05153-8.

7 **accept their feelings:** Alethea Desrosiers et al., "Observing Nonreactively: A Conditional Process Model Linking Mindfulness Facets, Cognitive Emotion Regulation Strategies, and Depression and Anxiety Symptoms," *Journal of Affective Disorders* 165 (August 2014): 31–37, https://doi.org/10.1016/j.jad.2014.04.024.

7 **more stable mood:** Matthew R. Pearson et al., "Mindfulness and Emotional Outcomes: Identifying Subgroups of College Students Using Latent Profile Analysis," *Personality and Individual Differences* 76 (April 2015): 33–38, https://doi.org/10.1016/j.paid.2014.11.009.

8 **slower to anger:** Kristin D. Neff and Roos Vonk, "Self-Compassion versus Global Self-Esteem: Two Different Ways of Relating to Oneself," *Journal of Personality* 77, no. 1 (February 2009): 23–50, https://doi.org/10.1111/j.1467-6494.2008.00537.x.

9 **Sinclair recounts how:** Safiya Sinclair, *How to Say Babylon: A Memoir* (37Ink/Simon & Schuster, 2023), 175–98.

9 **negative emotions exist:** Virgil Zeigler-Hill and Carolin J. Showers, "Self-Structure and Self-Esteem Stability: The Hidden Vulnerability of Compartmentalization," *Personality and Social Psychology Bulletin* 33, no. 2 (February 2007): 143–59, https://doi.org/10.1177/0146167206294872.

9 **is the modus operandi:** Jenna S. Thomas et al., "Compartmentalization: A Window on the Defensive Self," *Social and Personality Psychology Compass* 7, no. 10 (October 2013): 719–31, https://doi.org/10.1111/spc3.12061.

9 **they felt *more* rejected:** Zeigler-Hill and Showers, "Self-Structure and Self-Esteem Stability."

12 **"others treat you":** bell hooks, *All about Love: New Visions* (William Morrow, 2018), 58.

12 **all sides of ourselves:** Donnel B. Stern and Irwin Hirsch, *Further Developments in Interpersonal Psychoanalysis, 1980s–2010s: Evolving Interest in the Analyst's Subjectivity*, 1st ed. (Routledge, 2017), 140.

15 **"rather a defense against":** Maslow, *Toward a Psychology of Being*, 169.

17 **forms of love:** Erich Fromm, "Selfishness and Self-Love," in *Understanding Human Motivation*, edited by Chalmers L. Stacey and Manfred DeMartino (Howard Allen Publishers, 1958), 2, 3. https://doi.org/10.1037/11305-043.

17 **"Was his selfishness identical":** Erich Fromm, "Selfishness and Self-Love," 6.

17 **"approval and acceptance":** Maslow, *Toward a Psychology of Being*, 121.

19 **our inner wisdom:** Erich Fromm, *The Sane Society* (Holt Paperbacks, 1990), 164.

19 **aware of our unease:** Fromm, "Selfishness and Self-Love," 6.

19 **strong internal compass:** Hannah Arendt, "Eichmann in Jerusalem—I," *The New Yorker*, February 9, 1963, https://www.newyorker.com/magazine/1963/02/16/eichmann-in-jerusalem-i.

19 **were "terrifyingly normal":** Thomas White, "What Did Hannah Arendt Really Mean by the Banality of Evil?," *Aeon*, accessed December 23, 2025, https://aeon.co/ideas/what-did-hannah-arendt-really-mean-by-the-banality-of-evil.

19 **Stanford Prison Experiment:** "How Monsters Are Made," *Hidden Brain* podcast, December 2, 2024, https://www.hiddenbrain.org/podcast/how-monsters-are-made.

21 **very *essence* of well-being:** Anna Sutton, "Living the Good Life: A Meta-Analysis of Authenticity, Well-Being and Engagement," *Personality and Individual Differences* 153 (January 2020): 109645, https://doi.org/10.1016/j.paid.2019.109645.

25 **most thorough version:** Jennifer Crocker and Noah Nuer, "The Insatiable Quest for Self-Worth: Comment," *Psychological Inquiry* 14, no. 1 (January 2003): 31–34.

Chapter 2: The Theory That Changed Everything

28 ***worse* after compliments:** David R. Kille et al., "Who Can't Take a Compliment? The Role of Construal Level and Self-Esteem in Accepting Positive Feedback from Close Others," *Journal of Experimental Social Psychology* 68 (January 2017): 40–49, https://doi.org/10.1016/j.jesp.2016.05.003.

28 **got positive feedback:** Özlem Ayduk et al., "Consistency over Flattery: Self-Verification Processes Revealed in Implicit and Behavioral Responses to Feedback," *Social Psychological and Personality Science* 4, no. 5 (January 2013): 538–45, https://doi.org/10.1177/1948550612471827.

28 **sound of a beep:** Joanne V. Wood et al., "Positive Self-Statements: Power for Some, Peril for Others," *Psychological Science* 20, no. 7 (July 2009): 860–66, https://doi.org/10.1111/j.1467-9280.2009.02370.x.

29 **improves job success:** Samantha Krauss and Ulrich Orth, "Work Experiences and Self-Esteem Development: A Meta-Analysis of Longitudinal Studies," *European Journal of Personality* 36, no. 6 (July 2021): 849–69, https://doi.org/10.1177/08902070211027142.

29 **"The Secret Sorrows of Over-Achievers":** Alain de Botton, "The Secret Sorrows of Over-Achievers," The School of Life, accessed February 19, 2026, https://www.theschooloflife.com/article/the-secret-sorrows-of-over-achievers/.

30 **weight-loss intervention:** N. Lasikiewicz et al., "Psychological Benefits of Weight Loss Following Behavioural and/or Dietary Weight Loss Interventions: A Systematic Research Review," *Appetite* 72 (January 2014): 123–37, https://doi.org/10.1016/j.appet.2013.09.017.

33 **dubs "disintegration anxiety":** Heinz Kohut, *How Does Analysis Cure?* (University of Chicago Press, 1984): 16.

33 **positive events happened:** J. D. Brown and K. L. McGill, "The Cost of Good Fortune: When Positive Life Events Produce Negative Health Consequences," *Journal of Personality and Social Psychology* 57, no. 6 (December 1989): 1103–10, https://doi.org/10.1037//0022-3514.57.6.1103.

33 **treated them fairly:** Batia M. Wiesenfeld et al., "Is More Fairness Always Preferred? Self-Esteem Moderates Reactions to Procedural Justice," *Academy of Management Journal* 50, no. 5 (October 2007): 1235–53, https://doi.org/10.5465/amj.2007.20159922.

33 **"When I am complimented":** Kille et al., "Who Can't Take a Compliment?"

34 **waiting in the corners:** Máire B. Ford and Nancy L. Collins, "Self-Esteem Moderates Neuroendocrine and Psychological Responses to Interpersonal Rejection," *Journal of Personality and Social Psychology* 98, no. 3 (March 2010): 405–19, https://doi.org/10.1037/a0017345.

34 **physical and social pain:** Keiichi Onoda et al., "Does Low Self-Esteem Enhance Social Pain? The Relationship between Trait Self-Esteem and Anterior Cingulate Cortex Activation Induced by Ostracism," *Social Cognitive and Affective Neuroscience* 5, no. 4 (December 2010): 385–91, https://doi.org/10.1093/scan/nsq002.

35 **similar body state:** Antonio R. Damasio, "The Somatic Marker Hypothesis and the Possible Functions of the Prefrontal Cortex," *Philosophical Transactions of the Royal Society of London, Series B, Biological Sciences* 351, no. 1346 (October 1996): 1413–20, https://doi.org/10.1098/rstb.1996.0125.

35 **"window on reality":** Michael Pollan, *How to Change Your Mind: What the New Science of Psychedelics Teaches Us about Consciousness, Dying, Addiction, Depression, and Transcendence* (Penguin Press, 2018), 308.

38 **"woman poem" evocatively:** Nikki Giovanni, "Woman Poem," The Black Arts Movement, December 6, 2018, https://blackartsmovementumf.wordpress.com/nikki-giovannis-woman-poem/.

39 **obsess more over:** Clyde Hendrick and Susan Hendrick, "A Theory and Method of Love," *Journal of Personality and Social Psychology* 50, no. 2 (February 1986): 392–402, https://doi.org/10.1037/0022-3514.50.2.392.

39 **risk of breaking up:** Andrew Francis-Tan and Hugo M. Mialon. "'A Diamond Is Forever' and Other Fairy Tales: The Relationship between Wedding Expenses

and Marriage Duration," *Economic Inquiry* 53, no. 4 (March 2015): 1919–30, https://ideas.repec.org//a/bla/ecinqu/v53y2015i4p1919-1930.html.

39 **being more committed:** Vicki Ritts and James R. Stein, "Verification and Commitment in Marital Relationships: An Exploration of Self-Verification Theory in Community College Students," *Psychological Reports* 76, no. 2 (April 1995): 383–86, https://doi.org/10.2466/pr0.1995.76.2.383.

39 **saw them positively:** W. B. Swann et al., "Authenticity and Positivity Strivings in Marriage and Courtship," *Journal of Personality and Social Psychology* 66, no. 5 (May 1994): 857–69, https://doi.org/10.1037//0022-3514.66.5.857.

40 **we doubt ourselves:** Sandra L. Murray et al., "The Mismeasure of Love: How Self-Doubt Contaminates Relationship Beliefs," *Personality and Social Psychology Bulletin* 27, no. 4 (April 2001): 423–36, https://doi.org/10.1177/0146167201274004.

40 **equally positive impressions:** Sandra L. Murray et al., "When Rejection Stings: How Self-Esteem Constrains Relationship-Enhancement Processes," *Journal of Personality and Social Psychology* 83, no. 3 (September 2002): 556–73, https://doi.org/10.1037//0022-3514.83.3.556.

40 **might reject first:** Murray et al., "When Rejection Stings."

Chapter 3: Memories That Bleed

47 **toiled with rats:** Karim Nader et al., "Fear Memories Require Protein Synthesis in the Amygdala for Reconsolidation after Retrieval," *Nature* 406, no. 6797 (August 2000): 722–26, https://doi.org/10.1038/35021052.

48 **emotional memory may:** Joseph E. LeDoux et al., "Indelibility of Subcortical Emotional Memories," *Journal of Cognitive Neuroscience* 1, no. 3 (Summer 1989): 238–43, https://doi.org/10.1162/jocn.1989.1.3.238.

48 **record of events:** Greg Miller, "How Our Brains Make Memories," *Smithsonian*, May 2010, https://www.smithsonianmag.com/science-nature/how-our-brains-make-memories-14466850.

48 **no longer intact:** Daniela Schiller et al., "Preventing the Return of Fear in Humans Using Reconsolidation Update Mechanisms," *Nature* 463, no. 7277 (2010): 49–53, https://doi.org/10.1038/nature08637.

48 **revisit memories repeatedly:** James W. B. Elsey et al., "Human Memory Reconsolidation: A Guiding Framework and Critical Review of the Evidence," *Psychological Bulletin* 144, no. 8 (2018): 797–848, https://doi.org/10.1037/bul0000152.

49 **predict the world:** Mark Solms, "Reconsolidation: Turning Consciousness into Memory," *Behavioral and Brain Sciences* 38 (June 2015): e24, https://doi.org/10.1017/S0140525X14000296.

49 **striking feature of memory:** Hagar Gelbard-Sagiv et al., "Internally Generated Reactivation of Single Neurons in Human Hippocampus during Free Recall," *Science* 322, no. 5898 (October 2008): 96–101, https://doi.org/10.1126/science.1164685.

49 **ten negative memories:** Megan E. Speer et al., "Finding Positive Meaning in Memories of Negative Events Adaptively Updates Memory," *Nature Communications* 12, no. 1 (November 2021): 6601, https://doi.org/10.1038/s41467-021-26906-4.

50 **"database for self-esteem":** Veronika V. Nourkova and Darya A. Vasilenko,

"On the Advantage of Autobiographical Memory Pliability: Implantation of Positive Self-Defining Memories Reduces Trait Anxiety," *Memory* 26, no. 7 (August 2018): 869–81, https://doi.org/10.1080/09658211.2017.1420195.

50 **"a person's experience":** Heinz Kohut, *The Search for the Self: Selected Writings of Heinz Kohut: 1950–1978*, vol. 2, edited by Paul H. Ornstein (International Universities Press, 1988), 579.

50 **"suffer mainly from reminiscences":** Elizabeth Rottenberg, "Freud's Other Legacy," 2014, https://parrhesiajournal.org/wp-content/uploads/2024/02/parrhesia21_rottenberg.pdf.

51 **unproductive rumination, research finds:** Edward R. Watkins, "Constructive and Unconstructive Repetitive Thought," *Psychological Bulletin* 134, no. 2 (March 2008): 163–206, https://doi.org/10.1037/0033-2909.134.2.163.

52 **assesses attachment style:** Fatima Attar and Khadija Ouadi, "Content Validity and Reliability of the Adult Attachment Interview in a Sample of Moroccan Young Adults," *World Journal of Advanced Research and Reviews* 18, no. 1 (April 2023): 149–56, https://doi.org/10.30574/wjarr.2023.18.1.0534.

52 **from the grown-ups:** Carol George et al., "Adult Attachment Interview," unpublished manuscript, Department of Psychology, University of California, Berkeley (April 1996), 10.

53 **what's called *open* memories:** Denise R. Beike and Erin T. Wirth-Beaumont, "Psychological Closure as a Memory Phenomenon," *Memory* 13, no. 6 (August 2005): 574–93, https://doi.org/10.1080/09658210444000241.

53 **of all attachment styles:** Jichun Jessy Hao and Ross B. Wilkinson, "Adult Attachment and Self-Esteem: A Meta-Analysis," paper presented at the International Association for Relationship Research Biennial Conference, January 2014, https://doi.org/10.13140/2.1.4033.9846.

53 **a devastating memory:** Denise R. Beike et al., "How Emotional and Nonemotional Memories Define the Self," in *The Self and Memory*, edited by Denise R. Beike and James M. Lampinen (Psychology Press, 2004), 151–52.

54 **closed these memories:** Beike et al., "How Emotional and Nonemotional Memories Define the Self," 150.

54 **end of therapy:** Rhonda N. Goldman et al., "Depth of Emotional Experience and Outcome," *Psychotherapy Research* 15, no. 3 (July 2005): 248–60, https://doi.org/10.1080/10503300512331385188.

55 **too much emotion:** Richard D. Lane et al., "Memory Reconsolidation, Emotional Arousal, and the Process of Change in Psychotherapy: New Insights from Brain Science," *Behavioral and Brain Sciences* 38 (May 2015): e1, https://doi.org/10.1017/S0140525X14000041.

55 **"learn from experience":** Bessel van der Kolk, *The Body Keeps the Score: Brain, Mind, and Body in the Healing of Trauma* (Memories of Ages Press, 2021), 207.

56 **similar process:** Soljana Çili et al., "Impact of Imagery Rescripting on Adverse Self-Defining Memories and Post-Recall Working Selves in a Non-Clinical Sample: A Pilot Study," *Cognitive Behaviour Therapy* 46, no. 1 (January 2017): 75–89, https://doi.org/10.1080/16506073.2016.1212396.

57 **debilitating stage fright:** Joseph Murphy, *The Power of Your Subconscious Mind* (Martino Fine Books, 2011), 119.

57 **Ready to retreat:** Tom Frøkjær, "Quotes from and about Caruso," accessed February 18, 2026, https://www.enricocaruso.dk/quotes.php.

57 **endure strong emotions:** James L. McGaugh, "Emotional Arousal Regulation of Memory Consolidation," *Current Opinion in Behavioral Sciences* 19 (February 2018): 55–60, https://doi.org/10.1016/j.cobeha.2017.10.003.

57 **emotion recollected in tranquility:** William Wordsworth, "Preface to *Lyrical Ballads*," in *Lyrical Ballads*, edited by W. Wordsworth and S. T. Coleridge (Biggs and Co., 1800), xxxiii, https://anthology.lib.virginia.edu/work/Wordsworth/wordsworth-preface?view=pageImages.

58 **"they do feel like home":** Gloria Steinem, *Revolution from Within: A Book of Self-Esteem* (Back Bay Books, 2020), 38, 161–62.

58 **recommends voyages inward:** Steinem, *Revolution from Within*, 38, 161–162.

58 **"diving for pearls":** Steinem, *Revolution from Within*, 160–61.

59 **Actualizing, he argued:** Abraham H. Maslow, *Toward a Psychology of Being* (Wiley, 2000), 24, 298.

Memory Reconsolidation Exercises

61 **Reparenting:** Soljana Çili et al., "Impact of Imagery Rescripting on Adverse Self-Defining Memories and Post-Recall Working Selves in a Non-Clinical Sample: A Pilot Study," *Cognitive Behaviour Therapy* 46, no. 1 (2017), 75–89, https://doi.org/10.1080/16506073.2016.1212396.

63 **Meaning Making:** Speer et al., "Finding Positive Meaning in Memories of Negative Events Adaptively Updates Memory," *Nature Communications* 12, no. 6601 (2021), https://doi.org/10.1038/s41467-021-26906-4.

Chapter 4: Memories That We Don't Remember

68 **"a shadow in the brain":** Northwestern University, "How Traumatic Memories Hide in the Brain, and How to Retrieve Them," ScienceDaily, August 17, 2015, https://www.sciencedaily.com/releases/2015/08/150817132325.htm.

68 **composed of emotion:** Shayla Love, "Can You Feel Your Heartbeat? The Answer Says a Lot about You," *Vice*, February 3, 2020, https://www.vice.com/en/article/connection-between-heartbeat-anxiety.

68 **memory activates sensations:** Paul S. Foster et al., "Spreading Activation in Emotional Memory Networks and the Cumulative Effects of Somatic Markers," *Brain Informatics* 4, no. 2 (July 2016): 85–93, https://doi.org/10.1007/s40708-016-0054-2.

68 **most of the scars:** Jarvis Jay Masters, *Finding Freedom: Writings from Death Row* (Padma Publishing, 1997), 67–73.

70 **brain damage:** Antoine Bechara et al., "Double Dissociation of Conditioning and Declarative Knowledge Relative to the Amygdala and Hippocampus in Humans," *Science* 269, no. 5227 (August 1995): 1115–18, https://doi.org/10.1126/science.7652558.

70 **a third of women:** L. M. Williams, "Recall of Childhood Trauma: A Prospective Study of Women's Memories of Child Sexual Abuse," *Journal of Consulting and Clinical Psychology* 62, no. 6 (December 1994): 1167–76, https://doi.org/10.1037//0022-006x.62.6.1167.

71 **angry faces were:** J. S. Morris et al., "Conscious and Unconscious Emotional Learning in the Human Amygdala," *Nature* 393, no. 6684 (June 1998): 467–70, https://doi.org/10.1038/30976.

71 **"Reality denied":** Philip Kindred Dick, *Flow My Tears, the Policeman Said* (Houghton Mifflin Harcourt, 2012), 139.

71 **for autistic adults:** Freya Rumball et al., "Experience of Trauma and PTSD Symptoms in Autistic Adults: Risk of PTSD Development Following DSM-5 and Non-DSM-5 Traumatic Life Events," *Autism Research* 13, no. 12 (April 2020): 2122–32, https://doi.org/10.1002/aur.2306; Alice Shaam Al Abed et al., "Parvalbumin Interneuron Activity in Autism Underlies Susceptibility to PTSD-Like Memory Formation," iScience 27, no. 5 (April 2024): 109747, https://doi.org/10.1016/j.isci.2024.109747.

71 **implicit memory systems:** Vladimir Jovasevic et al., "GABAergic Mechanisms Regulated by miR-33 Encode State-Dependent Fear," *Nature Neuroscience* 18, no. 9 (September 2015): 1265–71, https://doi.org/10.1038/nn.4084.

72 **passionate love employ:** Hsuan-Chu Shih et al., "The Neurobiological Basis of Love: A Meta-Analysis of Human Functional Neuroimaging Studies of Maternal and Passionate Love," *Brain Sciences* 12, no. 7 (June 2022): 830, https://doi.org/10.3390/brainsci12070830.

72 **early attachment experiences:** Phillip R. Shaver and Mario Mikulincer, "Attachment Theory and Attachment Styles" (January 2008): 9, https://adultattachment.faculty.ucdavis.edu/wp-content/uploads/sites/66/2015/09/Shaver_2009_Attachment-Theory-and-Attachment-Styles.pdf.

73 **evidence of this:** Igor I. Galynker et al., "Distinct but Overlapping Neural Networks Subserve Depression and Insecure Attachment," *Social Cognitive and Affective Neuroscience* 7, no. 8 (November 2012): 896–908, https://doi.org/10.1093/scan/nsr074.

73 **the pithy phrase:** Ada McVean, "The History of Hysteria," Office for Science and Society, McGill University, July 31, 2017, https://www.mcgill.ca/oss/article/history-quackery/history-hysteria.

73 **rats got nervous:** Lynn Nadel, "Dorsal and Ventral Hippocampal Lesions and Behavior," *Physiology and Behavior* 3, no. 6 (November 1968): 891–900, https://doi.org/10.1016/0031-9384(68)90174-1.

75 **do mental exercises:** David C. Glass et al., "Psychic Cost of Adaptation to an Environmental Stressor," *Journal of Personality and Social Psychology* 12, no. 3 (July 1969): 200–210, https://doi.org/10.1037/h0027629.

77 **"own unimproved self":** Michael Pollan, *How to Change Your Mind: What the New Science of Psychedelics Teaches Us about Consciousness, Dying, Addiction, Depression, and Transcendence* (Penguin Press, 2018), 280–81.

77 **"never get better":** Bessel van der Kolk, *The Body Keeps the Score: Brain, Mind, and Body in the Healing of Trauma* (Penguin Books, 2015), 27.

78 **both explicit memory:** Dominique J.-F. de Quervain et al., "Glucocorticoid-Induced Impairment of Declarative Memory Retrieval Is Associated with Reduced Blood Flow in the Medial Temporal Lobe," *European Journal of Neuroscience* 17, no. 6 (2003): 1296–302, https://doi.org/10.1046/j.1460-9568.2003.02542.x.

78 **lowered heart rate:** Donna Bach et al., "Clinical EFT (Emotional Freedom

Techniques) Improves Multiple Physiological Markers of Health," *Journal of Evidence-Based Integrative Medicine* 24 (February 2019): 2515690X18823691, https://doi.org/10.1177/2515690X18823691.

78 **PTSD symptoms:** Peta Stapleton et al., "Emotional Freedom Techniques for Treating Post Traumatic Stress Disorder: An Updated Systematic Review and Meta-Analysis," *Frontiers in Psychology* 14 (August 2023), https://doi.org/10.3389/fpsyg.2023.1195286.

78 **significant decreases in depression:** Jerrod A. Nelms and Liana Castel, "A Systematic Review and Meta-Analysis of Randomized and Nonrandomized Trials of Clinical Emotional Freedom Techniques (EFT) for the Treatment of Depression," *Explore* 12, no. 6 (August 2016): 416–26, https://doi.org/10.1016/j.explore.2016.08.001.

78 **anxiety rates, too:** Morgan Clond, "Emotional Freedom Techniques for Anxiety: A Systematic Review with Meta-Analysis," *Journal of Nervous and Mental Disease* 204, no. 5 (May 2016): 388–95, https://doi.org/10.1097/NMD.0000000000000483.

78 **to 105 traumatized people:** Carl Johnson et al., "Thought Field Therapy—Soothing the Bad Moments of Kosovo," *Journal of Clinical Psychology* 57, no. 10 (October 2001): 1237–40, https://doi.org/10.1002/jclp.1090. See also for rebuttal, Rita Rosner, "Between Search and Research: How to Find Your Way Around? Review of the Article 'Thought Field Therapy—Soothing the Bad Moments of Kosovo,'" *Journal of Clinical Psychology* 57, no. 10 (August 2001): 1241–44, https://doi.org/10.1002/jclp.1091.

79 **electricity to organs:** David Feinstein, "Rapid Treatment of PTSD."

79 **cited a review:** Feinstein, "Rapid Treatment of PTSD: Why Psychological Exposure with Acupoint Tapping May Be Effective," *Psychotherapy: Theory, Research, Practice, Training* 47, no. 3 (2010): 385–402, https://doi.org/10.1037/a0021171.

79 **it was inconclusive:** Andrew C. Ahn et al., "Electrical Properties of Acupuncture Points and Meridians: A Systematic Review," *Bioelectromagnetics* 29, no. 4 (May 2008): 245–56, https://doi.org/10.1002/bem.20403.

79 **leading therapies for:** American Psychological Association, "PTSD Treatments," 2017, https://www.apa.org/ptsd-guideline/treatments.

80 **have similar benefits:** Thanos Karatzias et al., "A Controlled Comparison of the Effectiveness and Efficiency of Two Psychological Therapies for Posttraumatic Stress Disorder: Eye Movement Desensitization and Reprocessing vs. Emotional Freedom Techniques," *Journal of Nervous and Mental Disease* 199, no. 6 (June 2011): 372–78, https://doi.org/10.1097/NMD.0b013e31821cd262.

80 **memories less vivid:** Marcel A. van den Hout et al., "EMDR and Mindfulness: Eye Movements and Attentional Breathing Tax Working Memory and Reduce Vividness and Emotionality of Aversive Ideation," *Journal of Behavior Therapy and Experimental Psychiatry* 42, no. 4 (December 2011): 423–31, https://doi.org/10.1016/j.jbtep.2011.03.004.

81 **pattern of points:** Jackie Andrade et al., "Eye-Movements and Visual Imagery: A Working Memory Approach to the Treatment of Post-Traumatic Stress Disorder," *British Journal of Clinical Psychology* 36, no. 2 (May 1997): 209–23, https://doi.org/10.1111/j.2044-8260.1997.tb01408.x.

81 **and play Tetris:** Iris M. Engelhard et al., "The Impact of Taxing Working Memory on Negative and Positive Memories," *European Journal of Psychotraumatology* 1, no. 1 (December 2010), https://doi.org/10.3402/ejpt.v1i0.5623.

81 **draw a complicated shape:** Raymond W. Gunter and Glen E. Bodner, "How Eye Movements Affect Unpleasant Memories: Support for a Working-Memory Account," *Behaviour Research and Therapy* 46, no. 8 (August 2008): 913–31, https://doi.org/10.1016/j.brat.2008.04.006.

81 **recalling a trauma:** John S. Isaacs, "Numerical Distraction Therapy: Initial Assessment of a Treatment for Posttraumatic Stress Disorder," *Traumatology* 10, no. 1 (March 2004): 39–54, https://doi.org/10.1177/153476560401000104.

81 **memories degrade more:** Eva Kemps and Marika Tiggemann, "Reducing the Vividness and Emotional Impact of Distressing Autobiographical Memories: The Importance of Modality-Specific Interference," *Memory* 15, no. 4 (April 2007): 412–22, https://doi.org/10.1080/09658210701262017.

81 **why EFT works:** Wendy L. Comeau and Mark D. Holder, "Assessment of the Emotional Freedom Technique: An Alternative Treatment for Fear," *Scientific Review of Mental Health Practice: Objective Investigations of Controversial and Unorthodox Claims in Clinical Psychology, Psychiatry, and Social Work* 2, no. 1 (2003): 20; Rachel Rogers and Sharon Sears, "Emotional Freedom Techniques (EFT) for Stress in Students: A Randomized Controlled Dismantling Study," *Energy Psychology Journal* 7, no. 2 (2015): 26–32. https://doi.org/10.9769/EPJ.2015.7.2.RR.

Implicit Memory Reconsolidation Exercises (or What to Do When You're Triggered)

81 **Tetris:** Iris M. Engelhard et al., "The Impact of Taxing Working Memory on Negative and Positive Memories," *European Journal of Psychotraumatology* 1, no. 1 (July 2010): 1–8, https://doi.org/10.3402/ejpt.v1i0.5623.

84 **Adapted from:** Betty Moore-Hafter et al., *EFT International Free Tapping Manual* (EFT International, 2021), 12–18.

Chapter 5: Remember to Feel

90 **in regard to internalizing:** Peter Levine, *Waking the Tiger: Healing Trauma* (North Atlantic Books, 1997), 176.

91 **likelihood of disassociating:** Niels G. Waller and Colin A. Ross, "The Prevalence and Biometric Structure of Pathological Dissociation in the General Population: Taxometric and Behavior Genetic Findings," *Journal of Abnormal Psychology* 106, no. 4 (November 1997): 499–510, https://doi.org/10.1037/0021-843X.106.4.499.

91 **separated from their mothers:** John Bowlby, *Attachment and Loss*, vol. 2, *Separation, Anxiety and Anger*, chapter 1 (Basic Books, 1973): 8–11, https://pep-web.org/browse/document/IPL.095.0001A.

91 **regulate their emotions:** Janina Fisher, "The Treatment of Structural Dissociation in Chronically Traumatized Patients," 2023, https://janinafisher.com/wp-content/uploads/2023/03/structural-dissociation.pdf.

91 **calls "fault lines":** Fisher, "The Treatment of Structural Dissociation in Chronically Traumatized Patients."

92 **"communicate negative feelings":** Robert Karen, "Becoming Attached," *The Atlantic*, February 11, 1990, https://www.theatlantic.com/magazine/archive/1990/02/becoming-attached/308966.

92 **detached throughout their lives:** Bowlby, *Attachment and Loss*, 12.

92 **Although a meta-analysis found:** Ruben Vonderlin, et al., "Dissociation in Victims of Childhood Abuse or Neglect: A Meta-Analytic Review," *Psychological Medicine* 48, no. 15 (April 2018): 2467–76, https://doi.org/10.1017/S0033291718000740.

92 **helping us express:** bell hooks, *All about Love: New Visions* (William Morrow, 2018), 18–19.

92 **Jennette McCurdy reveals:** Jennette McCurdy, *I'm Glad My Mom Died* (Simon & Schuster, 2022), 42–43.

93 **dismissiveness from their moms:** Lissa Dutra et al., "Quality of Early Care and Childhood Trauma: A Prospective Study of Developmental Pathways to Dissociation," *Journal of Nervous and Mental Disease* 197, no. 6 (June 2009): 383–90, https://doi.org/10.1097/NMD.0b013e3181a653b7.

93 **mothers reported how much:** Kristina Oldroyd et al., "Social Antecedents to the Development of Interoception: Attachment Related Processes Are Associated with Interoception," *Frontiers in Psychology* 10 (April 2019), https://doi.org/10.3389/fpsyg.2019.00712.

93 **ask avoidant children:** Carol George et al., "Adult Attachment Interview," unpublished manuscript, Department of Psychology, University of California, Berkeley (April 1996).

94 **ghosted the therapist:** WUSF, "Jennette McCurdy Explains Why She's Glad Her Mom Died," November 8, 2022, https://www.wusf.org/2022-11-08/jennette-mccurdy-explains-why-shes-glad-her-mom-died.

95 **meta-analysis explored:** Emily J. Ozer et al., "Predictors of Posttraumatic Stress Disorder and Symptoms in Adults: A Meta-Analysis," *Psychological Bulletin* 129, no. 1 (January 2003): 52–73, https://doi.org/10.1037/0033-2909.129.1.52.

95 **fight or flee:** Levine, *Waking the Tiger*, 19–21.

95 **One study found:** Tracey J. Shors et al., "Inescapable versus Escapable Shock Modulates Long-Term Potentiation in the Rat Hippocampus," *Science* 244, no. 4901 (April 1989): 224–26, https://doi.org/10.1126/science.2704997.

96 **after being shocked:** Joanne Weinberg et al., "Shock-Induced Fighting Attenuates the Effects of Prior Shock Experience in Rats," *Physiology and Behavior* 25, no. 1 (July 1980): 9–16, https://doi.org/10.1016/0031-9384(80)90173-0.

96 **In fact, Levine argues:** Levine, *Waking the Tiger*, 146–147.

98 **energy mobilized:** Levine, *Waking the Tiger*, 20–21.

98 **we must overcome what:** Maria Popova, "How to Be Animal: An Antidote to Our Self-Expatriation from Nature," *The Marginalian*, July 10, 2023, https://www.themarginalian.org/2023/07/10/how-to-be-animal-melanie-challenger.

99 **involves paying attention:** Levine, *Waking the Tiger*, 98, 100, 120.

99 **let our body speak:** Levine, *Waking the Tiger*, 120.

99 **In that study:** Jay M. Weiss et al., "Attenuation of Gastric Lesions by Psychological Aspects of Aggression in Rats," *Journal of Comparative and Physiological Psychology* 90, no. 3 (March 1976): 252–59, https://doi.org/10.1037/h0088038.

100 **"space to move":** Eugene T. Gendlin, *Focusing*, 2nd ed. (Bantam Books, 1981), 86.

Somatic Exercises

104 **Tracking Exercise:** Peter Levine, *In an Unspoken Voice: How the Body Releases Trauma and Restores Goodness* (North Atlantic Books, 2010), 73–95; Peter Payne et al., "Somatic Experiencing: Using Interoception and Proprioception as Core Elements of Trauma Therapy," *Frontiers in Psychology* 6, no. 93 (April 2015): 1–18, https://doi.org/10.3389/fpsyg.2015.00093.

106 **Body Trust Exercise:** Gendlin, *Focusing,* 49–51.

Chapter 6: The Parts Who Own Our Memories

111 **parts of us:** Onno van der Hart et al., "Trauma-Related Dissociation: Conceptual Clarity Lost and Found," *Australian and New Zealand Journal of Psychiatry* 38, nos. 11–12 (November 2004): 906–14, https://doi.org/10.1080/j.1440-1614.2004.01480.x.

112 **"in the course of ten minutes":** Ben Blum, "Inside the Revolutionary Treatment That Could Change Psychotherapy Forever," *Elemental*, July 21, 2020, https://elemental.medium.com/inside-the-revolutionary-treatment-that-could-change-psychotherapy-forever-8be035d54770.

112 **Plato philosophized that the soul:** Blum, "Inside the Revolutionary Treatment That Could Change Psychotherapy Forever."

112 **point of therapy:** Stephen A. Mitchell, "Contemporary Perspectives on Self: Toward an Integration," *Psychoanalytic Dialogues* 1, no. 2 (1991): 130, https://doi.org/10.1080/10481889109538889.

113 **Renowned psychiatrist Harry Stack Sullivan:** Mitchell, "Contemporary Perspectives on Self," 129.

113 **call it an "emotional expertise":** Christine D. Wilson-Mendenhall and John D. Dunne, "Cultivating Emotional Granularity," *Frontiers in Psychology* 12 (December 2021), https://doi.org/10.3389/fpsyg.2021.703658.

113 **less likely to self-medicate:** Todd B. Kashdan et al., "Emotion Differentiation as Resilience against Excessive Alcohol Use: An Ecological Momentary Assessment in Underage Social Drinkers," *Psychological Science* 21, no. 9 (September 2010): 1341–47, https://doi.org/10.1177/0956797610379863.

113 **aggressive when provoked:** Richard S. Pond et al., "Emotion Differentiation Moderates Aggressive Tendencies in Angry People: A Daily Diary Analysis," *Emotion* 12, no. 2 (April 2012): 326–37, https://doi.org/10.1037/a0025762.

113 **less depression:** Emre Demiralp et al., "Feeling Blue or Turquoise? Emotional Differentiation in Major Depressive Disorder," *Psychological Science* 23, no. 11 (October 2012): 1410–16, https://doi.org/10.1177/0956797612444903.

113 **shape our reality:** Alan Lightman, *Einstein's Dreams* (Knopf Doubleday, 2011), 167–170.

114 **is happening now:** Phillip M. Bromberg, "'Speak! That I May See You,'" in *The Interpersonal Perspective in Psychoanalysis, 1960s–1990s*, edited by Donnel B. Stern and Irwin Hirsch (Routledge, 2017), 301, https://doi.org/10.4324/9781315471976-26.

115 **badgering the part:** Richard C. Schwartz and Martha Sweezy, *Internal Family Systems Therapy* (Guilford Publications, 2019), 14.

115 **"won the battle":** Richard C. Schwartz, *No Bad Parts: Healing Trauma and Restoring Wholeness with the Internal Family System Model* (Sounds True, 2021), 15.

115 **deep gash across:** Blum, "Inside the Revolutionary Treatment That Could Change Psychotherapy Forever."

115 **"I give up":** Blum, "Inside the Revolutionary Treatment That Could Change Psychotherapy Forever."

116 **"some kind of enemy":** Blum, "Inside the Revolutionary Treatment That Could Change Psychotherapy Forever."

116 **lackluster report cards:** NPR, "How 'Parts' Therapy Can Help You Heal," *Life Kit*, October 17, 2024, https://www.npr.org/transcripts/1210942202.

116 **"was fooling people":** Schwartz, *No Bad Parts*, 149.

116 **clients' mental health issues:** Tori Olds, "Memory Reconsolidation: How to Rewire Your Brain," accessed February 19, 2026, https://www.toriolds.com/memory_reconsolidation_ts4.

116 **"they would fight":** Schwartz and Sweezy, *Internal Family Systems Therapy*, 14.

119 **love a woman:** Erich Fromm, "Selfishness and Self-Love," in *Understanding Human Motivation*, edited by Chalmers L. Stacey and Manfred DeMartino (Howard Allen Publishers, 1958), https://doi.org/10.1037/11305-043.

121 **"rebuilding the life":** Patricia E. Deegan, "Recovering Our Sense of Value after Being Labeled: Mentally Ill," *Journal of Psychosocial Nursing and Mental Health Services* 31, no. 4 (April 1993): 7–9, https://doi.org/10.3928/0279-3695-19930401-06.

122 **"That changed my world":** Blum, "Inside the Revolutionary Treatment That Could Change Psychotherapy Forever."

122 **"That's not a part":** Schwartz, *No Bad Parts*, 22.

122 **sense of self:** Veronika V. Nourkova and Darya A. Vasilenko, "On the Advantage of Autobiographical Memory Pliability: Implantation of Positive Self-Defining Memories Reduces Trait Anxiety," *Memory* 26, no. 7 (August 2018): 869–81, https://doi.org/10.1080/09658211.2017.1420195.

123 **IFS therapy decreases PTSD:** Alexandra Comeau et al., "Online Group-Based Internal Family Systems Treatment for Posttraumatic Stress Disorder: Feasibility and Acceptability of the Program for Alleviating and Resolving Trauma and Stress," *Psychological Trauma: Theory, Research, Practice, and Policy* 16, suppl 3 (December 2024): S636–40, https://doi.org/10.1037/tra0001688; Hilary B. Hodgdon et al., "Internal Family Systems (IFS) Therapy for Posttraumatic Stress Disorder (PTSD) among Survivors of Multiple Childhood Trauma: A Pilot Effectiveness Study," *Journal of Aggression, Maltreatment and Trauma* 31, no. 1 (2022): 22–43, https://doi.org/10.1080/10926771.2021.2013375.

123 **depression:** Shelley A. Haddock et al., "The Efficacy of Internal Family Systems Therapy in the Treatment of Depression among Female College Students: A Pilot Study," *Journal of Marital and Family Therapy* 43, no. 1 (August 2016): 131–44, https://doi.org/10.1111/jmft.12184.

123 **internet addiction**: Mohammad Mehrad Sadr et al., "Design and Validation of a Therapy Program Based on the Internal Family Systems Model and Its Efficacy on Internet Addiction," *Journal of Psychological Science* 22, no. 121 (March

2023): 19–36, https://ifs-institute.com/resources/research/internet-addiction-and-efficacy-ifs.

123 **arthritis:** Nancy A. Shadick et al., "A Randomized Controlled Trial of an Internal Family Systems–Based Psychotherapeutic Intervention on Outcomes in Rheumatoid Arthritis: A Proof-of-Concept Study," *Journal of Rheumatology* 40, no. 11 (November 2013): 1831–41, https://doi.org/10.3899/jrheum.121465.

123 **But it didn't reduce anxiety or improve confidence:** Shadick, "A Randomized Controlled Trial of an Internal Family Systems–Based Psychotherapeutic Intervention on Outcomes in Rheumatoid Arthritis."

123 **decreased shame and guilt:** Hodgdon et al., "Internal Family Systems (IFS) Therapy for Posttraumatic Stress Disorder (PTSD) among Survivors of Multiple Childhood Trauma."

123 **increased self-compassion:** Comeau et al., "Online Group-Based Internal Family Systems Treatment for Posttraumatic Stress Disorder."

123 **healing attachment wounds:** Richard Schwartz, "An IFS Approach to Build Secure Internal Attachment," National Institute for the Clinical Application of Behavioral Medicine, 2025, accessed February 19, 2025, https://www.nicabm.com/program/p2-fb-ifs-schwartz.

123 **to ensure survival:** Bessel van der Kolk, *The Body Keeps the Score: Brain, Mind, and Body in the Healing of Trauma* (Penguin Books, 2015), 285.

124 **"a more effective therapist":** Carl R. Rogers, "Empathic: An Unappreciated Way of Being," *The Counseling Psychologist* 5, no. 9 (1975): 9, https://doi.org/10.1177/001100007500500202.

124 **the Self "impathy":** Stefanie Neubrand and Jens Gaab, "The Missing Construct: Impathy," *Frontiers in Psychology* 13 (October 2022): 9, https://doi.org/10.3389/fpsyg.2022.726029.

124 **better their sleep:** Michael Fitzgerald, "Cool, Calm, and Collected: The Associations between Self-Leadership and Adult Mental and Relational Health Outcomes," *American Journal of Family Therapy* 50, no. 1 (2022): 57–71, https://doi.org/10.1080/01926187.2020.1865218.

124 **embracing a spiritual side:** Richard Schwartz, "The Larger Self," accessed December 23, 2025, https://ifs-institute.com/resources/articles/larger-self.

124 **or God Within:** Schwartz and Sweezy, *Internal Family Systems Therapy*, 43.

IFS Exercises

127 **IFS Excercises:** Richard C. Schwartz, *No Bad Parts: Healing Trauma and Restoring Wholeness with the Internal Family System Model* (Sounds True, 2021); Richard C. Schwartz and Martha Sweezy, *Internal Family Systems Therapy* (Guilford Publications, 2019).

Chapter 7: Memories of Stigma

135 **Adam and Eve:** J. David Velleman, "The Genesis of Shame," *Philosophy and Public Affairs* 30, no. 1 (January 2001): 27–52, https://doi.org/10.1111/j.1088-4963.2001.00027.x.

135 **attacked a warehouse:** History.com editors, "Abolitionist Movement," October 27, 2009, https://www.history.com/articles/abolitionist-movement.

135 **people dying of AIDS:** Michael Specter, "How ACT UP Changed America," *The New Yorker*, June 7, 2021, https://www.newyorker.com/magazine/2021/06/14/how-act-up-changed-america.

135 **maladjusted to injustice:** Southern Methodist University, "Transcript of Dr. Martin Luther King's Speech at SMU on March 17, 1966," January 10, 2014, https://www.smu.edu/news/archives/2014/mlk-at-smu-transcript-17march1966.

136 **leaner government that:** Thomas Lemke, "'The Birth of Bio-Politics': Michel Foucault's Lecture at the Collège de France on Neo-Liberal Governmentality," *Economy and Society* 30, no. 2 (December 2001): 190–207, https://doi.org/10.1080/03085140120042271.

136 **first cropped up:** Sina Najafi et al., "The Invention of Failure: An Interview with Scott A. Sandage," 2002, https://cabinetmagazine.org/issues/7/najafi_serlin_sandage.php.

136 **what often happens:** Jean Baker Miller, *Toward a New Psychology of Women* (Beacon, 1976), 115–124.

136 **months of daily tears:** "The Things I Usually Keep to Myself," *Always Flying Solo*, July 30, 2020, https://alwaysflyingsolo.home.blog.

137 **chronically evaluating ourselves:** Karl Eriksson, "Self-Stigma, Bad Faith and the Experiential Self," *Human Studies* 42, no. 3 (April 2019): 391–405, https://doi.org/10.1007/s10746-019-09504-8.

137 **"I am what I am":** Ralph Ellison, *Invisible Man* (Vintage International, 1996), 230–31.

138 **worth required proof:** John E. Pachankis and Mark L. Hatzenbuehler, "The Social Development of Contingent Self-Worth in Sexual Minority Young Men: An Empirical Investigation of the 'Best Little Boy in the World' Hypothesis," *Basic and Applied Social Psychology* 35, no. 2 (March 2013): 176–90, https://doi.org/10.1080/01973533.2013.764304.

138 **wrecked exam curves:** Adam Chandler, "The Best Little Boy in the World—That's Me," May 6, 2013, https://www.nytimes.com/2013/05/07/opinion/the-best-little-boy-in-the-world-thats-me.html.

138 **"racism is distraction":** "Racism as Distraction: Aminatta Forna Writes about Toni Morrison," *Medical Humanities*, accessed February 19, 2025, https://medicalhumanities.georgetown.edu/media-and-scholarship/media/racism-as-distraction.

139 **"and a fulfillment":** Kahlil Gibran, "On Freedom," in *The Prophet* (Alfred A. Knopf, 1923).

140 **his groundbreaking study:** Shadd Maruna, *Making Good: How Ex-Convicts Reform and Rebuild Their Lives* (American Psychological Association, 2001), 73–84, https://doi.org/10.1037/10430-000.

140 **"doomed to deviance":** Maruna, *Making Good*, 74.

140 **"some other way":** Maruna, *Making Good*, 76.

140 **"dead somewhere":** Maruna, *Making Good*, 79.

141 **moment of collective forgiveness:** Maruna, *Making Good*, 158.

141 **insignificant and stupid:** Laurie Santos, "How to Build Resilience (with Ben Walter from 'The Unshakeables')," *The Happiness Lab with Dr. Laurie Santos*, April 29, 2025, podcast, https://www.pushkin.fm/podcasts/the-happiness-lab-with

-dr-laurie-santos/how-to-build-resilience-with-ben-walter-from-the-unshakeables.

141 **poignant story of an authority figure:** "The Revolution of Tenderness—Part 2," Tara Brach, June 11, 2025, 35:00–47:00, https://www.tarabrach.com/the-revolution-of-tenderness-part2-2.

142 **shrinking the gap:** Gregory M. Walton and Geoffrey L. Cohen, "A Brief Social-Belonging Intervention Improves Academic and Health Outcomes of Minority Students," *Science* 331, no. 6023 (March 2011): 1447–51, https://doi.org/10.1126/science.1198364.

143 **retrieval competition theory:** Kees Korrelboom et al., "The Effectiveness of Transdiagnostic Applications of Competitive Memory Training (COMET) on Low Self-Esteem and Comorbid Depression: A Meta-Analysis of Randomized Controlled Trials," *Cognitive Therapy and Research* 46, no. 3 (January 2022): 532–43, https://doi.org/10.1007/s10608-021-10286-6.

145 **we are environments:** Merlin Sheldrake, *Entangled Life: How Fungi Make Our Worlds, Change Our Minds and Shape Our Futures* (Random House, 2021), 17–18.

147 **shed the propaganda:** Peter Catapano and Rosemarie Garland-Thomson, eds., *About Us: Essays from the Disability Series of "The New York Times,"* 1st edition, with Andrew Solomon (Liveright, 2019), xv, xvii, 78.

Retrieval Competition Theory Exercise

149 **retrieval competition theory:** Kees Korrelboom et al., "Competitive Memory Training (COMET) for Low Self-Esteem in Patients with Personality Disorders: A Randomized Effectiveness Study," *Behavioural and Cognitive Psychotherapy* 39, no. 1 (2011), 1–19, https://doi.org/10.1017/S1352465810000469.

150 **This exercise was based:** Korrelboom et al., "Competitive Memory Training (COMET) for Low Self-Esteem in Patients with Personality Disorders; M. van der Gaag et al., "Initial Evaluation of the Effects of Competitive Memory Training (COMET) on Depression in Schizophrenia-Spectrum Patients with Persistent Auditory Verbal Hallucinations: A Randomized Controlled Trial," *British Journal of Clinical Psychology* 51, no. 2 (2021), 158–71, https://doi.org/10.1111/j.2044-8260.2011.02025.x.

Chapter 8: Psychedelic Memories

152 **protect this self:** "No Self (Anatta)," Lion's Roar, accessed December 23, 2025, https://www.lionsroar.com/buddhism/no-self-anatta.

152 **too-fixed story of self:** Robin L. Carhart-Harris et al., "The Entropic Brain: A Theory of Conscious States Informed by Neuroimaging Research with Psychedelic Drugs," *Frontiers in Human Neuroscience* 8, no. 20 (2014): 1–22, https://doi.org/10.3389/fnhum.2014.00020; Robin Carhart-Harris et al., "Canalization and Plasticity in Psychopathology," *Neuropharmacology* 226, no. 15 (2023): 1–14, https://doi.org/10.1016/j.neuropharm.2022.109398.

152 **To find certainty:** Robin L. Carhart-Harris, "How Do Psychedelics Work?," *Current Opinion in Psychiatry* 32, no. 1 (January 2019): 16–21, https://doi.org/10.1097/YCO.0000000000000467.

152 **kind of order:** Merlijn Olthof et al., "Destabilization in Self-Ratings of the Psychotherapeutic Process Is Associated with Better Treatment Outcome in Patients with Mood Disorders," *Psychotherapy Research* 30, no. 4 (November 2020): 520–31, https://doi.org/10.1080/10503307.2019.1633484.

152 **locked our brain:** R. L. Carhart-Harris et al., "Canalization and Plasticity in Psychopathology."

153 **calls an "ego tunnel":** Thomas Metzinger, *The Ego Tunnel: The Science of the Mind and the Myth of the Self* (Basic Books/Hachette Book Group, 2009), 6.

154 **a "one-way trip":** *Life*, "The Exploding Threat of the Mind Drug That Got Out of Control," Trippingly, July 23, 2020, https://www.trippingly.net/lsd-studies/life-magazine-march-25-1966.

154 **us lose ourselves:** Michael Pollan, *How to Change Your Mind: What the New Science of Psychedelics Teaches Us about Consciousness, Dying, Addiction, Depression, and Transcendence* (Penguin Press, 2018), 301.

154 **been "rusted stuck":** Pollan, *How to Change Your Mind*, 313–14.

155 **"prison of my brain":** Rosalind Watts et al., "Patients' Accounts of Increased 'Connectedness' and 'Acceptance' after Psilocybin for Treatment-Resistant Depression," *Journal of Humanistic Psychology* 57, no. 5 (June 2017): 528, https://doi.org/10.1177/0022167817709585.

155 **randomized controlled study:** Alan K. Davis et al., "Effects of Psilocybin-Assisted Therapy on Major Depressive Disorder: A Randomized Clinical Trial," *JAMA Psychiatry* 78, no. 5 (May 2021): 481–89, https://doi.org/10.1001/jamapsychiatry.2020.3285.

155 **"therapy on steroids":** Rosalind Watts and Jason B. Luoma, "The Use of the Psychological Flexibility Model to Support Psychedelic Assisted Therapy," *Journal of Contextual Behavioral Science* 15 (January 2020): 92–102, https://doi.org/10.1016/j.jcbs.2019.12.004.

155 **two and a half times more effective:** Allen Rubin and Miao Yu, "Within-Group Effect Size Benchmarks for Cognitive-Behavioral Therapy in the Treatment of Adult Depression," *Social Work Research* 41, no. 3 (September 2017): 135–44, https://doi.org/10.1093/swr/svx011.

155 **effective than antidepressants:** Jay C. Fournier et al., "Antidepressant Drug Effects and Depression Severity: A Patient-Level Meta-Analysis," *JAMA* 303, no. 1 (January 2010): 47, https://doi.org/10.1001/jama.2009.1943.

156 **other determining factor:** Theresa M. Carbonaro et al., "Survey Study of Challenging Experiences after Ingesting Psilocybin Mushrooms: Acute and Enduring Positive and Negative Consequences," *Journal of Psychopharmacology* 30, no. 12 (December 2016): 1268–78, https://doi.org/10.1177/0269881116662634.

156 **your mindset when:** Lucas F. Borkel et al., "Set and Setting Predict Psychopathology, Wellbeing and Meaningfulness of Psychedelic Experiences: A Correlational Study," *Expert Review of Clinical Pharmacology* 17, no. 2 (2024): 165–76, https://doi.org/10.1080/17512433.2023.2295997.

156 **builds off wisdom:** Daniel R. George et al., "Ancient Roots of Today's Emerging Renaissance in Psychedelic Medicine," *Culture, Medicine, and Psychiatry* 46, no. 4 (December 2022): 890–903, https://doi.org/10.1007/s11013-021-09749-y.

156 **Indigenous communities:** David Cox, "What Western Medicine Can Learn from the Ancient History of Psychedelics," September 11, 2024, https://www.bbc.com/future/article/20240910-the-ancient-history-behind-healing-trauma-with-psychedelics.

156 **reinstate the critical periods:** Romain Nardou et al., "Psychedelics Reopen the Social Reward Learning Critical Period," *Nature* 618, no. 7966 (June 2023): 790–98, https://doi.org/10.1038/s41586-023-06204-3.

156 **we experience as kids:** "Study Shows Psychedelic Drugs Reopen 'Critical Periods' for Social Learning," Johns Hopkins Medicine, June 14, 2023, https://www.hopkinsmedicine.org/news/newsroom/news-releases/2023/06/study-shows-psychedelic-drugs-reopen-critical-periods-for-social-learning.

156 **to these ailments:** Sabé et al., "Reconsidering Evidence for Psychedelic-Induced Psychosis: An Overview of Reviews, a Systematic Review, and Meta-Analysis of Human Studies," *Molecular Psychiatry* 30, no. 3 (2025): 1223–55, https://doi.org/10.1038/s41380-024-02800-5.

157 **can imprint itself:** Nardou et al., "Psychedelics Reopen the Social Reward Learning Critical Period."

157 **experiencing bad trips:** Carbonaro et al., "Survey Study of Challenging Experiences after Ingesting Psilocybin Mushrooms."

157 **took psilocybin with a friend:** Richard A. Friedman, "Psychedelics Open Your Brain. You Might Not Like What Falls In," *The Atlantic*, February 1, 2023, https://www.theatlantic.com/health/archive/2023/02/psychedelic-drug-therapy-effects-brain-neuroplasticity/672910.

158 **"bad country song":** Caleb Hellerman, "Hitting the Brain's Reset Button," PBS, December 1, 2016, https://www.pbs.org/wgbh/nova/article/ptsd-drug-treatment.

161 **of condensed experience:** Stanislav Grof, *Realms of the Human Unconscious: Observations from LSD Research* (Souvenir Press, 1979), 46–49.

161 **researchers speculate, allows:** Franz X. Vollenweider and Katrin H. Preller, "Psychedelic Drugs: Neurobiology and Potential for Treatment of Psychiatric Disorders," *Nature Reviews Neuroscience* 21, no. 11 (September 2020): 611–24, https://doi.org/10.1038/s41583-020-0367-2.

161 **to bubble up:** Max Wolff et al., "Learning to Let Go: A Cognitive-Behavioral Model of How Psychedelic Therapy Promotes Acceptance," *Frontiers in Psychiatry* 11 (February 2020), https://doi.org/10.3389/fpsyt.2020.00005.

161 **or enhanced memory:** C. J. Healy "The Acute Effects of Classic Psychedelics on Memory in Humans." *Psychopharmacology* 238, no. 3 (March 2021): 2, https://doi.org/10.1007/s00213-020-05756-w.

161 **the term *psychedelic*:** Janice Hopkins Tanne, "Humphry Osmond," *British Medical Journal* 328, no. 7441 (March 2004): 713, https://www.ncbi.nlm.nih.gov/pmc/articles/PMC381240.

161 **whole "sequences unroll":** Betty Grover Eisner and Sidney Cohen, "Psychotherapy with Lysergic Acid Diethylamide," *Journal of Nervous and Mental Disease* 127, no. 6 (December 1958): 533, https://doi.org/10.1097/00005053-195812000-00006.

161 **suppressing the parts:** Janina Fisher, "The Treatment of Structural Dissociation in Chronically Traumatized Patients," 2023, https://janinafisher.com/wp-content/uploads/2023/03/structural-dissociation.pdf.

162 **default mode network:** Pollan, *How to Change Your Mind*, 307.

162 **neural bumpers on:** Allison A. Feduccia and Michael C. Mithoefer, "MDMA-Assisted Psychotherapy for PTSD: Are Memory Reconsolidation and Fear Extinction Underlying Mechanisms?," *Progress in Neuro-Psychopharmacology and Biological Psychiatry* 84 (June 2018): 221–28, https://doi.org/10.1016/j.pnpbp.2018.03.003.

162 **inner therapist sprung:** Watts et al., "Patients' Accounts of Increased 'Connectedness' and 'Acceptance' after Psilocybin for Treatment-Resistant Depression," 550.

162 **"presence of something divine":** Watts and Luoma, "The Use of the Psychological Flexibility Model to Support Psychedelic Assisted Therapy."

162 **doesn't make you hallucinate:** Jerrold S. Meyer, "3,4-Methylenedioxymethamphetamine (MDMA): Current Perspectives," *Substance Abuse and Rehabilitation* 4 (November 2013): 83–99, https://doi.org/10.2147/SAR.S37258.

162 **deactivating your amygdala:** Feduccia and Mithoefer, "MDMA-Assisted Psychotherapy for PTSD."

162 **new positive meaning:** Felix Müller et al., "MDMA-Induced Changes in Within-Network Connectivity Contradict the Specificity of These Alterations for the Effects of Serotonergic Hallucinogens," *Neuropsychopharmacology* 46, no. 3 (November 2020): 545–53, https://doi.org/10.1038/s41386-020-00906-2.

162 **other psychedelics, like ayahuasca:** Antonio Inserra, "Hypothesis: The Psychedelic Ayahuasca Heals Traumatic Memories via a Sigma 1 Receptor-Mediated Epigenetic-Mnemonic Process," *Frontiers in Pharmacology* 9 (April 2018), https://doi.org/10.3389/fphar.2018.00330.

162 **and psilocybin, have been shown to have promise:** Watts et al., "Patients' Accounts of Increased 'Connectedness' and 'Acceptance' after Psilocybin for Treatment-Resistant Depression."

162 **can help people:** Feduccia and Mithoefer, "MDMA-Assisted Psychotherapy for PTSD."

162 **took a placebo:** Jianhua Yang et al., "The Efficacy and Safety of MDMA-Assisted Psychotherapy for Treatment of Posttraumatic Stress Disorder: A Systematic Review and Meta-Analysis from Randomized Controlled Trials," *Psychiatry Research* 339 (September 2024): 116043, https://doi.org/10.1016/j.psychres.2024.116043.

163 **cut in half:** Janna Lawrence, "'Like a Hug from Everyone Who Loves You'—How MDMA Could Help Patients with Trauma," *Pharmaceutical Journal*, October 15, 2018, https://pharmaceutical-journal.com/article/feature/like-a-hug-from-everyone-who-loves-you-how-mdma-could-help-patients-with-trauma.

165 **long-term changes:** Jordan Sloshower et al., "Psychological Flexibility as a Mechanism of Change in Psilocybin-Assisted Therapy for Major Depression: Results from an Exploratory Placebo-Controlled Trial," *Scientific Reports* 14, no. 1 (April 2024): 8833, https://doi.org/10.1038/s41598-024-58318-x.

166 **the metaphor of a fist:** Robert Kegan, *The Evolving Self: Problem and Process in Human Development* (Harvard University Press, 1982), 8.

166 **never an entity:** Kegan, *The Evolving Self,* 8.

166 **them they repressed:** Neşe Devenot et al., "Psychedelic Identity Shift: A Critical Approach to Set and Setting," *Kennedy Institute of Ethics Journal* 32, no. 4 (December 2022): 384, https://doi.org/10.1353/ken.2022.0022.

166 **"Ordinary personality is":** Devenot et al., "Psychedelic Identity Shift."

167 **emotions as weakness:** Rosalind Watts et al., "Patients' Accounts of Increased 'Connectedness' and 'Acceptance' after Psilocybin for Treatment-Resistant Depression," 520–64.

168 **"sketch of a dinner table":** Thomas C. Swift et al., "Cancer at the Dinner Table: Experiences of Psilocybin-Assisted Psychotherapy for the Treatment of Cancer-Related Distress," *Journal of Humanistic Psychology* 57, no. 5 (June 2017): 488–519, https://doi.org/10.1177/0022167817715966.

168 **like a spiral:** Hillevi Ruumet, *Pathways of the Soul: Exploring the Human Journey* (Trafford Publishing, 2006).

Takeaways

172 **time of this writing:** "Law and Politics," UC Berkeley Center for the Science of Psychedelics, accessed December 23, 2025, https://psychedelics.berkeley.edu/law.

Conclusion

174 **ever to become secure:** Sara H. Konrath et al., "Changes in Adult Attachment Styles in American College Students over Time: A Meta-Analysis," *Personality and Social Psychology Review* 18, no. 4 (April 2014): 326–48, https://doi.org/10.1177/1088868314530516.

177 **benefit the collective:** Mark E. Koltko-Rivera, "Rediscovering the Later Version of Maslow's Hierarchy of Needs: Self-Transcendence and Opportunities for Theory, Research, and Unification," *Review of General Psychology* 10, no. 4 (December 2006): 302–17, https://doi.org/10.1037/1089-2680.10.4.302.

177 **"All sorts of insights":** Koltko-Rivera, "Rediscovering the Later Version of Maslow's Hierarchy of Needs," 304.

177 **his 1967 address:** Koltko-Rivera, "Rediscovering the Later Version of Maslow's Hierarchy of Needs," 306–8.

178 **"transcending of itself":** Koltko-Rivera, "Rediscovering the Later Version of Maslow's Hierarchy of Needs," 304.

178 **aligned with thinking:** David Cox, "What Western Medicine Can Learn from the Ancient History of Psychedelics," BBC, September 11, 2024, https://www.bbc.com/future/article/20240910-the-ancient-history-behind-healing-trauma-with-psychedelics.

Index

About the Author

Photo © Dante Corinaldi (@don.visuals)

Dr. Marisa G. Franco is the *New York Times* bestselling author of *Platonic: How the Science of Attachment Can Help You Make—and Keep—Friends.* She holds a PhD in counseling psychology from the University of Maryland and works as a professor there currently. She writes for *Psychology Today* and has been a featured psychologist in *The New York Times* and on NPR and *Good Morning America*. Dr. Franco delivers talks about connection, belonging, and worth all over the country to private companies, universities, and nonprofit organizations. Her newest talk is titled "Self-Worth at Work: Helping Employees Thrive in Times of Uncertainty."

VISIT MARISA G. FRANCO ONLINE

drmarisagfranco.com
DrMarisaGFranco
DrMarisaGFranco
https://drmarisagfranco.substack.com